SLAUGHTERED

*How Inconsistent Lockdowns
Collapsed the Hospitality Industry
During COVID-19*

VINCENT TROPEPE

Copyright © 2021 by Vincent A. Tropepe

All rights reserved

Published in the United States of America

Library of Congress Cataloging –in- Publication Data

Tropepe, Vincent A. – 1st ed.

SLAUGHTERED

I. Restaurant Food Service

II. Current Affairs

III. Politics

Printed in the United States of America

Photography by Jessica Sterner

10 9 8 7 6 5 4 3 2 1

First Edition

To Caroline —
It was great to catch up with you.
Wishing you all the best

Love,
[signature]

SLAUGHTERED

How Inconsistent Lockdowns
Collapsed the Hospitality Industry
During COVID-19

VINCENT TROPEPE

DEDICATION

This book is dedicated to the dishwashers, bus boys, waiter staff, line cooks, executive chefs and owners, operators and investors. The book is further dedicated to those who lost their jobs, careers and also to those who lost it all. To those that came close to losing it all and for those that hung on during the most difficult times during COVID-19.

I firmly dedicate this book to you all.

Always remember – **it's up to you if the comeback is greater than the setback.**

Table Of Contents

Chapter One

Politics in the Food Industry

1

Chapter Two

Struggles of the Industry in the Middle of the Pandemic

20

Chapter Three

A Recipe for Disaster

47

Chapter Four

2009 Recession & COVID-19 and their Impact on the Hospitality Industry

75

Chapter Five

Government Response to the Hospitality Industry During COVID-19

117

Chapter Six

Politics and the Hospitality Sector in COVID Times

157

Chapter Seven

Politicians and their Hypocrisy

198

Chapter Eight

COVID-19 and Civil Liberties

212

Chapter Nine

Food & Culture

239

Chapter Ten

Concept of Free Enterprise

269

Chapter Eleven

Widespread Impact of the Restaurant Industry Shutdowns

289

Chapter Twelve

Input of Technology in the Restaurant Industry

301

Chapter Thirteen

The New Normal

349

Chapter Fourteen

An Act of Bio Terrorism?

360

Chapter Fifteen

Now and Beyond

373

PREFACE

From an early and impressionable age when I first started working in professional kitchens, it is a clear fact that there are differences between a good cook and a great chef. This difference ranges from technique, creativity, understanding one's ingredients and consistency in execution, kitchen leadership and standards. Consistency in all places of business, particularly in a food service establishment allows the public to consider it to be reliable and even safe.

However, when it comes to the worldwide COVID-19 pandemic, all we have received was mixed messaging, questionable information and yes inconsistencies in approaches to lockdowns from the leadership who we put in place.

By the time this book comes out, it's very likely that everyone will either know someone who had COVID-19 or even worse knows someone who lost somebody from COVID-19. But besides the significant priceless human casualties, the hardest hit business sector is the hospitality industry.

From closings and lockdowns, to reopening, to one mask to two, to outdoor seating, to no outdoor seating, to limited indoor seating and curfews changes to only name a few. The rules and regulations for both the public and business community have been thrown and it seems at times too difficult to bear and keep on top of.

In this groundbreaking book, *SLAUGHTERED! How Inconsistent Lockdowns Collapsed the Hospitality Industry During COVID-19*. I am proud to release this book that will discuss and reveal how the COVID-19 lockdown immensely collapsed the hospitality industry.

CHAPTER ONE

Politics in the Food Industry

COVID-19 outbreak has presented unprecedented circumstances before the fragile tourism and hospitality industry. The highly infectious novel corona virus continues to thwart the sector and raises serious questions about the present and future survival of the sector. This book addresses four important concerns, first, pertains to the major challenges that hospitality and tourism industry faces amid current conditions; and second relates to the vital learning for the industry. Thirdly the ripple effect the virus has had on the economy of the United States and also mentioning notable places in the United States affected by the pandemic. The book will further discuss the impact the government lockdown restrictions had an on owners and

CHAPTER ONE

employees in the hospitality industry and how the industry is recovering for the year 2021.

Time immemorial, the concept of hospitality is about receiving guests in a spirit of good will, especially strangers from other part of the land. Hospitality in its literal sense mean warmth, respect and even protection; it builds understanding and appreciation amongst different cultures and widens a person horizon about other countries and communities.

Hospitality means welcoming a guest and making them comfortable at your place by looking after their needs during their temporary stay. When we do and provide the above things as a service, business to anyone, with the help of products and services, for a price it becomes hospitality industry.

Hospitality industry can be defined and understood as an industry which provides facility for stay, food and complete related services for the comfort and leisure of the travelers and visitors.

Hospitality is the industry covering all the products and services that serve travelers, tourists and all types of

CHAPTER ONE

visitors. When you know tourism you also understand hospitality industry.

This industry is closely associated and a part of the tourism industry. it is a key part of the tourism industry value chain. This industry is mainly driven by growing tourism, yet it caters to both tourists and travelers.

Hospitality and Tourism industry are closely related and each plays an important role in development and growth of the other industry. Tourism brings revenue, growth and development for hospitality. On the other hand hospitality industry adds to the overall value and importance of tourism. It creates more tourism demand, makes it look more attractive, and adds the much needed comfort level for tourists and travelers. Without hospitality, tourism would be incomplete and will not achieve the growth.

The hospitality Industry value chain is a part of the tourism industry value chain. All of the services, segments, sectors and components of hospitality Industry broadly come under the tourism industry.

This is because hospitality is the very important segment of tourism. Hospitality majorly caters to the tourists and

CHAPTER ONE

travelers. The customers or the business of hospitality comes from tourism and also from travelling.

Yet, we need to look at the value chain of this industry because looking at hospitality through tourism is not that deep and detailed. Hospitality, although is an important part of tourism yet it is also an independent industry that serves and caters to all types of people including those who are not tourists.

The value chain is defined and structured across the two sectors or segments of hospitality industry i.e. accommodation sector and food & beverages sector or segment. Then it covers the sub-segments and types for each segment i.e. types of accommodation facilities and types of food & beverages services in hospitality.

There are two major segments of customers that come to hospitality and are served by this industry. These are customers for accommodation sector and customers for food & beverages sector or segment.

Five types of economic or social activities lead up to the hospitality industry. These are tourism activities, travelling activities, business activities, social activities and other various general or day to day activities.

CHAPTER ONE

This also helps us identify the customers of hospitality across its two main sectors and types, accommodation and food & beverages. All those people carrying out and involved in the above different types of activities are or can be the customers of hospitality.

The hospitality industry is quite similar to the tourism industry when it comes to the vastness of its value chain and the economic and social importance and impact. As we know that tourism industry is important for the economy and society of every country. Similarly, this hospitality sector is also very important economically and socially for a country, both as part of tourism and independently.

The hospitality industry supports boosts and drives economic activities and growth in a big way. It also is an important part of a country's social infrastructure, providing good support.

This industry through its two core sectors creates many other economic activities, helps and boosts activities, revenues and growth for many other industries.

The accommodation or the hotel industry carries out so many activities, also covering the food segment. It is a large industry and as it is labor intensive it is one of the

CHAPTER ONE

major employment generation industries. Besides this, it requires much equipment (like utensils, decorative, interiors, furniture, bed sheets, quilts, pillows, etc.), material and many other things.

So it boosts and drives directly the construction industry. And if we go into details of all the products or things that are used in hotels, restaurants, etc and make a comprehensive list then there would be hundreds of small medium and big industries or sectors which directly or indirectly benefit from this industry.

The hospitality industry is a labor intensive industry. This industry employs huge manpower. Hospitality industry requires a large manpower to provide the services to its customers and also to create these services and products. Hospitality is also therefore one of the largest employments generating industry.

Customer satisfaction is the utmost objective of this industry. Although every product, service and industry is always driven by customer satisfaction but in the hospitality industry the importance of satisfying is much more.

CHAPTER ONE

In the hospitality industry you need to constantly satisfy your customers and keep them happy always. It is believed that in this industry the time take to consume the services and products is long and vital. The customers are at your premise all through the time of their consumption. In fact, staying in itself is a part of the service and also a key part of consuming the services. So, the businesses need to ensure that the customer is happy and satisfied throughout the time of their stay at the premise and all throughout the consumption of the services.

To start with, the hospitality industry is a very vital aspect and component of the travel and tourism industry. As I said at the start, tourism and its industry would be incomplete without the hospitality services. Going for a holiday, vacation, to see a tourist destination, traveling for leisure or recreation or even for any other long type of travelling or journey you need hospitality services. Without it can be nearly impossible to have tourism.

Similarly, hospitality plays very important role in Meetings, Incentives, Conferencing, and Exhibition industry. MICE means travelling for business and events, and also involves recreation. MICE industry needs facilities

CHAPTER ONE

to host meetings, conferences. All this is provided by hotels, which are a critical part of hospitality. Besides this, travelers, and not specifically tourists need accommodation services. Food and beverages segment of this industry serves many people, even if they are not tourists or travelers.

The decade 2020 started with a much unsettling and unfortunate occurrence of new disease in the line of over 30 novel infections that the world has experienced in past 30 years. This time the name given to the new severe acute respiratory syndrome (SARS) outbreak was the novel corona virus. Later termed COVID-19, the disease represented an atypical pneumonia that started in China, and later spread across nations' the world over. Countries like United States of America, Brazil, India, Italy, Spain, France, South Korea, Italy, Iran and many more are experiencing unprecedented spread of the disease and life loss from past several months.

On December 8, 2019, the government of Wuhan, China, announced that health authorities were treating dozens of new virus cases, identified as corona virus disease 2019 (COVID-19) . Since then, COVID-19, a new strain of

CHAPTER ONE

SARS (SARS-CoV-2), has grown into a global pandemic and spreading across many countries. A highly transmissible respiratory disease, COVID-19 spreads through contact with other infected individuals, with symptoms such as fever, cough, and breathing problems. Transmission can also occur from asymptomatic individuals, with up to 40% of infected persons remaining asymptomatic. Other factors that facilitate infection include

(1) Speed and efficiency of COVID-19 transmission;

(2) Airborne transmission;

(3) Close contact between infected and non-infected individuals;

(4) Vulnerability of immune compromised individuals with specific underlying health conditions (e.g., hypertension, diabetes, cardiovascular disease, respiratory problems);

(5) Susceptibility of persons over 65; and

(6) Contact with persons who have traveled to locations with a high number of cases.

CHAPTER ONE

Critical global responses to control the spreading of the COVID-19 pandemic have included travel restrictions, shelter-in-place and social distancing orders. Most countries around the world have imposed partial or complete border closures, with travel bans affecting the majority of the world's population. With millions suddenly unemployed, uncertainty over economic recovery, and global fears of continuing COVID-19 spread and its future waves, the hospitality industry was among the first industries affected, and it will probably be among the last industries to recover. On 20 January 2020, the United States reported its first COVID-19 confirmed case. In February and through March 2020, the pandemic began to exact unprecedented economic and social consequences. Since public health concerns started to escalate in mid-February 2020, U.S. hotels have lost room revenues. As of 3 June 2020, six out of ten hotel rooms remain empty across the country. Since August 2020, almost half of the hotel industry employees are still not working, and five out of ten rooms are empty.

Hospitality, which was rather a part of the culture, emerged as a huge business opportunity. A lot of people started building hotels and they incorporated more and more

CHAPTER ONE

facilities. Innovations in transportation systems enabled more and more people to travel. Some people saw the opportunity and jumped into the hotel business. That is why in the early to mid 20th Century, a lot of giant hotel chains started doing their business. The industry had become more competitive than ever. In the year 1919, Conard Hilton opened his first hotel in Texas. Later on, Conard also bought the Ellsworth Statler's chain of hotels in the year 1954. Marriot (est. 1927), Sheraton (est. 1937) and Hyatt (est. in 1957) also emerged as giant players in the industry.

Cars became extremely popular in the mid 20th century. Intercity traveling became more convenient because of the well-connected network of roads. These factors favored the growth of Motels. The word motel is made up of "Motor and Hotel". Motels were small 10×10 Ft wooden cabins for the travelers to take rest during the night journeys. These motels were built alongside the main highways to host more and more people who might want to take rest for a few hours or stay overnight during their journey. The concept of the motel was well received and they grew exponentially in numbers in a later stage. The motels were affordable and convenient and that is the reason why the concept of Motels was well received.

CHAPTER ONE

While it all started with providing only a place for sleeping, the traditional hospitality industry has evolved to become what we see today. Despite all the changes the industry saw, the customer has always been the center. It is consistently evolving to become more advanced. In this new century, the hotels reached the new heights, literally. Some of the tallest hotels were built in the 21st century. The technological advancements in the engineering made it all possible. Hotel Fairmont Makkah and Burj al Arab are some examples of it.

Founded in the year 2008, Airbnb opened up a new segment in the hospitality industry. It acts as a marketplace connecting people who wanted to rent their property with those who want to rent it. Since more and more people are traveling for business or for leisure, this gives them a very convenient and affordable option. Also, there has been seen a great hike in the number of solo travelers globally. These solo travelers not much bothered about the amenities. They don't mind sharing spaces. They love meeting and interacting with locals as well as fellow travelers. And that is why concepts of youth hostels and home-hospitality have become new trends. The Internet helps a lot to such hospitality businesses. People can see the availability,

CHAPTER ONE

photos, and reviews from other users. Today, we can browse through all our possible option for staying in any part of the world. We can know about services and amenities. Not only we can reserve our stay but we can also pay in advance. The recent trends in the evolution of hospitality industry favor the construction of hotels which has a classic historic touch integrated with modern services.

The hotel industry has always contributed largely in terms of revenue for any healthy economy. The modern hotel industry in 1960 valued around $3 Billion, which crossed the mark of $25 Billion in the year 1990. These numbers went down due to attacks of 9/11 and recession in the early 2000s. But the industry and its people stood strong and got back its lost pace soon in the new decade. Today, the hotel industry is worth more than $500 Billion providing jobs to 4.5 million people.

However, in the 21st century, hospitality also refers to a portion of the service industry which includes restaurant, hotels, sporting events, entertainment, cruises and other tourism related entity. The hospitality industry is not just important to the society but also to the economies of a

CHAPTER ONE

country, its customers and people seeking employment in such areas of service.

The hospitality industry provides essential services that includes lodging and food for travelers, visitors, whether they are travelling for reasons of necessity, relaxation, leisure or luxury and thus essential to individual customers and to businesses as well.

Another importance of the industry economically is the jobs it created. According to the KTNs Knowledge and Transfer Global Networks, global Survey it revealed that in 2017, the hospitality industry accounted for 313 million jobs worldwide, which translates to 9.9% of total employment and 20% of all global net jobs in the past decade.

The United States Labor Statistics accounted for 16.78 million people working in the hospitality industry and leisure industry as of December 2019. According to the Department of Commerce, the United State travel and Tourism Industry generated over $1.6 trillion in economic output in 2017, supporting 7.8 million United States jobs. Travel and tourism exports accounted for 11 percent of all United States exports and nearly a third i.e. (32 percent) of

CHAPTER ONE

all United States services export. The United States leads the world in international travel and tourism exports and ranks third in terms of total visitation.

The American political history has been strongly distinguished by sectional patterns of behavior, in which the citizen of a particular geographical region, at all levels of society, have felt themselves united against the opposing interests of other sections of the society.

The influence of politics upon the hospitality and tourism sector is of striking effect. Almost unlimited are the ways in which governments impact the administration of hospitality and tourism output, whether by the process of regulating commerce, business and real estate development , cultural and historic care strategies and taxation conduct. The government may also be engaged in spending general funds on the advancement of attractions that are privately owned and operated. The majority of political issues that directly influence the industry emanate at the state level. Within state legislatures, there are two major key means for having industry's concern represented. The first is through finding the entryway of legislators. Industry representatives give detailed report to legislators and their staff the

CHAPTER ONE

significance of hospitality and tourism, and ensure they understand the multitude bills they will consider.

The other more direct means of affecting legislation is to elect officials from the hospitality and tourism industry. These newcomers can educate and influence their legislative peers concerning the importance and weaknesses of the sector, recommend and advocate for legislations beneficial to hospitality and tourism, and alter or prevent legislation that may pose imminent danger to the industry.

The National Restaurant Association estimated that the industry could lose $240 billion in sales by the end of 2020 as the result of the pandemic and predicts that as many as 100,000 locations could close this year. According to a data from the U.S. Bureau of Labor Statistics, employment in food services and drinking places has declined by 2.3 million since February 2020s.

The Heroes Act includes $120 billion for a fund to help revitalize independent restaurants and bars. The Independent Restaurant Coalition in 2020 was lobbying hard for Congress to act quickly, warning that 85 percent of its members could be forced to shut down by the end of the yea 2020r. "Without passage of this restaurant relief program, there is no light at the end of the tunnel," restaurateur Andrew Zimmern told the Washington Post.

Streateries, "ghost kitchens" (kitchens without a storefront preparing meals for delivery only) and the explosive growth of delivery services have helped many restaurants stay afloat. The public is embracing these options, and according to a new survey from Deloitte, the pandemic has accelerated innovation and consumer demand that can help restaurants generate more revenue even after indoor dining can resume safely.

However, new COVID-19 cases have been trending steadily upward since September 2020 and outbreaks are expected to worsen by winter. As federal aid for restaurants hangs in the balance, state legislators are looking for ways to support this important element of local economies.

District of Columbia B23-0942 amends an earlier program to allow restaurant "streateries," extending the registration validity date from April 30, 2021, to Dec. 31, 2021. The intention of the amendment is to assure restaurant owners that investments in the equipment needed to operate streateries successfully will be worthwhile, and to signal

CHAPTER ONE

support for this "vital engine of economic activity" throughout the pandemic.

S72, a Louisiana bill, provides a one-time refundable tax credit to restaurants and bars affected by the COVID-19 pandemic. The credit will equal the amount of any state license or permit fee for any month, or portion thereof, during which they were forced to close due to emergency public health proclamations.

A4765 in New Jersey would make it a third-degree crime, punishable by a fine of $15,000, for a restaurant employee to spit into the food or drink of a law enforcement officer. Employers would be required to suspend a worker charged with this crime and would face civil penalties if they fail to do so.

Pennsylvania H2860, the Hospitality Industry Restoration Act, establishes standards for restoring indoor service during the pandemic. One hundred percent occupancy would be allowed if a county has experienced no incidents of COVID-19 transmission in the past 14 days. Lower rates of occupancy would be determined on the basis of the number of cases per 100,000 residents: less than 10 for 75 percent occupancy, between 10 and 99 for 50 percent

CHAPTER ONE

occupancy, and 100 or more for 25 percent. The bill also sets forward the testing method required to determine case rates.

S9046A, a New York bill, sets limits on the fees that third-party delivery services can charge to restaurants during the declared public health emergency. It forbids such services from charging an amount greater than 20 percent of an online purchase, plus card processing costs, for any combination of fees, commissions, delivery charges, etc. The delivery fee itself may not exceed 15 percent of the cost of an online order. Moreover, delivery services may not reduce compensation to workers as a result of these changes

CHAPTER TWO

CHAPTER TWO

The Thrive & Struggle of the Industry in the Middle of the Pandemic

As the global tourism industry is under sway of the novel Corona virus, and the world still remains with a limited medical capacity to threat the pandemic, despite the creation of vaccines and with its only weapon of precautionary measures, masks, gloves and lockdown, a part of hospitality industry develops new stratagems and applies new tactics to survive the upcoming financial debacle. The almost worldwide lockdown, the brutal impact of mass cancelations caused by the virus spread, and the people's significantly reduced willingness to travel

CHAPTER TWO

produce major upheavals in the tourism economy. The purpose of this study is to systematize the problems and opportunities in the hospitality industry in a pandemic. For this study there has been applied the secondary research methodology with several pieces of literature such as scientific journal articles, preprint papers, government documents, data from global organizations and mass media data etc., but no primary research was conducted. As the phenomenon is still ongoing, there is not yet the significant number of published papers about the opportunities in the hospitality sector. The main findings of the present study are demonstrating that, although this situation makes tourism highly vulnerable, the sector is also in a unique position to contribute to broader and just recovery plans and actions. Significant conclusions are the vulnerability of the travel sector and travel restrictions' effects on hospitality industry, the appearance of a new form of hotel clients - 'quarantine guests', and the need of new survival strategies on hotel industry based on virtualization and domestication.

As the novel corona virus declared a pandemic outbreak, stocks entered the bear market in January 2020, but that decline did not last long and losses were quickly

CHAPTER TWO

compensated. January's and February's declines were, generally, in the Asian markets, especially in China. Despite the strict measures taken into account in China, it was impossible to prevent the global spread of virus, so the stock markets at the global level collapsed. The stock markets further declined when the World Health Organization announced corona virus as a global pandemic on January 30, 2020, and a public health emergency is of international concern. In early March of 2020, the brutal drawdown in global financial markets probably indicates that the global economy is on a path to recession. The pandemic has also led to increases in stock-price volatility, decreases in nominal interest rates, and leads to contractions of real economic activity, as reflected in the real

A rapid spread of the novel corona virus (2019-nCoV) since the first case that occurred in December 2019 in Wuhan, Mainland China, led to a significant reduction in almost all global tourism. Despite the creation of vaccines against the coronavirus and still limited medical capacity to treat the disease the planet seems to face an economic shock by declining export and tourism revenue in a large scale due to restricted export policies and travel bans.

CHAPTER TWO

Tourism, the world's largest service sector industry, has been badly battered, as summer vacations seem to be off the table this year. Covid19 has led to some changes in the touristic consumer behaviors and also has generated risk, uncertainty and fear. The travel and tourism industry came to a complete halt, and the spread of the novel coronavirus demonstrates once again the tourism sector vulnerability to various types of crises, such as epidemics, terror, natural disasters, economic or political crises. The coronavirus has changed the world forever in every imaginable respect and has impacted heavily on the worldwide travel-tourism demand and the hospitality industry, one of the world's largest employers. Correspondingly, the world is now experiencing a temporary de-globalization, and by virtue of the heavy travel restrictions and the suspension of international travel, geographical barriers between places have re-emerged, relative distances have increased and remote places have again become truly remote.

Tourism and hospitality industry thrives on the patterns of visitations and considerable efforts are placed by decision makers to attract visitors to support the sector and enhance the multiplier effect from the industry. But due to the ongoing situation travel restrictions are being observed at

CHAPTER TWO

national and international levels. These travel bans, border closures, events cancellations, quarantine requirements and fear of spread; have placed extreme challenges on tourism and hospitality sectors. Air travel, for instance, has been regarded as an amplifying and accelerating factor for influenza and this segment has witnessed significant curtailments as the need of personal safety and survival has become pivotal. It has also prominently reduced the need for leisure travel and search for hedonistic getaways. Despite the enormous blow, the sector is salvaging resources and ways to remain afloat for now, be it sturdier negotiations with suppliers for mutual sustenance, extensive cost reduction practices, or minimum mandatory period for accommodation bookings when visiting tourism destinations. Correspondingly, accommodation providers have extended support, mostly at some price, for those needing isolation during quarantine period and to those who are involved in treating COVID patients and cannot return to their usual place of residence. These initiatives, for now, indicate the ad hoc coping mechanisms adopted by the industry and appear to remain in place until some stability is attained.

CHAPTER TWO

Several researchers agree that air connectivity is one of the outstanding factors for the tourism development in the global level. In addition, the connectivity brought by air transport is indispensable for the conveyance of people and goods, especially in places where surface transport networks are underdeveloped. Regarding the significance of air connectivity to tourism development, researcher Van Houts in 1984 argues that while mass tourism was possible by other means of transport, the great step forward was achieved by developments in commercial aviation. In other words, international approachability by air is required for developing any tourism destination and for integrating into the worldwide economy. More than fifty percent of all tourists arrive to their destinations by air and with their spending contribute to a 285 million jobs in global air transportation industry. As the worldwide economy is becoming more and more intertwined, the aviation industry is one of the fastest transportation sectors. Commercial airlines transported more than 4.5 billion passengers in 2019 and were expected to generate more than 580 billion U.S. dollars in global revenue in 2020. Air transportation also plays a significant role in tourism, contributing to economic growth, especially in developing countries. The number of global tourist arrivals escalated from 1.32 billion in 2017 to 1.4 billion in 2018; more than a half of tourists chose to reach their destination by air.

The mobility trend at the global level has been rising over the last ten years at a pace that is faster than the global world population growth. However, air traffic flows have been shaped at the regional and national scale by shocks due to economic crises, terrorism or political instability. In addition, the aviation industry has shown strong dependency on the past pandemic outbreaks, such as 2003 SARS or 2015 MERS, with effects that had repercussions at the regional and international scale. Since the corona virus global outbreak, the air industry is undergoing the worst crisis in its history. Business Insider in 2020 said "The impact of this new crisis is more serious than the 9/11 terrorist attacks, the 2008 financial crash and virtually every other history-altering event of the jet age combined".

As reported by the International Business Information System (IBIS) World market research, during the corona virus crisis, the airline revenues lose about $1.6 billion per day, while the aviation industry is typically worth around $825 billion per year in the worldwide economy. While

CHAPTER TWO

landed the air industry cannot generate cash, cannot repay debts and cannot remunerate its own equity (European Investment Bank, 2020). Despite the $58 billion bailout that the U.S. President signed for the aviation industry, CAPA Centre for Aviation alerts that the majority of global airlines are being threatened with bankruptcy due to the current pandemic.

Since early February 2020, fifty-nine airline companies have limited or suspended flights to mainland China, and several other countries such as the United States, Italy, Russia and Australia, have imposed travel restrictions, issued by governments. In the middle of April 2020, the region with the most drastic air traffic reduction globally was the Persian Gulf. Skies are usually congested with wide-body planes serving the three major hub airports there, which then connect to Europe, Asia, and Australia. In recent weeks, Emirates and Etihad have grounded all aircraft, except for a few repatriation flights departing the United Arab Emirates. Qatar continues to fly passengers, while some cargo plans also operate. According to World Aware (2020), the result is an almost-empty airspace, with fewer than fifty airplanes in the skies at any one time, that

CHAPTER TWO

is, around 300 aircraft fewer compared with the previous year.

In the agreement with Official Airline Guide (OAG, 2020), Europe has seen the most extensive contraction of air services of any world region in the period of March-May 2020. While the European countries, including the United Kingdom, France, Ireland, Spain and Italy, are in the process of easing their lockdown conditions, there is a lot of caution and air travel, especially international air travel, continues to be widely restricted. In May 2020, the number of scheduled flights operating was down by 68% compared to the same week of 2019. Furthermore, a lot of countries continue to maintain restrictions on arrivals of air travelers, and also in many markets appear to have stabilized frequency reductions (OAG, 2020).

A recent report suggests that self-isolation could lead to an increase in consumers' searching their future holidays. A survey found that 55% of the US consumers, who usually travel five or more times per year, say they may or will likely purchase a future holiday while confined to their homes during the COVID-19 outbreak, while for frequent business travelers, this figure rises to 61% (E consultancy,

CHAPTER TWO

2020). On the other hand, as specified by the managing director of Hospitality and Tourism International Consulting (HTI Consulting), a possible timeline is between one and two years for the hospitality industry across Africa and the Middle East to reach pre-corona virus levels (Travel Daily News, 2020).

As long as the planet confronts the realities of the worldwide pandemic, there is an opportunity to rethink what tourism will look like for the decades ahead. As hospitality, travel and tourism industries work to recover from the coronavirus crisis, stakeholders' decisions must be grounded on creditable scientific authentication. It is also significant to remember that COVID-19 is not the first disaster of its kind to strike the tourism industry, as in 2003 SARS brought similar effects. A come-back to pre-pandemic growth patterns requires time and depends on the depth and extent of the recession sparked by the novel corona virus.

As businesses catalyze outstandingly both in helping society get through a financial crisis and in creating innovations that shape the society after an emergency, there arises a principal issue: how will the current crisis modify the future society? While it seems hard to predict the future, it is more feasible to develop understanding of what is ahead by analyzing current trends. There have already been observed considerable changes in business practices, and the new global norm is to work from home.

As maintained by Vivek Wadhwa (Foreign Policy, 2020) it is very possible that the next leap forward will come from the virtual reality, which is advancing at a breakneck speed. Activities such as family vacations, business meetings, and leisure activities will increasingly move into the virtual world. In the past decades, e-Tourism, as an area of scientific research, has evolved into a sizeable body of knowledge with the focus on theory and information technology development oriented towards the core issues in tourism.

In short, it can be argued that the coronavirus has accelerated technology trends almost in all the human activities. During the pandemic, technologies are playing an important role as they keep the society functional in times of quarantines and lockdowns. Technological applications such as virtual reality could be significantly useful for promotion strategies of travel destinations after the travel restrictions period.

The hospitality industry is facing an existential crisis, because of the coronavirus spread and the global lockdown. This pandemic creates panic among the public, which contributes to a decrement trend in the tourism industry. As the coronavirus pandemic spreads around the world, many hotels are starting to advertise quarantine packages to guests. Lockdown as an extended practice adopted by a number of countries around the world produces the need to self-isolate for a lot of people. So, several hotels earn money by offering their rooms to people who want to self-isolate due to the spread of the pandemic.

Although this situation makes tourism highly vulnerable, the sector is also in a unique position to contribute to broader and just recovery plans and actions. All over the world, tourism represents development opportunities, promotes solidarity and understanding beyond borders, while domestic tourism also helps to foster cohesion within nations (DUNC, 2020). Chains and boutique hotels alike are offering quarantine packages for those interested in selfisolation (Boutique Hotel News, 2020). Thailand's 'A-

CHAPTER TWO

One' Hotel group is one of the first to offer a self-isolation package within its doors. Bangkok and Pattaya hotels offer full board packages to Thais or other residents seeking to isolate in their hotels, with the various towels, linens and other essential services handled separately by special staff. Rates for these packages have been slashed by 20% as the hotel hopes to gain traffic during an industry wide downturn. With few people traveling right now, Thailand's A-One Hotels Group is employing a new tactic to attract bookings by offering a self-quarantine package at its Bangkok and Pattaya hotels. These full-board packages are targeted at Thais or residents who wish to isolate themselves for 14 days. Meals are delivered to the rooms on trolleys, while dishes, cutlery and bed sheets used by guests in self-isolation will be separated for special handling. A special team will provide daily housekeeping services and help monitor the conditions of the guests under quarantine. Should any of these guests become unwell or develop any coronavirus symptoms during their stay at the hotel, they will be immediately sent to the several hospitals located in the hotel's vicinity, according to the company's director. These packages are priced very competitively with rates slashed by 20%. This risky

CHAPTER TWO

strategy is a first reaction to the challenge that faces the global hospitality industry. This policy seems to be followed by other hotel industry companies around the world; the Dorsett chain of hotels, for example, is selling a two-week or 27-day quarantine package at nine locations, according to the (Wall Street Journal). Guests must have their temperatures checked twice a day to see if they're exhibiting symptoms of the virus, which include fever. They can order meals through online food delivery services or through the hotel's concierge.

Some of Hong Kong's high-end hotels are offering similar packages as well. The Park Lane Hong Kong has a 14-day package that runs for $2,525 and includes three meals a day. In Singapore, some hotels are offering reduced rates to people who need to quarantine. The Fairmont Singapore has a two-week package with a daily rate of about half the hotel's usual rate (The Real Deal, 2020). At the same time, Asset World Corp has announced the temporary closure of five hotels in Bangkok from March 26 to April 15 to reduce the risk of spreading the Covid19 disease. The five hotels closed are: Bangkok Marriott Marquis Queen's Park Hotel, DoubleTree by Hilton Sukhumvit Bangkok Hotel, Le

CHAPTER TWO

Meridien Bangkok Hotel, The Okura Prestige Hotel Bangkok and the Bangkok Marriott Hotel the Surawongse.

In Australia, the Novotel Sydney Brighton Beach (2020), a resort-style 4.5-star hotel, which belongs to Accor Hotels Group, is offering an extended stay discount of 40% off the best available rate for bookings of 14 nights or more. The promotion comes with several perks, including a complimentary room upgrade, an all-inclusive room service package and complimentary Wi-Fi & parking (The Points Gay News, 2020). According to the hotel, self isolating guests will be provided with fresh linens and amenities on request, delivered to their door, and left outside for collection, and also common areas of the hotel are frequently and thoroughly cleaned and disinfected to the most stringent standards, paying special attention to high touch-point areas.

In Switzerland, the 'Bijou Hotel & Resort' made up of repurposed luxury apartments, advertises them as "quarantine apartments" on its COVID-19 service page. Furthermore, this hotel invites all healthcare workers fighting the corona virus and need a break to stay at 'Le Bijou' free of charge (Le Bijou, 2020). This strategy could

CHAPTER TWO

bring future benefits to the company, as the literature shows that relationship marketing, focused on transactional tactics, such as trips and holiday gifts, is possible to be a major instrument for hospitality enterprise development

In South Africa, the National Corona virus Command Council announced risk-adjusted strategy regulations which became effective from March 27, 2020. All domestic and international travel remains prohibited as well as interprovincial movement but in exceptional circumstances. All hotels and establishments remain closed. The only exception is about accommodating international tourists who remain in South Africa, or providing accommodation for essential services people (Official COVID-19 Recourse Centre for South African Tourism, 2020). The only chance to stay open for the hotels in South Africa is to be appointed as quarantine facilities. These accommodations establishments must be approved by the Department of Health as appropriate. In Greece, as well, despite the governmental decision ordering the temporary closure of the country's hotels, those establishments which could offer accommodation to medical and healthcare personnel, armed forces, the EU officials, foreign students, impacted individuals, education staff, asylum seekers or refuges,

CHAPTER TWO

were excluded from the ban. The Hellenic Chamber of Hotels chose fifty among those that expressed interest (Greek City Times, 2020).

Thus, summarizing the above, it can be noted that even in very difficult times of travel restrictions and almost no tourism activity, some hospitality companies exploit the potential of the current situation adapting to a changing business environment, create and provide new packages for the new kinds of clients.

The restaurant business provides ample opportunities for creative people, individuals who love to serve, passionate cooks, budding entrepreneurs, food and wine lovers and gracious hosts, but the restaurant forum for these activities must be treated as any other business if it is to support those dreams and aspirations. Let us look at reasons why people own restaurants:

1. OWNING A RESTAURANT LOOKS LIKE A QUICK WAY TO GET RICH: Some may look at the prices on menus and the cost of that steak in their local grocery store and come to an immediately conclusion that restaurants make money hand over fist. The truth is – if a restaurant is on their game, controlling costs, training staff

CHAPTER TWO

and managing vendors they might make 5-6% net. Unfortunately, most restaurants are not that astute. Restaurants are faced every day with waste, spoilage, theft, rising prices of raw materials and a struggle to convince their staff that every penny counts.

2. IF I OWNED A RESTAURANT I COULD ENJOY HAVING MY FRIENDS VISIT AND BE DAZZLED BY MY HOSPITALITY: Owning a restaurant is where you are able to clearly separate TRUE friends from people who are looking for an opportunity for a "deal". "I know the owner" are four words that every server, bartender and chef dreads hearing.

3. I LOVECOOKING AND HAVE BEEN TOLD BY MANY PEOPLE THAT MY FOOD IS SO GOOD THAT I SHOULD OPEN A RESTAURANT: there is a significant difference between cooking for family and friends and bumping those numbers up to 100 plus every night of the week. If you are the owner – no matter how much you like to cook, you will not have the time to do so, nor should you. Cooking is the fun part – you are an owner now and must dedicate your time to running the business

CHAPTER TWO

(marketing, accounting, hiring and evaluating staff, customer relations, problem solving, training, etc).

4. IT WILL BE SO MUCH FUN BEING A HOST AND WELCOMING GUESTS TO MY RESTAURANT EXPERIENCE: Yes, hospitality can be enjoyable, but first and foremost it is hard work. You must be bright, positive and understanding every minute of every day. Most guests are nice people who appreciate what you and your staff do, but there is a 5% group that will eat up most of your time and energy. These are the ones who always find fault, know more than you, start with a negative attitude and leave with an even greater one. They still need to be served with a smile.

5. I LOVE FOOD AND WILL HAVE AN OPPORTUNITY TO EAT LIKE A KING OR QUEEN EVERY DAY

6. I AM A PEOPLE PERSON AND WILL ENJOY HIRING AND WORKING WITH PEOPLE WHO HAVE DEDICATED THEIR LIVES TO FOOD AND SERVICE: There are many of those dedicated disciples of the restaurant business. These are the people that you should always try to hire and develop, but finding them is

CHAPTER TWO

not always easy. Additionally, no matter how focused a person is on food and service – they will have bad days and guess what: their attitude becomes your problem to solve. As a restaurant owner you will spend as much if not more time on human resource issues than you do on serving the guest.

7. OWNING A RESTAURANT IS A PUBLIC SERVICE THAT GIVES GUESTS AN OPPORTUNITY TO ENJOY AN EXPERIENCE THAT MIGHT NOT BE AVAILABLE OTHERWISE: well, yes – you are in the business of creating an experience and this is what people do seek out. It will be that "experience" that brings them back and builds your reputation as a restaurateur. This is a noble objective, but never lose sight of the fact that you are running a business, not a non-profit organization. The experience is your responsibility, but so is maintaining a financially successful business that allows the experience to continue.

The restaurant business provides ample opportunities for creative people, individuals who love to serve, passionate cooks, budding entrepreneurs, food and wine lovers and gracious hosts, but the restaurant forum for these activities

CHAPTER TWO

must be treated as any other business if it is to support those dreams and aspirations

Because of the fluid situation with COVID-19 and the increasing number of cases in South Carolina and other states, things are difficult on many fronts.

With the initial shutdown, locally owned restaurants faced many issues. There was wasted food due to the short notice of the shutdown. Labor costs continued, which quickly led to layoffs and terminations. Rent and utilities still had to be paid. Government funds designated to help restaurants were difficult to come by and often went to corporations, like Shake Shack and Ruth's Chris, rather than the small businesses they were meant to help. Loopholes prevented some locally owned restaurants from getting financial help as quickly as they needed it.

Once restaurants started to reopen in May 2020, outside dining was OK with social distance, and indoor dining opened soon after with limits on the number of people and required spacing between tables. This challenged many locally owned restaurants because fewer customers were allowed inside. It is hard for an already small 50-seat restaurant to be limited to 15 seats and still pay its bills,

CHAPTER TWO

labor costs and increased food prices stemming from limits in the supply chain.

Unfortunately, as the pandemic continues, the uncertainty of what will happen tomorrow has caused many owners to question how much longer they can stay open without their full capacity of customers.

The biggest challenges right now are;

1. A situation that changes almost daily with the virus and infection rates.
2. Fear of the virus keeping people from going out to eat.
3. The difficulties of keeping restaurants open with such a small number of customers. There are break-even numbers of customers and meals sold that allows restaurants to stay open and many restaurants have not been hitting that "sweet spot" for months.
4. Shortage of staffs. Some restaurants are operating at only 50 percent capacity. Having enough people for shift is a constant struggle.
5. Supply shortages

CHAPTER TWO

Curbside pickup and delivery are a good short-term fix for casual dining restaurants, fast-casual restaurants and limited-service restaurants. However, despite the fact that delivery containers and procedures have improved over the years, it still is not an option for some menus where food temperatures and presentation needs to be precise to ensure quality.

The concern is that many restaurants are not — or were not — set up for curbside pickup or delivery because of their menu and the perish ability of the food, or the fact that they used the restaurant as part of the experience of their brand. For example, Planet Hollywood is a restaurant that uses its environment and movie memorabilia as a part of the overall meal experience.

Some restaurants have very large dining rooms with rent based on the overall size of the restaurant, so switching to curbside and delivery alone is cost-prohibitive. Rent would not decrease, yet the underutilized space does not bring in revenue.

Other restaurants' food would diminish in quality if they delivered it. For example, Ruth's Chris' steaks may not be able to make the 20-minute drive to your house with the

CHAPTER TWO

same level of quality you would get in the restaurant. Upscale and fine dining restaurants count on the level of service and quality of the food as integral components of the dining experience. Picking up food curbside or having it delivered does not compare to the dining room experience.

Food trucks and fast-food restaurants are doing very well, all things considered. With food trucks, the main challenge is to try to keep people socially distanced while waiting in line. Fast-food restaurants are already set up for success in this environment because about 70 percent of their business occurred through the drive-thru before COVID-19. They have mastered the drive-thru, double lane drive-thru and takeout orders. Over the past 20 years, many fast-food restaurants decreased the size of their dining rooms. I believe that fast food and other segments will decrease indoor dining room size even more as time goes on.

Home delivery meal services also have been successful during this time and I believe the trend will continue. The customer gets pre-portioned meals with fresh ingredients delivered to their home, helping them make fresher and healthier meals than they can get from some of the other dining options.

CHAPTER TWO

Many casual dining chains, such as Texas Roadhouse, have set up drive-thru and pickup areas in their parking lots to accommodate the changing requirements.

The restaurant industry is integral to many businesses. Food production, farming, the trucking industry, paper products production, fishing, food manufacturing and virtually everything we do is impacted by changes to the restaurant industry.

With the shutdown of restaurants in March and April, the demand for food products dried up. Products were expiring on the shelves of restaurants, and vending machines were left empty because no one was going out. Grocery stores had limited hours and high demand for certain items such as toilet paper, sanitizing wipes, canned goods and paper products. But in other parts of the food chain, there was no longer a need for things like school system milk cartons, plates for fine dining restaurants and large quantities of cooking oil.

Food cannot be saved indefinitely and therefore production had to stop on many products until more was known about the pandemic and the potential reopening of restaurants. A

CHAPTER TWO

system that normally worked without fail had finally broken down due to the pandemic.

Despite the fact that many people miss going out to eat; the restaurant industry will be slow to recover due to the inconsistencies in following COVID-19 protocol, as well as the moving target we are facing related to regulations and clear guidelines.

The big question remaining is who can survive for the long haul? Large chain restaurants have deeper pockets and a better ability to survive financially. But the small, independently owned businesses have the advantage of being able to change their menu and marketing options much faster than the larger companies.

The biggest challenge right now is not knowing when the pandemic will end. With numbers not showing any sign of decreasing, it is hard to know when, or if, to roll back new regulations. Despite the fact that COVID-19 is not a food-borne illness, the restaurant industry has taken a substantial hit.

One step we can all take to help our favorite restaurants weather this storm is to follow health safety regulations to reduce the spread of the virus and continue to support local

CHAPTER TWO

restaurants by frequenting their pick-up, delivery and socially distant dining options.

CHAPTER THREE

A Recipe for Disaster

The hospitality industry has undoubtedly been affected by COVID-19. During the spring, as lockdown restrictions, shelter-in-place orders and regulations were put into effect, businesses were prohibited from operating. Tourism has continually been impacted and for some hotels, it no longer made sense to continue normal operations. While some industries had it better than others, every single one has felt the effects of COVID-19 to a certain effect. The restaurant and hospitality industry has suffered a particular hard blow

CHAPTER THREE

because of customer shortage caused by the lockdown across the United States.

The restaurant and hospitality industry was possibly hit the hardest. With 7.5 million jobs lost in February 2020 which is nearly 40% of all industry jobs. Unsurprisingly the restaurant industry has lost more workers than any other. That's mainly because it lost the most customers as well.

The layoffs were a tactical move by the restaurant and hotel owners, meant to help them save money. However, this didn't seem to help their situation a lot, because since the beginning of the pandemic , hotels around the United States have lost more than $46billion. At the end of 2020, the industry grossed 50% less than it did in 2019. Industry employees even got it worse. According to the United States Labor Statistics, industry workers lose around $1.7 billion every week in payment and tips. Currently 9 out of 10 restaurants are not operating at full capacity and 65% of owners feel like the situation will remain the same for quite some time.

Another key factor affecting the industry market despite the ease on the lockdown include the decrease in tours and travels as most flight are getting cancelled. Key companies

CHAPTER THREE

of the hospitality industry that are getting affected in the industry include Burger King Corp, Choice Hotels International Inc, Domino Pizza, Inc., Expedia Group, Four Seasons Holdings Inc., Intercontinental Hotels Group PLC, KFC Corp., Marriott International Inc., McDonalds Corp., and Walt Disney Co.

Investors are helping shore up distribution networks by injecting cash into distributors to keep products flowing. Franchisees are being offered more generous payment terms. Every player in the fragile ecosystem is facing a threat, and the industry is pulling together to shore up each part of the system.

"Inventory is going to be a big issue for us," said Thomas Keller whose restaurant group includes the French Laundry Napa Valley and Per Se in Manhattan. "How do we help shore up our suppliers, many of whom are also independent business people, who have been impacted by our closure? Can we use PPP money to pay our suppliers to resupply our restaurants? Like us, their revenue has dropped to zero. How can we make sure they survive?"

Amidst their own pain, restaurateurs are helping others in their communities by lending their physical spaces and staff. Keller's ad hoc restaurant in Yountville, Calif. delivers food to homebound elderly in the area, providing inexpensive, three-course meals for those on unemployment, and uses its facility to host a small food bank.

In conjunction with the nonprofit Rethink Food, New York City's Eleven Madison Park, a three-Michelin-starred restaurant ranked as the top restaurant in the world in 2017, transformed into a commissary kitchen preparing 3,000 meals daily for community members facing hunger. When Orange County, California's public schools closed, Slapfish, a fast-casual seafood chain, immediately launched a carryout, kids-eat-free policy. Other restaurateurs are organizing consortiums of their suppliers to curate subscription boxes of artisanal food sold online.

California declared a state of emergency just as a cruise ship returning to the state from Hawaii was being held off the coast of San Francisco because of reported passengers displaying COVID-19 virus symptoms. Across the country, many consumers are playing it safe and staying home, while there are still others that are continuing normal day-to-day operations. Businesses are also being prudent and

CHAPTER THREE

restricting non-essential travel and activities. Due to the fear of community spread through travel and group environments, one of the industries feeling the most immediate impact is Hospitality/Travel. Resorts and hotels that were booked by excited vacationers and corporate conference-goers are receiving calls to postpone plans or cancel entirely. This is hitting their bottom line in a big way.

When New York Governor Andrew Cuomo blocked enforcement of state and local bans on indoor and outdoor dining in San Diego County on the 14th of December 2020, Superior Court Judge Joel Wohlfeil cited a lack of evidence that restaurants following COVID-19 safeguards, such as occupancy limits and physical distancing, posed a significant public health risk. Politicians and public health officials tend to assume that dining out is an important source of corona virus transmission. But while the evidence is limited and mixed, data from New York, Minnesota, and California suggest that restaurants' role in the epidemic has been exaggerated in at least some parts of the country. New York Governor. Andrew Cuomo, who allowed indoor dining in New York City to resume at the end of September, shut it down again in December. Yet the

CHAPTER THREE

statewide contact tracing data that Cuomo released on December 11 indicate that restaurants account for a very small share of COVID-19 infections. According to Cuomo's numbers, which are based on 46,000 cases since September, just 1.4 percent of infections were traced to "restaurants and bars." That finding is similar to data from Minnesota, where Gov. Tim Walz banned indoor and outdoor dining at a time when 1.7 percent of COVID-19 cases were associated with restaurants. The percentages reported for retailers, gyms, and "hair & personal care" in New York were even tinier: 0.6 percent, 0.14 percent, and 0.06 percent, respectively. But all of these sources paled in comparison with "household/social gatherings," which accounted for 74 percent of the cases.

Cuomo's numbers did not indicate what share of the cases associated with restaurants and other businesses involved customers rather than employees. But data from Los Angeles County—the most populous local jurisdiction in the country, with 10 million residents—shed some light on that question. The Los Angeles County Department of Public Health reports 500 COVID-19 clusters involving three or more laboratory-confirmed cases in nonresidential settings. About 40 of those (8 percent) involved restaurants,

CHAPTER THREE

with the number of cases ranging from three to 12. But all of the cases involved employees rather than diners.

In late October, by contrast, Los Angeles County Public Health Director Barbara Ferrer said "we've...seen somewhere between 10 and 15 percent of our cases being connected to a dining experience." A month later, the ABC station in Los Angeles reported, based on county data, that "restaurants have been linked to less than 4% of corona virus outbreaks in non-residential settings." The difference between "cases" and "outbreaks" may explain some of that gap. But during a press briefing on November 23, Ferrer conceded that estimating the contribution of particular infection sources is an iffy proposition. "I wish we could answer this question," she said. "I think people would feel better if we could say with certainty where people got infected, but we just can't."

California Gov. Gavin Newsom banned indoor dining in Los Angeles County at the beginning of July. In November 2020 the county imposed a ban on outdoor dining that was blocked earlier in December 2020 by Superior Court Judge James Chalfant, who said it was "not grounded in science, evidence, or logic." But by then, Los Angeles County was

CHAPTER THREE

subject to a state ban on outdoor dining that kicks in when a region's available ICU capacity drops below 15 percent.

California Health and Human Services Secretary Mark Ghaly has admitted that the ban was not based on evidence that outdoor dining was playing a significant role in spreading COVID-19. Ghaly said the policy is "not a comment on the relative safety of outdoor dining" but is instead aimed at discouraging Californians from leaving home.

Judge Wohlfeil did not merely question the ban on outdoor dining. He said neither San Diego County nor state officials had presented any evidence that indoor dining, when operated in compliance with occupancy limits and other COVID-19 safeguards, was contributing to the local spread of the disease either.

The San Diego County Health and Human Services Agency reports that "bars and restaurants" accounted for 9.2 percent of "potential community exposure settings" mentioned by people who tested positive for COVID-19 in interviews conducted from June 5 to December 12. But the agency does not break out restaurants as a separate category, and it adds this caveat: "Potential community exposure settings

CHAPTER THREE

are defined as indoor or outdoor locations in which cases came within 6 feet of anyone who was not a household member for at least 15 minutes during the 2-14 days prior to symptom onset, even if the case wore a mask or facial covering. Potential exposure settings are places case-patients visited during their exposure period, not confirmed sources of infection. Persons may have visited more than one location."Most people (54 percent) did not mention any potential exposure settings, while less than 5 percent mentioned "group gatherings." The latter result is surprising, given that New York found "household/social gatherings" accounted for three-quarters of cases. Although people might be reluctant to admit getting together with members of other households, it is not clear why they would be especially reluctant in San Diego County. Maybe New York's contact tracers are simply better at eliciting that information.

The evidence implicating restaurant dining in the spread of COVID-19 is largely indirect. A study of 10 states that the Centers for Disease Control and Prevention published in September 2020, for example, found that people who tested positive for COVID-19 in July were more than twice as likely as control subjects who had tested negative to report

CHAPTER THREE

visiting a restaurant in the two weeks prior to symptom onset. "Exposures and activities where mask use and social distancing are difficult to maintain, including going to places that offer on-site eating or drinking, might be important risk factors for acquiring COVID-19," the researchers concluded.

The study found "no significant differences" between cases and controls with regard to several other possible risk factors, including shopping, spending time in an office, visiting a salon, going to a gym, visiting a bar or coffee shop, attending church, using public transportation, and gathering with others in a home, whether the number of people was fewer or greater than 10. So if this study implicates restaurants, it also seems to absolve those other settings, which many politicians believe are risky enough to justify government restrictions. The finding regarding social gatherings is especially puzzling in light of New York's data.

A PLoS [Public Library of Science] one study published in October looked at interstate differences in case numbers and trends during the early stages of the epidemic last spring. The researchers found that "early social distancing

CHAPTER THREE

restrictions, particularly on restaurant operations, were correlated with increased doubling times"—i.e., how long it took for the number of confirmed cases to double.

Again, these projections counterfactually assume that restaurants and other businesses will operate as they did prior to the pandemic. They also focus on public "points of interest," meaning they exclude the private gatherings that New York found accounted for the vast majority of infections. The fact that restaurants and gyms following COVID-19 precautions accounted for a very small or negligible share of cases traced in New York suggests that such businesses can operate without contributing much to the spread of COVID-19.

Restaurants may be a more significant source of virus transmission in other jurisdictions. In Houston, where restaurants have been allowed to operate indoors at 75 percent of capacity since mid-September (compared to 25 percent in New York City prior to previous ban), 8.7 percent of people who tested positive for COVID-19 have reported restaurants as a potential source of exposure in interviews During her presentation in October, Ferrer claimed that in Louisiana, "25 percent of cases had their

CHAPTER THREE

origins in bars and restaurants." That figure, which was reported in August, excludes outbreaks in "congregate settings" such as nursing homes and prisons, which together account for a large share of infections. Leaving out those sources, according to the latest data from Louisiana, restaurants have accounted for 7 percent of cases.

California Health Line notes that contact tracing varies widely across the country and is woefully inadequate in many places, which makes it hard to get a handle on the role that restaurants (or other sources) are playing in virus transmission. State and local restrictions on restaurants also vary widely, which compounds the difficulty. In the absence of better data, politicians continue to issue edicts that wreck businesses without any confidence that it will do much good.

The City News Service on the 15th of December 2020 reported that 11 senators ask Governor Gavin Newsom. They include senators from both sides of the aisle, including several Southland law makers, are asking Gov. Gavin to move restaurants into "essential" category and permit them to reopen statewide, despite the current public health lockdown.

CHAPTER THREE

" We ask that you immediately reclassify the restaurant industry as criticaL Infrastructure before more damage is done," the letter says. "As it isbecoming obvious to Californians, these essential businesses do more thanSimply provide a place to eat. Restaurants are active participants in local neighborhoods, providing meals to senior citizens and working with foodbanks to feed families struggling to put food on their tables."

The National Restaurant Association said restaurant and food-service sales were $240 billion below its 2020 pre-pandemic forecasts.

The association hopes 2021 will be a year of rebuilding, with trends like off-premise dining and delivery continuing to gain in importance as consumer preferences shift. As at January 2020 Corona virus New York City Restaurants Resume Indoor Service At 25% Capacity

Plastic 'house' tents are set outside a restaurant on the Upper West Side as the city continues the re-opening efforts following restrictions imposed to slow the spread of corona virus on November 01, 2020 in New York City.

More than 110,000 eating and drinking establishments closed last year, either temporarily or for good, and 2.5

CHAPTER THREE

million restaurant industry jobs disappeared, according to a new report that tallies the devastating toll of the pandemic.

"If one looks at the industry in terms of actual sales volume level at the end of 2020, it was down at 2014 levels. In other words, the industry has been set back six years of sales growth," said Hudson Riehle, senior vice president research at the National Restaurant Association, as the trade group releases its annual look at the state of industry.

The report, which surveyed 6,000 operators and 1,000 adults, said restaurant and food-service sales came in at $659 billion last year — that's $240 billion lower than its pre-pandemic projections for the year of $899 billion in total sales.

"2020 was certainly the worst year for the restaurant industry in its history," said Riehle senior vice president research at the National Restaurant Association.

However, he noted that the Covid-19 crisis prompted operators to get creative with new forays into technology and delivery, and many are hoping the second half of 2021 will bring an opportunity for a rebound as consumers have pent-up demand.

CHAPTER THREE

"It's important to think of 2021 as the year of transition," he said. "Recovery for the industry will definitely take time."

The group is projecting a bounce back in food and beverage sales in 2021 to $731.5 billion, still far below where things stood before Covid-19 hit the industry.

The report comes as states like California start to lift restrictions on dining that have limited operators to takeout and delivery, but with the rate of new Covid-19 cases still unacceptably high, the threat of new restrictions lingers even as vaccinations are rolling out.

The report said decades of restaurant experience didn't guarantee success as consumers and state and local governments reacted to the virus. Most of the restaurants that closed for good in 2020 were legacy operators in their communities, according to the survey. On average, these restaurants were in business for 16 years, and 72% of those that shuttered said it was unlikely they'd open another restaurant in the months or years ahead.

"I think all of us have become masters of emotional elasticity, oscillating between hope and despair," said Philippe Massoud, owner and chef at ilili and ilili Box in

CHAPTER THREE

New York City. "This roller coaster of emotion has really been taxing on a lot of us."

Massoud has been in business for 14 years, so he's withstood other economic downturns such as the Great Recession. But his Lebanese-Mediterranean restaurant has been ravaged by the pandemic. Sales were down 80% last year.

Massoud has gone from 165 employees to under 20, and has spent some $70,000 to set up a safe outdoor dining area at his Fifth Avenue location, which he hopes to open soon. At best, he said, it will take two years to recoup his lost sales. At worst, he projects five, as he relies on takeout and delivery.

He received a Paycheck Protection Program loan and is awaiting news on his second-draw loan application. He's also hopeful the government may do more for restaurants. He said without the help he's received so far, he wouldn't have made it. He's most concerned for his workers and eager to see if pent-up demand will bring tourism back to the city.

"We are hoping that our leaders in Washington, D.C., will either convert the PPP for the restaurant industry as grants

CHAPTER THREE

like the Restaurants Act, so that we're not carrying this big ball of liabilities for the next couple of years," he said. "This is going to [need to] be hand-in-hand marching to resurrect and save our cities, our neighborhoods. ... Not doing so would be a catastrophe."

Restaurants that had the most success were able to adapt quickly and innovate to offset the blow of limited operations. Leaning into off-premise sales and using technology to cater to delivery has given restaurants a lifeline. Sales of alcohol to-go were another way to boost sales amid dining restrictions.

Large operators including Starbucks and Chipotle have also continued to rely on to-go and off-premise offerings, and accelerated new store formats like drive-thru and pick-up as the pandemic altered consumer preferences.

The shift is likely for good, as its adoption has happened across all ages, Riehle senior vice president research at the National Restaurant Association said. He added that off-premise traffic pre-pandemic was at about 60%, and that has jumped to about 80% today.

"The convenience-driven market remains a very, very important drive for industry growth," he said.

CHAPTER THREE

In response to this major health issue, resort operators should be planning with their teams for the possibility of two scenarios: 1) if their resort gets infected with the virus; and 2) potential loss of income from diminished travel as a result of the fear (or reality) of virus spread.

With regards to resort health, I came across this helpful guide for the hospitality industry, published by the Department of Health and the Health Protection Agency in collaboration with the Department for Culture, Media and Sport, Visit Britain, the British Hospitality Association and Leisure safe. It provides a lot of common-sense guidance on what you can do to protect your employees and your guests to prevent the spread of flu viruses, such as: washing hands frequently; avoiding touching eyes, mouth and nose; and use soap and water to clean frequently used surfaces.

The information contained in this document can help expand disaster preparedness plan, if these recommended measures aren't built into it already. Most disaster recovery plans include such items as data recovery, property loss, safety and the like, but few cover this type of event. It is important at this point to review the recovery plan in place and add action items in the event a resort is affected, either

CHAPTER THREE

directly or indirectly, by the virus. It is likely that all resorts will feel effects from a decrease in the traveling public, if they have not already.

With regard to the impact on business revenue, resort owners and management should check with their insurance provider, inquiring what their policy defines as "major disasters" and business interruption coverage. For example, according to the Association of State and Territorial Health Officials, a flu pandemic can qualify as a major disaster if it can be considered a natural catastrophe, as that term is defined for purposes of the Robert T. Stafford Disaster Relief and Emergency Assistance Act of 1988 (a.k.a. the Stafford Act). Pandemic influenza and other communicable diseases are defined as emergencies eligible for coverage under the Stafford Act. But let's hope we don't get to that point! The Insurance Services Office (ISO) is an insurance advisory organization that can be a resource as well by providing statistical and actuarial information to businesses.

Another point to consider is that many travel insurance companies may not consider this a coverable event, as a traveler at this point should know of the potential for

CHAPTER THREE

interruption. Resorts should advise their patrons and owners to check their personal travel insurance policies closely, if they have them.

In the short term, resort owners and operators should consider the need for a line of credit to help finance potential inadequate cash flow as a result of the downturn in business. They should also evaluate contracts and prioritize expenditures, cutting out those non-essential costs while trying to monetize inventory through collaborative efforts with neighboring resorts and external service providers and wholesalers. A strategic planning session with key stakeholders on how the impacts might affect the resort is most assuredly a prudent idea. Also, consider offering incentives for people to drive to the resort, such as waiving parking fees or offering discounts. As existing flights and routine travel routes continue to get modified or cancelled, driving as a means of vacation travel seems to be increasing. In the longer-term, expenditures such as major capital projects can be put into abeyance until business begins to pick up again.

Barriers to rebuilding restaurant staffing begin with ensuring the safety of restaurant workers; including the

CHAPTER THREE

need to take into account the ages and pre-existing conditions of current and prospective employees. Restaurant owners must also provide flexibility in scheduling due to childcare needs and the possibility that summer programs and schools may be closed until September or later. Some employees may be reluctant to return because the combination of state unemployment benefits and the federal supplement of $600 per week, that became available until at least August 1 2020, increased their earnings beyond their pre-COVID compensation. On the other hand, given massive unemployment across the nation, if offered a return to work, many may respond positively, concerned about competition for their positions from others seeking work.

Many other restaurant employees, particularly front-of-house tipped workers, earned more while working than receiving unemployment compensation and want to return quickly, but are concerned their income will drop because of less-than-capacity restaurants. Thin industry margins make raising restaurant employee wages nearly impossible absent increased menu prices, which customers hard hit by the crisis are likely to reject.

CHAPTER THREE

More tip jars and prominent space on checks for voluntary staff appreciation contributions will likely be part of restaurants' initial response and, as the economy recovers, menu prices will likely increase. Addressing employees' concerns will be critical—successful restaurateurs know that treating their employees well is the best way for them to ensure that customers' concerns about safety are front of mind in every aspect of service while maintaining high standards for hospitality.

Restaurant implementation of highly variable federal, state, local, and industry operating guidelines may provide confidence, especially to more vulnerable employees. In kitchens, many tightly designed for workers to multitask across different cooking and prep stations, close proximity of workers is of concern. In dining and restroom areas, in addition to wearing masks or face shields, vigilance will be required about cleaning and sanitizing. Management effectiveness at controlling numbers and flow of customers and enforcement of local requirements, such as requiring customers to wear masks when not eating, will impact the perception and reality of employee safety.

CHAPTER THREE

When planning to reopen dine-in locations, operators are identifying new staff positions, including "concierges" to manage entry and employees assigned to sanitize tables, chairs, and restrooms.

Anecdotally, early experiences from states opening up show some people crowding in and refusing to wear masks. Employees who are returning to work have found working conditions, including wearing masks, to be difficult. On Cape Cod in Massachusetts, an ice cream store shut down after one day after teenage staff members were verbally harassed by customers frustrated by long lines and wait-times due to new safety protocols.

Throughout the crisis, restaurants and regulatory authorities have discussed game plans for reopening. Prominent features of these plans include reconfiguring floor plans to enable physical distancing while acknowledging that the oft-cited six-foot rule may not be practical for restaurant dining, utilizing transparent screens or other physical barriers to demarcate table separation, limiting the number of individuals at each table, expanding outdoor seating, health and safety training and staggered shifts for employees, more flexible sick day policies, frequent and

CHAPTER THREE

more rigorous sanitation of all surfaces, touch-free interactions between customers and wait staff, scanning QR codes, single-use menus or contactless, mobile-device ordering and payment, wait staff screening and gloving, and many more.

Guidelines coming from local municipalities and state governments rankle some restaurant operators. While important, Paul Brown said, "it would be nice if those guidelines were a bit more consistently applied. It's a real challenge. We maintain a 32-page document for each of our restaurant chains that contain different parameters for every local municipality. We have to update it nearly every day as things change. It's almost impossible to operate a restaurant like that, and consumers are confused—they don't know how to behave."

Adoption of specific reopening protocols and rigorous and consistent adherence to those protocols will signal restaurants' commitment to customer and employee safety. Although necessary, protocols alone will likely not be sufficient to enable restaurants to meet the most important prerequisite of successful reopening—restoration of customer confidence and trust while maintaining the

CHAPTER THREE

hospitality that is an essential part of the restaurant experience.

Rebuilding that confidence and trust needs to begin with empathy and respect for restaurant employees who will be a new contingent of frontline workers in the fight against COVID-19 as well as the culture carriers and custodians of the restaurant experience. Notes Keller: "The most important thing we are all facing is really the confidence and comfort that our guests are going to have when they come back to our restaurants. That's going to be our biggest hurdle, regardless of the guidelines that the government is giving us. Are you really going to want to go to a restaurant? Until people get comfortable with that, nothing's going to happen."

Until COVID-19 struck, Americans spent more for away-from-home food than for at-home consumption. Restaurants had been the space, in addition to home and the workplace, where relationships have been formed, incubated, and maintained.

What is clear, however, is that for the industry to recover, restaurants must incorporate health and safety measures into a hospitable environment, staffed by well-trained and

CHAPTER THREE

appropriately incentivized employees whose interactions with customers induce them to return.

Consumer polls, conducted in May 2020 by The Washington Post, researchers at the University of Maryland, and Morning Consult, revealed that only 26 percent of Americans believe restaurants should reopen, and merely 18 percent felt comfortable returning to restaurants to eat. In a consumer survey undertaken by Datassential also in May 2020, 75 percent of consumers said safety was more important than visiting their favorite restaurant and 64 percent said they will definitely avoid eating out. Customers with higher risk tolerances have patronized restaurants in states that have begun to reopen but in numbers below those necessary for restaurants to return to profitability. Takeout business continues to grow, but more slowly than hoped.

Consumers are growing weary of cooking all of their own meals. People are resilient in their desire to eat out, and perhaps a bit bored with what's in their refrigerators, so eager to enjoy some of their dining occasions prepared by someone outside their own homes.

CHAPTER THREE

Changes in consumer needs and habits will also affect restaurant usage. Restaurants located in or near office complexes suffered as office occupancy reduced, and will continue to feel the negative impact. Consumers heading to offices may have now grown accustomed to coffee or breakfast at home and in the future may be working increasingly from home. Previously, site selection strategies for restaurants focused on density of both working and residential population—depending on the concept, the relative density of each provided key input for predictive models. For those concepts that placed more weight on the density of working population, such as in urban areas, those selection projections may now be compromised.

Another critical factor that will impact the industry is the sheer number of unemployed Americans overall and the cadence of their return to employment across all parts of the economy. With their real disposable income severely impacted, discretionary purchases from restaurants may be reduced. Moreover, when employed, consumers have less time for meal preparation and turn to away-from-home solutions; when unemployed, free time enables more home cooking.

CHAPTER THREE

With the many regulations imposed on the restaurant industry over the past eight years by the Obama Administration, it's no secret the two didn't exactly share a love affair. Overtime, menu labeling and increased minimum wage regulations were just a few areas where the administration and restaurateurs often butted heads.

Many were hoping things between the industry and the government would be a little less strained under a Donald Trump presidency, but it's safe to say their relationship status could still be classified as "Complicated."

That's because while many restaurant executives, as well as the National Restaurant Association and the National Retail Federation, have shown support for the president Trump's focus on business owners and his nomination of CKE's CEO Andy Puzder as his labor secretary, others are concerned with some of Trump's decisions. Now that a new President has emerged, what lays the fate of the restaurant industry? Only time would eventually tell.

CHAPTER FOUR

The 2009 Recession & the COVID-19 and the Impact on the Hospitality Industry

Disruption from Corona virus has been especially significant for the restaurant industry. The economic slowdown, public markets in distress, supply chains interrupted, tourism coming to a halt, consumers staying at home (which for many translates to a lower disposable income), and huge uncertainty can have long-lived effects for many restaurant businesses. A global economic downturn is impacting businesses across the world, though there is a case to be made for why recessions are ultimately good for the restaurant industry.

CHAPTER FOUR

This reveals the importance of having contingency and crisis plans in place (and, frankly, how common it is for chains to under-invest in the planning process). Ignoring macro risks is riskier than ever. Great corporate planning is about more than financial forecasts — and the more thorough it is, the less a CEO has to keep him or her awake at night.

Between 3.1b–5.4b people in the world are projected to get the corona virus (between 40%–70% of the population) within a year, according to a Harvard University epidemiologist

With a mortality rate of 3.4% (according to the World Health Organization), between 105m–184m people could die from the virus

This death rate is unprecedented since World War II, where some 75m people died — this means that corona virus could be anywhere from 40%–145% more lethal

By comparison, food borne illness affects 770m globally every year (and half of food borne illnesses are estimated to be associated with restaurants), though it kills approximately 500,000 people

CHAPTER FOUR

The average American knows 600 people, which means that on average — 20 people you know may die

Some estimates put global dine-in traffic for full-service restaurants down 89% year-over-year as of March 18th (comparisons are daily)

According to the First National Bank of Omaha (FNBO), 49% of Americans live paycheck-to-paycheck and one-third of the population is a $400 expense away from financial hardship (and having to either borrow or not be able to cover an unexpected cost)

The average foodservice worker, making $10/hour, could lose up to $400 of income — assuming they miss 5 days of work with sickness

At the start of the 2008 financial crisis (September–November '08), the S&P500 restaurant stock index lost $26b in market cap; between February 19–28, 2020 (when the worst of the corona virus fears impacted the market) the loss was $42b

Global stock markets lost $6t in less than a week after the effects of corona virus began to ripple throughout industries

CHAPTER FOUR

According to the National Restaurant Association, there are more than 15.3m restaurant industry employees in the U.S. alone, servicing roughly one million foodservice establishments.

Labor costs represent an average of 30% of standard unit-level revenue for most restaurants; any reduction in revenues has a dramatic impact on the P&L at a unit-level

According to the Travel and Tourism Research Association More than 170m Americans visit some type of eatery every day.

Social distancing recommendations which have been issued by both federal and local governments around the world reduce demand drivers for restaurants (including movie theaters, concert venues, etc.) further impact the industry

Naturally, many Americans will be planning to stay home and restrict dining out, so we can expect to see plenty of empty restaurants, but delivery drivers are not the salvation — rather, they're the pollen bees of the virus, as they fly from delivery to delivery, potentially spreading sickness among families contained in their homes

CHAPTER FOUR

Publicly traded restaurants in the U.S. lost $152b in market capitalization in 42 days (from February 10 to March 23); that's equivalent to: 2.9 times the current total market cap of airlines, or 2.2 times the market cap of hotels, motels, and cruise lines, or 2.5 times the market cap of the clothing industry

This crisis represents an opportunity to develop new ways to mitigate risk. Some solutions will come from new food safety and sanitation programs (food handling, preparation, packaging, etc.), but alternative formats and technological developments — even applications from other industries — will be critical to navigating the waters to find a profitable way forward. Restoring some of the core tenets of hospitality, including empathetic listening, can also be a benefit to the industry in the longer term.

The ruthless march of COVID-19 throughout the globe is first and foremost a human tragedy, affecting the health of hundreds of thousands of people. The consequences of measures taken worldwide to curb the pandemic are having a growing impact on the global economy. This article aims to offer key highlights on the impact being felt by the industry due to factors including, but not limited to, the migratory nature of the hospitality work force and the pause on global travel, tourism and restaurant services.

The unprecedented growth of the travel industry leading into 2020 made 2008 crash look like an anomaly. And while a shocked and stuttering economy under the strain of corona virus might seem overwhelming, it's not unprecedented. In addition to the 2008 crash, the travel industry also experienced fallout after 9/11, SARS, MERS, and Swine Flu before coming back stronger.

Will the same happen with corona virus? Or could the pandemic prove a game-changer in a world that's shuttering its doors to mass travel and tourism? Here's a breakdown of then and now, and what to look for as we navigate through the crisis and towards recovery.

The dictionary definition of a recession is a period when economic output contracts for two straight quarters. The National Bureau of Economic Research's Business Cycle Dating Committee, which makes the official U.S. determination, uses a different approach, considering factors such as inflation-adjusted GDP, employment, industrial production and income. The International Monetary Fund, in designating recessions on a global scale,

CHAPTER FOUR

looks at several indicators including a decline in inflation-adjusted per-capita GDP that's backed up by weakness in industrial production, trade, capital flows, oil consumption and unemployment.

Eventually, yes—recessions follow expansions, and vice versa. The real questions are when the recession hits, how long it lasts and how severe it is.

The so-called Great Moderation, a roughly 25-year period of relative stability around the globe beginning in the mid-1980s, spawned the view that modern-day recessions don't happen without an unexpected economic shock like a sharp increase in oil prices—a cause of U.S. downturns of the 1970s and 1980s—or accumulated imbalances like the massive buildup in the subprime-lending industry that preceded the Great Recession of 2007-2009. A global pandemic that stifles travel, shutters businesses, cancels sports events and sends stock markets into freefall certainly has the potential to be that kind of economic shock.

Economists at Goldman Sachs Group Inc. and Morgan Stanley believe so, and the debate is shifting to how long and deep the slump of the economy as a result of the pandemic will be . The economies of Japan, Germany,

CHAPTER FOUR

France and Italy were already shrinking or stalled before the virus outbreak, and as of March, China was on course for what could be its first quarterly contraction in decades. As the virus spreads, the threat grows of a phenomenon economists refer to as a feedback loop—a vicious cycle in which a country that starts to recover domestically then suffers diminished demand from abroad as other nations succumb, prolonging the downturn. The International Monetary Fund has counted only four global recessions tracing back to 1960, compared to the 11 counted in the U.S. since World War II by National Bureau of Economic Research.

An increasing number of economists believe the almost-11-year U.S. expansion is coming to an end, with many expecting the economy to contract in the second quarter, which ends on June 30. Uncertain times may lead to widespread hiring freezes and job losses—especially among those that work in transportation or the hospitality industry. All of that means the main engine of the U.S. economy, consumer spending, may crumble. Not everyone agrees. The U.S. Treasury secretary, Steven Mnuchin, said on March 15 that he expects the corona virus pandemic will slow growth but not tip the U.S. economy into recession.

CHAPTER FOUR

Its duration, for one thing. The 2007-2009 recessions lasted 18 months, making it the longest since the Great Depression. The recession of 1980, by contrast, lasted just six months. Other measures of a recession's severity are how much the economy contracts and how bad unemployment gets. The worst recessions tend to be those paired with some sort of collapse in the financial system, as happened in the U.S. in 1929 and 2008. Another driver of a recession's severity is how broadly the economy suffers a contraction. The relatively short and mild 2001 recession, for instance, was largely confined to the tech sector, with modest fallout to the rest of the economy.

Back in 2008, the travel industry had been in recovery mode since 9/11. It faced an uphill battle as domestic and international travelers were regaining their confidence in travel. Airline and flight bookings were still struggling from 9/11 and didn't return to previous levels until July 2004. The airline industry wasn't truly profitable again until 2006. When the 2008 Great Recession hit, the travel and lodging industry had recovered for just a few years.

Fast forward to late-2019 and 2020 and the landscape is much different. Before the corona virus outbreak, the

CHAPTER FOUR

travel industry had experienced rapid growth with few signs of slowing down. Research from Deloitte found that US hotel guest bookings grew from $116 billion to $185 billion between 2009 and 2017 with unprecedented growth expectations for 2020 and beyond. Compared to 2008, in 2020 the industry wasn't just licking its wounds, it was roaring.

The travel industry started pivoting during the 2008-2009 recession. Hotels worked to cut their bottom lines and operational costs to wait out the recession. In the following years, the global economy slowly recovered and travel dollars were flowing again, as house-holds regained solid financial footing. Also during this time, we saw smart phones being adopted by the average consumer. All of a sudden, apps made it easier for would-be travelers to find deals. Smartphone's and social media also created the 'travel influencer' trend. Travel was promoted to individuals across every socio-economic class – which helped fuel the expansion.

For the vacation rental industry, 2008 marked a pivotal point: Airbnb was born. The company embraced the uncertain financial climate by marketing to an emerging

CHAPTER FOUR

travel consumer who valued experiences and price points over hotel comfort. In the years after, the tech giant popularized the vacation rental industry to the masses, further boosting the travel industry's recovery. The vacation rental home market grew nearly five times over since 1999.

The recovery was a bit of a mixed bag of variables. Sure, the longest bull market in history helped bring money in the industry. However, advances in technology and social media also played a key role.

Although travel confidence had recovered from 9/11 fears and the world was traveling again, the 2008 crisis dramatically curbed discretionary spending. People lost jobs and the households not affected by layoffs or a repossession realized they had stretched themselves thin on cheap credit. They bootstrapped to deleverage their finances from credit. Back then, the hospitality industry suffered because travel dollars simply weren't there to grab.

In 2020, things appear to be different. For starters, the coronavirus makes it near impossible to travel overseas as more countries are closing their borders and airlines cancel

CHAPTER FOUR

flights. Would-be travelers are sheltering in place, self-quarantining, or avoiding domestic travel to save their health and money. To make matters worse for the travel industry, the lockdown caused an unexpected chain reaction of layoffs, furloughs and salary cuts as businesses struggle with the uncertainty surrounding the pandemic. So unlike 2008, we're not just dealing with reduced spending. Potential guests simply can't travel.

However, the slumps are always accompanied by consistent, upward growth. Of course, the past events weren't crippling pandemics that shut down travel completely. We're also far from being out of the woods with corona virus. However, China is reporting an uptick in travel since COVID-19 has started to abate. People want a break, especially after the stress of living in lockdown. And so, China could offer a glimmer of hope for the travel industry. Just a reminder: we have to be careful with a singular point of data. We could still see roller coaster losses until a corona virus vaccine is developed, and faith in travel is restored.

The grim data and predictions don't indicate that all hope is lost for our industry. Airbnb is lobbying for stimulus

CHAPTER FOUR

packages for hosts and vacation rental property managers to find some relief and stay afloat during the pandemic.

Additionally, the US corona virus stimulus bill could also offer hosts and vacation rental managers unemployment assistance. The bill would protect those hit with a COVID-19 diagnosis, or if their family receives such a diagnosis. Hosts deemed sole proprietors that report vacation rental income could also receive small business loans to cover the interest on mortgage payments, rent, and utility bills.

Platforms like Airbnb are already evolving to the crisis with options like, "More Flexible Reservations" and extended their extenuating circumstances policy worldwide to help soothe travelers' concerns. VRBO is strongly encouraging guests to offer traveler credits or full refunds.

Unfortunately for vacation rental managers that rely on foreign travel, the situation is complicated compared to 2008. Back then, you could find creative marketing tactics to convert the few potential travelers out there. But now, and because of current border closures, there's just no way to get travelers from their home country to your vacation rental.

CHAPTER FOUR

This could create a rippling effect in the industry as hosts and owners find themselves in a real estate predicament. As previously mentioned, the last 12 years were good for the industry. Many vacation rental owners and managers took advantage of the boom to boost their portfolio, often through cheap credit. Unfortunately, without income, those booming portfolios quickly become liabilities. Luckily, we're seeing some North American lenders offer mortgage deferral options which might give owners and managers that little bit of leeway to stay afloat.

Despite the corona virus pandemic, some vacation rental property managers are holding steady during corona virus with long-term bookings. Domestic travelers that aren't under lockdown are looking for a quiet place to practice social distancing and get away from the grim reality of their cities. Wooded cabins and homes in tranquil, remote areas are also a reprieve for travelers. Even in some cities affected by outbreaks, we're seeing bookings here and there with budget travelers looking for a deal. Everything may be closed, but the change of scenery seems to attract them nonetheless.

CHAPTER FOUR

The 2020 vacation rental industry is much more sophisticated and developed than it was in 2008. As soon as people can travel again. Unlike 2008 which relied heavily on booking platforms, they now have direct booking sites, social media, and paid ads. When the recovery happens, the industry will be better positioned to take advantage of increased economic activity. But what will the light at the end of the tunnel look like for the hospitality industry?

Domestic travelers from afar: the global economic downturn will put a pinch on household budgets. At first, we're likely to see local domestic travel (nearby towns or neighboring states), but eventually, we'll see domestic travels going from one coast to another. This will be a sign the average traveler is reconsidering traveling again.

Social media influencers: some of these famous personalities' entire livelihoods depend on their ability to travel. They'll be the first to travel in order to get their businesses back up. Once you see some of them in foreign countries, expect the average traveler to follow a few months later.

Tradeshows and conferences: once we see them sprout back up, it'll be a sign that travel is ready to boom again.

CHAPTER FOUR

The vacation rental industry may be the first to benefit from these travelers as companies restrict spending, limiting expensive hotel stays.

The unknowns related to COVID-19 are vast because the virus isn't just a singular event in time. Infections are hitting remote and vulnerable areas around the world. Even the experts don't know if the virus will come back in waves. There could also be long-term economic aftershocks that we can't predict.

What's for sure is that we'll likely continue to see bills and proposals that help bail out the industry and keep it from irreversible damage. It's safe to assume the travel industry and vacation rental property sector will change forever. However, if past recessions and trends hold true, the end result is the same. Over time and with innovation, the travel industry adapts to a world we can't possibly imagine and finds new ways to thrive

Accounting for the unprecedented travel restrictions, the United Nations World Tourism Organization expects that international tourists went be down by 20% to 30% in 2020, when compared to the last year. To put this into context, they also drew a comparison from the SARS

CHAPTER FOUR

outbreak in 2009, which led to a decline of just 0.4% of the international tourist market. The hospitality industry accounts for 10% of the global GDP.

Disruptions to production, initially in Asia, have now spread to supply chains across the world. All businesses, regardless of size, are facing serious challenges, especially those in the aviation, tourism and hospitality industries, with a real threat of significant declines in revenue, insolvencies and job losses in specific sectors. Sustaining business operations will be particularly difficult for small and medium enterprises.

In India: The hospitality industry is likely to be hit hard. Experts suggest that domestic hotel companies will face a weak Q4 FY20 and a weaker Q1 FY21. March has borne the brunt of many large-scale cancellations across the corporate, MICE and leisure segments. Tier 2 and tier 3 hotel markets in India continue to witness a small erosion in business for now. Occupancies in at least the first half of March 2020 were only partially lower despite the spread of the virus in some states,

In Europe: Industry experts have attempted to predict the effect upon the global hotel industry for 2020, estimating a

CHAPTER FOUR

profit decline of 11-29%. The Kaiser Health News (KHN), which represents bars, cafés and hotels, has said that the emergency measures to limit the spread of the virus are already causing a serious impact. Cancellations have risen by almost half - the KHN survey found that hospitality owners believe that they could make losses of 33% due to the emergency measures put in place by the government.

In China: Compared to 2019 figures, occupancy is down by as much as 68%. As China was the first market to deal with the corona virus, it is also the first to show signs of stabilization. As per data, 87% percent of the country's hotels are now open and occupancy is beginning to rise.

Other countries: Hotels across the U.S. are experiencing unprecedented booking cancellations due to the pandemic, which could eliminate up to four million posts (this accounts for 50% of all hotel jobs in America). The average occupancy in Italy is down by 96% ; the United Kingdom is down by 67%.

The World Travel & Tourism Council warned the COVID-19 pandemic could lead to a cut 50 million jobs worldwide in the travel and tourism industry. As per an Oxford economics study, Asia is expected to be the worst affected

CHAPTER FOUR

and data suggests the industry could take many months to recover.

Following travel bans, border closures and quarantine measures, many workers cannot move to their places of work or carry out their jobs which had effects on incomes, particularly for informal and casually employed workers. Given the current environment of uncertainty and fear, enterprises are likely to delay investments, purchases of goods and the hiring of workers. As per data, the impact on the Indian hospitality industry could render a majority of the people in hospitality in India, jobless. As a result of this pandemic, the Indian tourism industry is looking at pan India bankruptcies, closure of businesses and mass unemployment.

It's never been easy to make money in the restaurant industry. A highly fragmented sector dominated by 70 percent independent owners and operators, the average restaurant's annual revenue hovers around $1 million and generates an operating profit of just 4-5 percent. A financially sustainable business model for small independents is often elusive.

CHAPTER FOUR

So when a crisis of the magnitude of the COVID-19 global pandemic forces restaurants to close, and their revenue drops to zero overnight, things get particularly dire. Unlike the oligopolistic airline industry, where a few large firms can easily band together to lobby for government support, the concerns of restaurant owners and the unique realities and concerns of their industry remain largely unaddressed by government programs designed to help small businesses.

Two months into the pandemic, 40 percent of America's restaurants were shuttered and 8 million employees out of work—three times the job losses seen by any other industry. While some restaurants began reopening in May and June, most featured only takeout, delivery, or outdoor dining options due to local restrictions. The number of diners in June remained down more than 65 percent year over year, and the National Restaurant Association projected an industry revenue shortfall of $240 billion for the year.

Second-order effects of restaurant closures ripple through the American economy, bringing economic pain to farmers, fishermen, foragers, ranchers, manufacturers, and other

CHAPTER FOUR

producers who supply the industry. Equally hit are supply chain partners who move goods across the country.

Coming into 2020, the restaurant industry was thriving. Within a few short months, we now see an industry back on its heels, massively disrupted by an external force so unprecedented it is almost unfathomable.

The severity of this business interruption will continue to endure and be further complicated by the mandate of many local governments that dine-in capacity be limited to 25-50 percent even after restaurants are permitted to reopen. It's still an open question how skittish the American public will be about returning to one of its favorite past times.

As a result, the restaurant industry that emerges from the global pandemic will likely look fundamentally different from the one that existed in early March. How will the COVID-19 crisis change the landscape of the industry, and what do restaurants need to do to survive? And, what should consumers, desperate to return to their favorite restaurants but wary about whether it is safe to do so, expect?

CHAPTER FOUR

Restaurants are universally labor intensive—by any productivity metric they rank among the least productive industries. Labor is required to both produce food in the kitchen and serve to consumers in the dining area. On average, restaurants spend 30 percent of their revenue on labor. With increasing focus on fair wages and legislated wage increases, restaurants may easily exceed that average.

Moreover, restaurants spend roughly equivalently for cost of goods sold (COGS). Independent restaurants typically purchase without the ability to hedge or otherwise lock in pricing, and so are at the mercy of supply-price fluctuations.

A third cost challenge for restaurants is occupancy. Locations are generally leased on a triple net fixed rent basis, occasionally with an additional percentage rent above a specified revenue threshold. Normatively, the industry seeks to spend no more than 10 percent of revenue on occupancy costs, but when entering leases, restaurateurs may well be optimistic about their projected revenue and therefore agree to a fixed rent expense that winds up exceeding that percentage of actual revenue. Other

CHAPTER FOUR

expenses—insurance, credit card processing, marketing, utilities, repairs—mount up.

Assuming adequate working capital upon opening, a restaurant's cash from daily sales is used to pay for supplies previously purchased as well as for payroll, rent, and other expenses. As a result, restaurants typically operate with modest cash reserves. If revenue is disrupted, accrued payables as well as payroll and rent remain to be settled. When JPMorgan Chase sampled almost 600,000 businesses in 12 representative industries, restaurants had the lowest cash buffer.

Various segments of restaurants experienced the crisis differently. Those previously adept at drive-through and takeout service weathered the storm well while others, reliant on dining-in, faced total loss of revenue. At the outset of the crisis, most restaurants had only two to three weeks of operating reserves and those reserves were quickly exhausted. With no end date in sight of mandatory closures, owners moved quickly to furlough or layoff almost all staff, maintaining skeleton crews. Thomas Keller, whose restaurant group includes the French Laundry in Napa Valley and Per Se in Manhattan,

CHAPTER FOUR

employed 1,200 staff in his 13 restaurants, but by mid-March staffing was reduced to 18 employees across all restaurants. Many of whom were long-term employees who felt like family, were furloughed or laid off. Some owners kept their kitchens running solely to provide meals for their staff, fearful they might find themselves unable to feed themselves.

In 2012, the World Economic Forum published an assessment of plausible risks facing the industry. It assessed the risk of pandemics at 11 percent, below both a global energy shortage (19 percent) and labor shortages (17 percent).

As governments mandated closures, many restaurateurs looked to their business interruption insurers for relief. Some were dismayed to find that they had purchased policies with virus exclusions, leaving them uncovered for any losses due to the pandemic. Others, including Keller's group, had coverage for viruses, but their claims were still rejected by their insurers. Along with a number of well-known chefs and restaurateurs, Keller is leading a group named BIG (Business Interruption Group) to wage a legal, political, and public relations effort to mandate payment for

CHAPTER FOUR

policies with no virus exclusion and federal support for payment under policies with exclusions.

A lot of people expressed frustration with government aid programs, such as the US CARES Act and its Paycheck Protection Program (PPP) enacted in late March. Although designed to help small businesses with forgivable loans to encourage keeping employees on the payroll, the program disappointingly failed to address needs unique to the restaurant industry.

For example, eligibility for full loan forgiveness was predicated on using loan proceeds for an eight-week period which ended on June 30 2020 with maintenance of both wage levels and the number of employees at the same level as the comparable 2019 period. Moreover, 75 percent of loan proceeds were required to be used for payroll, at odds with an industry norm of payroll expenses totaling approximately 30 percent of revenue. As of mid-May 2020, restaurants that were open had reduced staffing for takeout and delivery only and the prospects for returning to full employment by June 30 were dim given the constraints imposed by capacity caps.

CHAPTER FOUR

Overall, it may be that the nature of hotels and restaurants will change to leaner and more efficient operations, where a balance between smart and skilled labor is sought after. Due to fear, a large part of the labor force is seeing a domestic-mass immigration, which means a majority of the front line staff at hotels will have moved back to their native areas. Temporary work forces will be the first to shrink, after which the impact will be felt by permanent employees as hospitality companies may be hard-pressed to cut costs. This may lead to a large number of people changing their industry to go where the cash flow is quicker. This global exodus could have a severe impact on the talent pool and may not recover until confidence is reinforced by employers and governments alike. Only through a compassionate approach taken by businesses can the workforce be saved.

With the incumbent lay-offs, it is possible to offer up skilling opportunities to front-line staff, so as to beef up their resumes and increase their probability in securing a job at the time of the market up-turn. This could curb mass-migration to the other industries that could increase the gestation period of the hospitality market's recovery phase by reducing specialized workforce. In this scenario, the

CHAPTER FOUR

training and up skilling of a replacement batch would take a longer time to recover – causing companies innumerable issues. However, innovative methods can be applied to aid the market in boosting and preserving the numbers for when the market finally normalizes.

Creating opportunities for hotel employees to add value to their skill-sets could build confidence in hotel companies, as layoffs can be expected by all major and minor hotel companies. Hyper-local hotels may see the largest number of layoffs due to the popular asset-light model, where large number of operating units, scattered across countries, could be written off all at once. This will bleed out a vast number of hospitality employees into an already difficult market. Individuals who can upgrade their skill sets by way of enrolling in specialty-specific courses could benefit greatly.

Offering routes such as 'Recognition of Prior Learning' opportunities to qualified hospitality front-line professionals could accelerate the process in re-skilling individuals, hence preparing them for roles in hotels and other hospitality-related operations in an environment where lean, yet skilled operations will be required.

CHAPTER FOUR

It is too soon to know when and how the industry and the economy will emerge from the pandemic. But sometimes a major crisis becomes a turning point where industries emerge stronger than before. Companies that focus on the health of their employees and customers, that deliver the meals and dining experience that consumers crave, that manage their capital wisely and look after the corporate health of their business, these are the companies that will uncover opportunities amidst the carnage that this crisis has brought.

Interestingly, during the Great Recession of 2007-2009, the number of eating and drinking locations did not decrease. Why? A large number of newly unemployed people, lacking other employment options, opened their own restaurant businesses. Whether the nature of this crisis has similar effects remains to be seen.

Intensive focus on restaurant and food handling safety will no doubt yield product innovation in packaging, no-touch technology for ordering, paying, restrooms, and even entry and exit from restaurants, and cleaning and sanitizing protocols and products. Air circulation within restaurants will also be examined. This process has already begun. For

CHAPTER FOUR

example, MASS Design Group, a non-profit collective founded a decade ago in response to epidemic outbreaks, is currently working with restaurateurs Jody Adams, Jaime Bissonnette, and Ken Oringer on case studies developing spatial strategies for their Boston and Cambridge restaurants, taking into account, among other things, entry and exit points, delivery and takeout, traffic patterns, physical barriers, and air flow. MASS has made its case studies and guidelines available as open source documents.

The foundational model for restaurant operations will also be examined. How will the future value proposition for consumers reconcile with the financial sustainability of restaurants and the well-being of employees? Will consumers be willing to pay more to help ensure fair wages and restaurant viability overall?

At the same time, restaurants may turn increasingly to technology, including the use of robotics, to improve labor efficiency.

Restaurants will need to address every aspect of fixed costs. Will restaurants be able to structure or restructure leases to make rent a variable expense linked to sales performance?

CHAPTER FOUR

Will consumers' use of takeout, curbside pickup, and delivery during the pandemic carry over to a post-pandemic time? If so, opportunities abound for restaurant operators to reduce brick and mortar dine-in access in favor of ghost or virtual kitchen capability that reduces significantly both capital investment and occupancy costs.

During the crisis, many localities adjusted regulations to permit restaurants to include alcoholic beverages with takeout, curbside, and delivery orders. Consumers have appreciated that convenience, which, if continued, provides an enhanced revenue source for restaurants.

The cost of third-party delivery commissions has been the bane of restaurants pre-COVID. Some localities, including New York City, have sought to cap those fees. The viability of the economics of third-party delivery for both restaurants and the delivery providers' post-COVID will continue to be addressed, with opportunities for lower-cost entrants to emerge.

Prior to COVID-19, the number of restaurants per capita had reached a record high; the industry would likely have seen a culling of locations even in the absence of the crisis. "I think you're going to see a lot of restaurants close and

CHAPTER FOUR

not come back, particularly those chains that don't have strong differentiation in the marketplace," said Pascal. "There's been a lot of capacity and many businesses hanging around for the last decade that probably shouldn't have survived." The elimination of excess capacity could improve profitability and growth potential of those remaining and create white space for new restaurant concepts to emerge.

During the crisis, many restaurants, while closed, have linked their supply chain to their patrons in order to help mitigate the impact of the crisis on their vendors, distributors, farmers, and other suppliers. If that continues post-pandemic, it may help provide more stable demand and pricing for both restaurants and the supply chain.

The trends that have reshaped (and are still reshaping) the industry despite Covid-19

- Digitalized guest experiences & Contactless Technology

Apps, in particular, are increasingly important in the way hoteliers manage the services they provide to their customers and can now control many aspects of the guest cycle and experience.

CHAPTER FOUR

Needless to say, the trend towards digital and contactless services has gained new momentum in 2020. Traditionally customer-facing services are being given an overhaul, thanks to the more widespread use of technology-assisted options, such as mobile check-in, contactless payments, voice control and biometrics.

Consumers who have become accustomed to unlocking their smart phones and laptops using facial and fingerprint recognition will soon come to expect the same convenience in accessing their hotel rooms, say. Unfortunately for the establishments looking to welcome them, however, these upgrades may be costly to install and maintain. If you want to stay ahead of the curve, we recommend you dig deep and make the investment.

- Personalization

Today's guests have grown to expect to be recognized and treated as individuals. Establishments are going the extra mile to personally greet their guests, while tools such as Mailchimp and Zoho have made personalized e-mail marketing accessible to the masses, ensuring highly target audience-specific communications. Far beyond simply adding the customer's name to email greetings, data

CHAPTER FOUR

provides insight into past buying habits, enabling hotels to tailor their offers and promotions and automatically provide similar services to previous stays.

- Experience economy & essentialism

Customers request extreme personalization, unique experiences, and so on. This could very well lead to the death of the travel agent and the rise of the independent traveler.

Travel guilt is real. Minimalism has reinvigorated the otherwise somewhat dusty saying "less is more". Travelers are decreasingly seeking lavish displays of wealth, preferring instead to spend wisely, purposefully and make a positive impact on the world. Unique experiences that give back to local communities in meaningful ways are in demand, as are niche properties, adventurous holidays and relaxation retreats.

- New Hospitality skills & asset management

The asset-light approach has become prevalent in the industry. The separation between the management of operations and real-estate assets now allows hospitality

CHAPTER FOUR

companies to focus on their core business, thus improving efficiencies.

It however induces additional complexity and potential agency problems, explaining the emergence of new types of jobs, such as asset managers.

In addition, new job profiles have emerged following the increasing complexity of the hospitality industry. In parallel, the need for quantitative competencies (for forecasting, budgeting, etc.) has also increased.

- Solo Travelers

In the age of mindfulness, many have embraced the meditative value of spending time alone and venturing out into the big wide world unencumbered, interacting and making friends to whatever degree suits. In an effort to make solo travelers feel comfortable, barriers between hotel staff and guests are being lowered, interior design choices made to evoke a sense of homeliness and an informal atmosphere cultivated. This, along with a less stark divide between guests and locals, encourages a feeling of hotel community.

- Generations X and Y

These new generations have different requirements and needs compared to older generations. A respondent said "Older generations think about hotels and car rentals. Younger generations think about Airbnb and Uber."

- Sustainability

Last but not least, a hospitality trend that is both current and a hallmark of recent years: "sustainability" once again assumes rank no. 10. A natural extension of avoiding disposable plastics, eliminating unnecessary paper consumption thanks to opt-in receipts and reducing food waste, more far-reaching ethical and environmental considerations are shaping decisions made at the hospitality management level. Decisions about things as simple as which towel rails to install during renovations have now have disproportionate repercussions when implemented at scale. Simple eco-friendly switches include replacing miniature toiletries with larger, locally sourced dispensers, choosing ethically produced bedsheets made from organic materials and reducing energy consumption with smart bulbs, etc. Vegetarian and vegan options also harbor well-known environmental advantages.

People are becoming increasingly sensitive to environmental and social issues. A respondent said that this "has to be considered in branding, but beware of green-washers: consumers are now well-aware that window-dressing exists, and they will not buy it."

- Virtual & augmented reality

Following on from the orientation towards visually appealing content, it seems only natural that businesses in the hospitality industry should seek to capitalize on features such as virtual tours, conjuring up a digital environment for consumers to picture themselves in. Videos providing 360-degree views of restaurant ambiance, sweet little café terraces enveloped in greenery or hotel beachfront locations, for instance, are just the ticket to make an establishment stand out this year. As ever, keeping the access threshold low is necessary to reaching as broad an audience as possible with virtual reality material: making content accessible on a variety of devices, without the need for a VR headset.

Once on site, guests should be able to whip out their trusty sidekick – their smart phone – and simply point it at real-world artifacts to summon up additional information.

CHAPTER FOUR

Augmented reality uses graphical or informational overlays to enhance in-situ environments. Once they have downloaded the respective app, guests can use this tool to access restaurant opening times, reviews or interactive tourist information maps or even create user-generated content.

- Automation & technology

This broad, sweeping category speaks to the technological developments that have been seen to reduce waiting times, "outsource" menial tasks to robots and use big data to optimize processes, for example. AI-powered chat bots have proven to be a customer service asset both during the booking process and in responding to the recurring questions on the protective measures pertaining to COVID-19.

Hotel operations more generally are increasingly shaped by the use of management systems to monitor and optimize revenues, customer relationships, property, channels and reputation. Mobile, cloud-based and integrated solutions are especially sought-after. Not to mention the rising importance of integrated messaging, predictive analytics, customer profiling and middleware, which seeks to connect any disparate systems.

It seems what has undeniably been a very challenging situation for many an industry in 2020 has yielded benefits that will be felt for years to come.

Other innovations

Continuous education

Hosting online classes in order to make up for lost time during this period could be highly advantageous for students and institutions. This would allow institutions to re-group and conduct live sessions, ensuring some cash flow and reducing the stress on their respective plans for their cohorts. Modern Learning Management Systems allow the hosting and remote delivery of their content via a simple self-learning approach or a one-to-many classroom style delivery. Technology that is currently available to us allows for a lot of creative methods to ensure continuity in learning that will surely see the light of day as necessity always breeds innovation.

What does the future of hospitality hold? Overall, our faculty suggests the need for hoteliers to properly embrace

CHAPTER FOUR

the above-mentioned trends and understand what's at stakes. Six dimensions came out from our survey:

- Standardization can no longer be the norm.

It is becoming critical to personalize and tailor the services to the needs and preferences of the travelers.

- To create value, focus on niche markets.

More customization and specialization may enable increased value creation for hospitality companies. But be careful, as a respondent said, as this requires to genuinely think about the value proposition of your offer and not "simply branding and rebranding".

- Exploit technology as an accelerator for business.

Technology will be at the core of the hotel experience both in room, before and after the trip. This will lead to the development of new concepts and more innovation in the industry and contribute to the emergence of an ever more individualized offer.

CHAPTER FOUR

- **Social responsibility is a moral and an economic obligation.**

The impact of global warming can today be considered a major risk for both corporations which may lose in revenues and profits and society as a whole. It is thus critical for governments but even more so for corporations to become more sustainable: "not just green, but real sustainable business models".

- **Develop more responsive and resilient business models.**

"Tourism, despite ever-growing flows of travelers, will become riskier and more prone to crises" as the number of travelers steadily continues to grow. This will be accompanied by increased regulation as a response to a disproportional increase in tourist flows in some places (e.g. Venice or Barcelona).

Widespread lockdown and upturned work and childcare schedules have afforded delivery services new importance this year. No longer content with (always) ordering the usual go-to pizza, Chinese or Indian takeaway, however, consumers are now looking to take things up a notch. Not wanting to forego the frills of fine dining, they are now

CHAPTER FOUR

looking to emulate the experience at home. F&B outlets are making this possible by incorporating drinks deliveries and offering extras: atmospheric candles, QR-code playlists and unexpected freebies. Whilst hotels have played their part in supporting local medical needs and turning hotel rooms into alternative work spaces for those tired with working from home.

- **Manage talents actively.**

The days of long-lasting employee retention as well as passive, hierarchical management styles are definitely gone. "Attracting, developing and keeping the right talent into and within the hospitality industry remain a core challenge."

While, as seen above, the consensus revolves around the need for the industry to evolve in order to better adapt to the current environment, some respondents were more 'extreme' and suggested that hotel rooms, as we know them today, "will become a thing of the past".

These respondents refer to the impact of the sharing economy and the tendency of today's customers to avoid traditional hotels. They believe that adjustments in the

CHAPTER FOUR

offer, like the ones listed above, are not sufficient and that the industry has to truly reinvent itself.

This standpoint is reinforced by the increasing importance of technology in the hospitality industry and the power that technology firms are acquiring.

CHAPTER FIVE

The Government Response to the Hospitality Industry during COVID-19

There is an obviously urgent and irrefutable need for social distancing today across the breadth of the United States during the new corona virus pandemic. The sacrifices necessary amid this public health emergency, however,

CHAPTER FIVE

impact some workers and their families and business owners and their families more than others. The U.S. restaurant industry is perhaps the most apt case in point.

Many cities and states took a decisive step to curb the spread of the corona virus by ordering bars, restaurants, and social gatherings, such as weddings and other celebrations often hosted or catered by restaurants, to shutter. There is early evidence that the cities that took this step at the outset are finding success in "flattening the curve" of the outbreak. Closing restaurants and encouraging people to stay home is saving lives, yet millions of workers and owners in the restaurant industry are sacrificing their livelihoods. For those few restaurants and staff still serving food and drink through limited carry-out and delivery services, they are risking their health, too, and will be even more exposed to becoming infected with COVID-19, the disease with no cure spread by the new corona virus, as governments in states and cities begin cautiously to allow sit-down service.

The restaurant industry had been one of the fastest-growing sectors of the U.S. economy, growing by 30.2 percent since the end of the Great Recession of 2007–2009, compared to

CHAPTER FIVE

18.6 percent for the rest of the private-sector economy.1 This growth has occurred in nearly every region of the country, both urban and rural, which makes it unusual in that many other industries tend to grow in single or a few similar regions (think the high-tech sector) and benefit those regions exclusively. The restaurant industry's total revenue in 2019 was $863 billion, representing 4 percent of our country's Gross Domestic Product. It was projected to grow by $36 billion in 2020.

In just the first full month of the pandemic, in March 2020, the U.S. economy shed 714,000 private-sector jobs, 58.5 percent of which were concentrated in the restaurant industry alone (417,300 jobs lost). The National Restaurant Association estimates that "more than 8 million restaurant employees have been laid off or furloughed since the beginning of the corona virus outbreak in March," or about two-thirds of all workers in the sector.4

The industry consists mostly of small businesses. And the restaurant workforce, though large, is disproportionately composed of low-wage workers, thus finding ways to help restaurant workers maintain their jobs or reclaim them as the pandemic lessens its grip on the nation and the

CHAPTER FIVE

economy begins to recover will help mitigate income inequality. Restaurants, though, are very "high touch" services firms—factors that, all together, leave restaurant establishments and their workers almost uniquely vulnerable to the corona virus and COVID-19.

What's more, restaurants are an important part of the fabric of economic life across the country. The restaurant industry consists of many kinds of businesses, from nationwide chains to regional chains to single metropolitan eatery chains to individually owned restaurants and bars.5 In the United States, the industry employs more than 11.8 million workers at more than 657,000 establishments. An estimated 5 million to 7 million chefs and line cooks, dishwashers, hosts, servers, bussers, and bartenders are predicted to lose their jobs during this pandemic. They work primarily at restaurants with less than 50 employees, according to the National Restaurant Association. And most of these restaurants are not chain establishments but individual establishments operated by single owners without dependable and quick access to savings or other financial streams to carry them through a prolonged or even a relatively short recession.

CHAPTER FIVE

In late March, Congress passed the Corona virus Aid, Relief, and Economic Security, or CARES, Act, which provided more than $2 trillion to stimulate our national economy. It includes $349 billion for loans to small businesses backed by the U.S. Small Business Administration and processed by local and national lenders. Despite this historically high amount of financial relief, it was not enough not by a long shot to help the U.S. restaurant industry weather the sharp collapse of its revenues, enable its workers to remain in the workforce, and prepare both owners and workers to help power the economic recovery.

The Small Business Administration's Paycheck Protection Program is out of funds as of mid-April 2020, with "accommodation and food service borrowers" garnering only the fifth-highest amount of stimulus money despite its legions of small business proprietorships. Because the industry already laid off or reduced the hours of most of its workforce prior to the distribution of the stimulus funds from the CARES Act, the financial aid may well have come too late to save most U.S. restaurants or their workers' jobs. The additional $380 billion in rescue funding for small businesses passed by Congress two

CHAPTER FIVE

weeks ago, with stipulations that the funding flow toward less-sizable small businesses may help. But even this new funding is expected to disappear in days.

This issue brief closes with three broad policy recommendations. As the U.S. restaurant sector struggles to find its footing amid the continuing menace of COVID-19 over the course of 2020 and into 2021, policymakers should:

Ensure that any future stimulus funds or other federal support for the industry focus on giving priority to smaller businesses with fewer than 100 employees, which is the firm-size limit that best targets aid to restaurants and gives independently owned businesses a better chance.

Continue to support policies that require businesses to expand "high-road" employment practices to ensure the restaurant industry not only comes back, but also comes back in a way that is more equitable and sustainable

Put in place pandemic economic resiliency plans that can reduce uncertainty in this crisis and better prepare for future public health emergencies that afflict this most "high touch" of high-tech services sectors

CHAPTER FIVE

A sector so important to the economic and social lifeblood of our nation can help power an economic recovery swiftly and sustainably. But this will only happen if federal support ensures these mostly small businesses get a fair shake and their workers gain the workplace protections and more equitable wages they need to become more productive workers and more stable consumers amid the recession and into the economic recovery.

A profile of the restaurant workforce across the United States

To understand the impact that the corona virus pandemic and ensuing recession will have on restaurant workers, it is first critical to understand more about who makes up the restaurant workforce in the United States. Even in the absence of a public health crisis, the restaurant industry employs a relatively low-wage and economically vulnerable workforce, with high job turnover and seasonal or shift work that does not always add up to a full-time livelihood. The age of the restaurant workforce skews younger than the national average, but significant proportions of these workers are over 30 years old (45 percent). Of these older workers, half (50.8 percent) have

CHAPTER FIVE

children in their homes. The industry also disproportionately employs women and people of color.

The median annual income of full-time workers in the restaurant industry is half of that of workers in other sectors. Because average wages in the sector are significantly lower than the rest of the economy, restaurant workers have difficulty putting savings aside for emergency situations. As a result, restaurant workers are more than 2.5 times as likely to live in households with incomes below the poverty line and are more likely to receive government food assistance.11

One aspect of the restaurant workforce that is more difficult to quantify with government statistics is the degree to which workers in the restaurant industry are undocumented immigrants. While the number varies from city to city, it is widely acknowledged that undocumented immigrants are an essential component of the workforce, especially in the lower-paid, back-of-house occupations, including cooks and dishwashers. One study estimated that undocumented workers make up between 8 percent and 10 percent of the entire restaurant workforce, which would be more than 1

CHAPTER FIVE

million workers.12 These workers are especially vulnerable because they are not eligible for Unemployment Insurance.

Additionally, restaurant workers are less likely to receive benefits such as employer sponsored health insurance (46.1 percent versus 71.6 percent for the entire U.S. workforce).13 Overall, the restaurant workforce is clearly more vulnerable than the overall labor force.

The structure of the restaurant industry across the United States

Although the U.S. restaurant industry is large overall, it is made up of hundreds of thousands of individual establishments spread throughout every community in the country. It contains a variety of restaurant types, ranging from single-establishment hot dog stands to Michelin-starred palaces of gastronomy, and from national fast-food chains owned by publicly traded Fortune 500 companies to regional fast-casual, full-service chains often owned by the same big firms.

All restaurants have been hurt by the public health crisis sparked by the new corona virus, but some have been hit harder than others. Therefore, it is important to understand the details of the structure of the restaurant industry. The

CHAPTER FIVE

overall restaurant sector—North American Industry Classification System NAICS 722-food service and drinking places, in U.S. Census Bureau data parlance—includes more than 657,000 establishments across three different industries: special food services, which includes caterers and food trucks, with 44,000 employees in 2018, the most recent year for which complete data are available; drinking places, with 40,000 employees; and restaurants, with 572,000 employees. The restaurant sector is evenly split between fast-food (251,000) and full-service establishments (250,000).

The stay-at-home orders and public health emergency laws enacted by 42 states and the District of Columbia mandated that all in-person dining be shut down. These measures disproportionately hurt full-service restaurants and bars, which have either shut their doors entirely or are scrambling to convert their operations to take-out or delivery only. Fast-food establishments are still allowed to operate drive-through service and take-out functions, but with so many office workers working at home and people encouraged to leave the house as little as possible, these establishments have also struggled.

CHAPTER FIVE

Although no statistics are available yet to understand exactly how much revenue has been lost in these sectors, a recent study shows a drop in hours worked as much as 70 percent. This is probably because small businesses make up the heart of the restaurant sector. Small business owners lack the capital reserves to carry the bulk of their workers amid such a sharp shock to their revenues. This means the vast majority of restaurants with fewer than 50 employees, alongside even smaller establishments with fewer than five, 10, 20, or 25 employees, comprise more than two-thirds of all restaurants.

The bulk of the workforce in the restaurant industry, however, is employed in restaurants that have between 20 and 100 employees. Employment within the full-service industry skews toward slightly larger establishments.

While government data sources yield a detailed picture of establishment sizes and employment, they cannot tell how many establishments are parts of larger firms that may own or operate a chain of restaurants. Chains can either be national or operate in a single metropolitan area, but they are more likely to have the financial strength to recover from the crisis faster. According to data from the business

CHAPTER FIVE

listing database Reference USA, chain restaurants make up approximately 35 percent of all establishments while 65 percent are independently owned, standalone operations.

Yet just two large, publicly traded national chains—Shake Shack Inc. and Ruth's Hospitality Group, Inc, the owner of the Ruth's Chris steakhouse chain—together received nearly $100 million in SBA loans from the Paycheck Protection Program.19 This is indicative of how the ownership structure of restaurants is critical for inequality. Although these two companies quickly returned the funds, the public outcry underscores how small, independently owned restaurants are both more vulnerable in the crisis, and also more important for the economic recovery.

First, given that independent owners make up 65 percent of all establishments, they clearly employ the plurality of restaurant workers. Second, independent restaurants are most likely owned by local entrepreneurs. This means that their profits are re-spent in their local economies, rather than being siphoned off to distant shareholders. Lastly, research has shown that labor standards are higher in cities that are dominated by small, independent restaurants rather than large chains. Anecdotally, restaurants that have been

CHAPTER FIVE

recognized as leaders in promoting high-road business practices tend to be small locally-owned establishments that are deeply embedded in their communities.20

These breakdowns are critical for federal and state and local policymakers to understand, not just to deploy corona virus recession economic relief most effectively but also to ensure the restaurant industry emerges on the other side of the recession with a stronger and more equitable workforce and still robust small-business-owned establishments.

How the federal government assistance can help small businesses and their workers

Given the mandatory closure or partial shutdowns of restaurants across the country, there is a serious possibility that millions of workers will lose their livelihoods and hundreds of thousands of small businesses will close. The restaurant industry, like other high-touch, face-to-face service industries, is important because of its sheer size and its outsized importance in powering a swift economic recovery. The federal government, through the CARES Act, is spending the bulk of the stimulus funds to create a multiplier effect throughout the economy, putting money into the hands of workers, families, and businesses to boost

CHAPTER FIVE

overall economic activity amid the sharp downturn. Shuttered and severely limited restaurant service across the country, however, curtails the potential multiplier effects for local economies.

Gauging how the CARES Act stimulus money flows into the different parts of the restaurant sector nationwide over the course of April and in the following months will be key to grasping how much additional stimulus funding will be needed from the federal government in the legislative package expected to pass Congress. And getting a handle on how many establishments survive and how many workers the remainder of the establishments manage to re-employ will go a long way toward knowing how steep the economy's decline, and how swift its recovery, will be.

The $2.2 trillion CARES Act spending package has several provisions that have the potential to help the restaurant industry. First, nearly all workers and their families will be eligible for the one-time $1,200 stimulus checks (given their low incomes), which will help in the short run with basic expenses such as rent and food—though that funding is estimated to only cover about two weeks' worth of expenses for the average household.21 Workers who were

CHAPTER FIVE

laid off will also benefit from the expanded Unemployment Insurance payments and the relaxation of job-searching requirements to access the UI funds. Restaurant workers accounted for close to 60 percent of all workers who lost their jobs in March, nearly 420,000, according to the U.S Bureau of Labor statistics, and account for the bulk of the 459,000 jobs lost in the broader leisure and hospitality category of jobs. When the data for April are released this week, the number of jobs lost will be especially grim.

Then, there's the stimulus money that is supposed to help these workers' employers rehire them in the coming months. The CARES Act funded $349 billion in forgivable loans for small businesses as part of the Small Business Administration's Paycheck Protection Program. (There also is a smaller pool of funds from the SBA in the form of Economic Injury Disaster Loans—which provide loans up to $10,000 with less paperwork.) Congress then added another $380 billion in funding to the PPP two weeks ago.

The Paycheck Protection Program is the main mechanism for supporting small businesses, including restaurants. Here are the program eligibility requirements for small businesses:

CHAPTER FIVE

They must have fewer than 500 employees.

They must have been open and in business on February 15, 2020.

They must make a "good faith" assertion that they were affected by the corona virus pandemic, which will be straightforward for most restaurants as they were ordered to close their dining rooms by state or local emergency orders.

They need to apply for a loan through a local financial institution.

All of this additional funding is either disbursed or expected to be disbursed quickly, yet understanding the parameters of the program remains important. Restaurants that meet these criteria are eligible to take out a loan for an amount determined by their prior year's payroll expenses during the "baseline" period of February to June 2019. If a business's total payroll for this period was $200,000, for example, then that is the maximum amount of the loan. Businesses can use the money to hire back workers, pay rent, or pay utilities for an 8-week period after the loan is taken out. These amounts would be forgiven from the principle.

CHAPTER FIVE

The goal of the Paycheck Protection Program is to keep people on the payroll. Yet the number of people who will be considered "on the payroll" will be counted at the start of the loan, and the business is not penalized if it has already laid off workers prior to applying for the loan. Any amount that is not used for qualified forgivable expenses—payroll, which must account for 75 percent of expenses, alongside rent and utilities would then be treated as a loan with interest rates not to exceed 1 percent.

This policy is meant to be a lifeline for businesses that were forced to close and incentivizes businesses to maintain an attachment to their workforces so that after stay-at-home orders are lifted, companies can recover more quickly. But, as is quickly becoming clear, these terms for the SBA loans are unrealistic for the vast majority of small business-owned restaurants.

Issues with the Paycheck Protection Program for restaurants

Because the restaurant industry is not monolithic, the loans from the Small Business Administration provided under the CARES Act may not be able to help prevent total catastrophe for individual restaurant owners or companies.

CHAPTER FIVE

While the agency's Paycheck Protection Program can, in principle, be a useful tool for restaurants, anecdotal evidence on the early rollout of the program highlights several potential pitfalls for small, independently operated restaurants. (Actual data on the plight of restaurants since the swift beginning of the corona virus recession last month may not be available and reliable for many months to come, given the chaos the restaurant sector is experiencing and the still unknowable number of restaurants that will fail.)

Still, broad trends are evident. First, the rolling appropriations by Congress for the Economic Injury Disaster Loans and Paycheck Protection Program loan programs are already exhausted , and yet so many restaurants that are independently owned and very small establishments benefited far less relative to size of their economic burdens.

Second, the larger businesses and the franchises of large corporations have an advantage in applying for these loans because they have more well-established relationships with big banks. The program, in its initial phase, operated on a "first come, first served" basis, which means the majority

CHAPTER FIVE

of the funding was likely gone before the smaller restaurants ever succeed at getting the attention of a bank and applying successfully. The second phase sets aside $30 billion for smaller lending institutions so that more of the Paycheck Protection Program funds get to smaller and more ethnically diverse firms. It's unclear at present how well that targeted lending will flow toward small restaurant establishments.

Third, there is a concern that because restaurants have been forced to close their dining rooms, they will be unable to apply these funds to forgivable payroll expenses. The reason: There is little work to be done presently and perhaps not until well into the summer or even longer, depending on how the spread of the corona virus plays out across cities and regions of the nation and how individual state and municipal governments decide when to allow restaurants to fully reopen. Because the terms of the loans require that 75 percent of the forgivable expenses be paid to workers, there is little money available for other expenses.

There is no reason to have, say, five waiters, several bartenders, and a full kitchen staff on the payroll if the only business that can be done is limited take-out ordering. The

CHAPTER FIVE

75 percent rule for employees means restaurant businesses basically become "pass through" entities for their employees to receive salaries provided by the federal government, which was clearly the intent of the law but which leaves restaurants, particularly smaller restaurants unable to pay the other expenses they need to pay to stay in business.

To be sure, the Paycheck Protection Program could at least give restaurant owners the ability to retain or rehire some of their workers and then find other work for their staff on a temporary basis, such as deep cleaning or minor remodeling. But the designated lending still leaves the owners largely unable put the funds to use to not just stay in business but to also prepare their establishments for probably a very different world for them and their employees when stay-at-home orders are gradually lifted around the country.

Helping restaurants reverse the corona virus recession and drive an economic recovery

From the inception of the novel new corona virus and the rest of 2020 spilling over to 2021, the restaurant industry is going to come haltingly back to life around the country.

CHAPTER FIVE

Depending on the course of the corona virus pandemic this spring and summer, public health decisions will determine when restaurants are allowed to reopen. And even then, a wary public may not return in force to restaurants until a vaccine is available and widely administered.

What's more, after restaurants are allowed to reopen, how they are allowed to do so will be important too. Will "safe distancing" limit the number of patrons? Will carry-out and delivery services become more mainstay businesses? Will food preparation lines, as well as front-of-house bar and restaurant seating, have to change for public health reasons? Finally, will restaurants be expected to test and trace their workers and their customers for signs of infection?

At this point of the corona virus pandemic, restaurateurs are only now beginning to think about how to answer these questions. Policymakers should not be just thinking about them but also considering how the ingrained economic inequality across the restaurant industry can be ameliorated now, so that this key sector can help power an economic recovery that is more equitable and thus more sustainable.

CHAPTER FIVE

First, Congress needs to provide additional support to small businesses through an expansion of the Paycheck Protection Program. Given that the current allocations for this program and the Economic Injury Disaster Loan program are all but tapped out, it is essential to provide additional funding. But policymakers should consider adjustments to the program to make sure the aid are better targeted to businesses most in need, especially restaurants.

For restaurants, these reforms might include a prioritization of funding for smaller businesses. This would entail either lowering the employment size cut-off from 500 to 100 employees—more than 90 percent of restaurants have fewer than 100 employees—or setting aside separate funding pools for different business sizes or industry sectors. Congress also could consider loosening or eliminating the 75 percent threshold for payroll expenses for these small restaurants to allow more of them that don't have the ability to add back their front-of-house staff during the stay-at-home orders to stay afloat.

Second, policymakers should continue to support policies that require businesses to expand high-road employment practices. The current crisis in the restaurant industry and

CHAPTER FIVE

the probable restructuring that will need to take place during the recovery is a time to think about what steps can be taken to ensure the restaurant industry not only comes back but also comes back in a way that is more equitable and sustainable.

Before the corona virus recession hit, there were steps being taken by local governments, labor organizing groups and even restaurant owners to improve wages, benefits, and working conditions in the restaurant sector. Hundreds of cities have raised their minimum wages and a few, such as San Francisco, now require businesses to provide paid leave and pay into healthcare plans.

These efforts are helping to demarcate a clear line between low-road and high-road business practices in the restaurant industry. Policymakers should keep this in mind when they will hear calls from some employers to reduce minimum wage requirements in the face of the current crisis. Instead, policymakers should consider how to help restaurant owners and their workers alike prepare for the recovery in ways that improve their resiliency and create more equitable and sustainable business practices.

CHAPTER FIVE

Making the restaurant industry strong and resilient before the next pandemic sweeps the nation

Policymakers need to begin considering how to develop a resiliency plan to ensure that restaurants and small businesses in general can bounce back after future pandemics or epidemics in this most high touch of high-touch services sectors. One thing these twin public health and economic crises reveal is that the United States has no real national strategy or local plans in place for resiliency in the face of pandemics. Communities in hurricane-prone areas have disaster plans on the books. The federal government has encouraged and funded "resiliency" planning in the wake of major hurricanes. And cities such as San Francisco have emergency plans in place in the event of a major earthquake.

This kind of preparation for natural disasters is now a major subfield of research in urban planning. While the new corona virus is not purely a natural disaster, there are no existing insurance programs to help businesses or workers in the high-touch service economy during this type of crisis. Given what we are all witnessing right now, what

CHAPTER FIVE

lessons can we learn that might help avoid some of the painful economic outcomes in future pandemics?

First, Congress may have to deal with the controversy over insurance companies not covering the pandemic as a legitimate business interruption claim. The federal government can act in two different ways to make sure that effective business interruption insurance coverage is in place for the next public health emergency. The government can use its regulatory powers to ensure that pandemics are covered under existing business interruption insurance policies. But if the losses claimed under this program would bankrupt insurance companies, then the federal government could set up and support financially a more robust business interruption insurance program specifically for public health disasters. Under such a program, businesses would pay some amount each year that goes into a pool for a time when a public health emergency forces them to close. Insurance carriers would be backed by the federal government, which already backs the national flood insurance program.

Second, policymakers need clearly defined and communicated government plans at the state and local

CHAPTER FIVE

levels in place for the next pandemic. Public health policymakers need to develop guidelines for when businesses in the services sector are expected to shutter their doors should they find themselves trying to get ahead of the curve of a future nascent pandemic, which, of course, did not happen in 2020 with the new corona virus pandemic. And they need to plan for how and when service-sector businesses can reopen should a future pandemic get ahead of public health officials.

Right now, different states and cities and even regions are trying to game this problem out. If there had been had a plan in place, then there would be less uncertainty among businesses that are wondering now if they should plan for 2 weeks of closure or a year. Clearly, the nature of the public health crisis will dictate the specifics of reopening, but the corona virus experience will likely lead to lessons of what works and what does not.

The U.S. restaurant industry ended 2020 with 2.5 million fewer jobs and more than 110,000 eating and drinking establishments were either temporarily closed or shut down for good, the National Restaurant Association says in a report.

CHAPTER FIVE

Job Losses: The majority of restaurants and bars that closed in 2020 were "well-established" businesses that have been operating for an average of 16 years, the restaurant association said in its report titled "2021 State of the Restaurant Industry." Unfortunately, 16% of restaurants that closed in 2020 had been operating for at least 30 years.

On average, a restaurant that closed employed 32 people, while 17% of restaurants kept at least 50 people employed.

Nearly three out of four restaurant owners who closed their business for good have no immediate desire to open a new restaurant in the months ahead. Only 48% of owners plan on staying in the food industry in some capacity in the months and years ahead.

State of the Industry Today: The restaurant and foodservice industry entered 2020 on track to represent 10% of all payroll jobs in the economy, according to the association. But 62% of fine dining operators and 54% of family dining and casual dining operators indicate their staff levels are more than 20% below normal in early 2021.

Approximately 2 million fewer 16 to 34-year-olds are working in the industry today compared to pre-pandemic levels.

CHAPTER FIVE

"Restaurants were hit harder than any other industry during the pandemic, and still have the longest climb back to pre-coronavirus employment levels," the report stated.

Menu Innovation for 2021: Restaurant owners continue to adapt their menu items to stay relevant in the consumer's mind. Half of casual and family dining operators and 63% of fine-dining operators are offering fewer items on the menu today compared to pre-pandemic.

Consumers want to transact with restaurants that offer a simplified menu with a good selection of comfort foods and/or restaurants with healthier options, according to the report. The availability of alcohol was also highlighted as an important addition to a take-out menu.

Pent Up Demand: There is "no doubt" that consumers want to return to restaurants as it represents an "integral part of our social fabric." Nearly nine out of 10 adults enjoy going to restaurants and 85% of them saying dining out is a better way to spend their time than cooking and cleaning at home.

"Restaurants are the cornerstone of our communities, and our research shows a clear consumer desire to enjoy restaurants on-premises more than they have been able to during the pandemic," said Hudson Riehle, senior vice president of National Restaurant Association's research and knowledge group.

"We've also found that even as the vaccine becomes more available and more social occasions return to restaurants, consumers will continue to desire expanded off-premises options going forward. Both will continue to be important for industry growth. With more than half of adults saying that restaurants are an essential part of their lifestyle, we are confident that, with time, the industry is positioned for a successful recovery" Hudson Riehle, senior vice president of National Restaurant Association's research and knowledge group said.

On the 26th day of January 2021 the National Restaurant Association released its 2021 State of the Restaurant Industry Report, which measures the impact of the corona virus pandemic on the restaurant industry and examines the current state of key pillars including technology and off-premises, labor, and menu trends across segments based on a survey of 6,000 restaurant operators and consumer preferences from a survey of 1,000 adults. The report also provides a look at the path to recovery for chains,

CHAPTER FIVE

franchises, and independents and the year of transition ahead.

Key findings regarding the impact of corona virus on the restaurant industry include:

Restaurant and foodservice industry sales fell by $240 billion in 2020 from an expected level of $899 billion.

As of December 1, 2020, more than 110,000 eating and drinking places were closed for business temporarily, or for good.

The eating and drinking place sector finished 2020 nearly 2.5 million jobs below its pre-coronavirus level.

"As we approach the one-year mark of pandemic-related dining restrictions, we know that virtually every restaurant in every community has been impacted. Amid an ever-changing landscape of dining restrictions and widespread closures, restaurants found ways to adapt, keep people employed, and safely serve our guests," said Tom Bené, President & CEO of the National Restaurant Association. "While we still have a long way to go, we are confident in the resilience of the industry's workforce, operators, suppliers, and diners. The year ahead will be critical as we

CHAPTER FIVE

continue to advocate for much-needed recovery funds to help get our industry back on track. Working together as one, I am confident in our ability to continue safely serving our guests and supporting our communities."

Accelerated Development and Adoption of Technology and Off-Premises

State and local mandates forced operators to make developments to streamline or enhance off-premises and contactless capabilities, and many restaurants across all segments have become more efficient as a result. The pandemic induced a widespread adoption of technology and off-premises use among groups that may not have otherwise engaged in off-premises. Takeout and delivery have become a part of people's routines with 68% of consumers more likely to purchase takeout from a restaurant than before the pandemic and 53% of consumers that say takeout and delivery is essential to the way they live. Other key takeaways include:

64% of delivery customers prefer to order directly from the restaurant and 18% prefer to order through a third-party service.

CHAPTER FIVE

72% of adults say it's important their delivery orders come from a location that they can visit in person—as opposed to a virtual kitchen space.

Legacy Businesses Lost

Of restaurants that closed for good in 2020, the majority were well-established businesses and fixtures in their communities. These operators had been in business, on average, for 16 years, and 16% of them had been open for at least 30 years. Additional data on these businesses include:

They employed an average of 32 people; 17% employed at least 50 people before they closed.

72% of restaurant owners who closed for good say it's unlikely they'll open another restaurant concept in the months or years ahead.

Only 48% think they'll stay in the restaurant industry in some form in the months or years ahead.

Devastating Year for the Restaurant Workforce

The restaurant and foodservice industry were projected to provide 15.6 million jobs in 2020 representing 10% of all

CHAPTER FIVE

payroll jobs in the economy. The impact of the pandemic has caused staffing levels to fall across all restaurant and foodservice segments with restaurant employment below pre-pandemic levels in 47 states and D.C. Key figures on the restaurant workforce include:

62% of fine dining operators and 54% of both family dining and casual dining operators say staffing levels are more than 20% below normal.

There are nearly two million fewer 16-to-34-year-olds in the labor force, the most prominent age cohort in the restaurant industry workforce.

Restaurants were hit harder than any other industry during the pandemic, and still have the longest climb back to pre-coronavirus employment levels.

Streamlined Menus with Comfort Food and Alcohol to Go

While restaurants continue to optimize and streamline operations, their menus prove no exception with 63% of fine dining operators and half of casual and family dining operators saying they have fewer items on the menu than before the pandemic. Consumers are equally influenced to

CHAPTER FIVE

choose one restaurant over another if the restaurant offers a good selection of comfort foods and/or dishes on the healthier side, but the availability of diet-specific fare such as vegan or gluten-free plays a lesser role in restaurant-choice criteria. The availability of alcohol to go with takeout orders, however, is an influence in restaurant choice.

Restaurants are meeting these demands with 1 in 5 family and casual dining operators adding comfort items and 7 in 10 full-service operators adding alcohol to go since March 2020. Consumers are also finding new ways to enjoy their favorite restaurants such as embracing bundled meals, restaurant subscription services, and meal kits. Key data points on food and beverage trends include:

38% of on-premises and 33% of off-premises customers say their restaurant choices will be influenced by whether the menus include the comfort foods they crave.

38% of on-premises customers say healthy choices would impact their restaurant choice.

35% of off-premises customers—with millennial leading the category at 53%—are more likely to choose a restaurant

CHAPTER FIVE

if it offers the option of including alcoholic beverages with the to-go order.

Pent-Up Consumer Demand Remains High

There is no doubt consumers are ready to return to restaurants. Restaurants are an integral part of our social fabric, and 6 in 10 adults say restaurants are an essential part of their lifestyle. In late April 2020, 83% of adults said they were not eating on-premises at restaurants as often as they'd like, a big jump from the 45% reported in January 2020. Baby boomers really want to return to restaurants, beating out Gen Z adults and millennial who say they are not eating on-premises at restaurants as often as they'd like. Additional data that validate pent-up demand include:

88% of adults enjoy going to restaurants and 85% of them say going out to a restaurant with family or friends is a better way to spend their leisure time than cooking (and cleaning) at home.

Nearly 8 in 10 adults say their favorite restaurant foods deliver flavor and taste sensations that just can't be duplicated in the home kitchen.

CHAPTER FIVE

A majority of adults across all generations say they are not eating at restaurants as often as they would like.

"Restaurants are the cornerstone of our communities, and our research shows a clear consumer desire to enjoy restaurants on-premises more than they have been able to during the pandemic. We've also found that even as the vaccine becomes more available and more social occasions return to restaurants, consumers will continue to desire expanded off-premises options going forward. Both will continue to be key for industry growth," said Hudson Riehle, Senior Vice President, Research and Knowledge Group, National Restaurant Association. "With more than half of adults saying that restaurants are an essential part of their lifestyle, we are confident that, with time, the industry is positioned for successful recovery."

"If a restriction goes in place and changes restaurant dining capacity to a more restrictive number, we see an immediate change in the data," said Neil Russell, vice president of corporate affairs at Sysco, during a Jan. 15 webinar hosted by the Center for Food Integrity.

Restrictions are likely to remain in place for months, even as the coronavirus (COVID-19) vaccine begins rolling out

CHAPTER FIVE

across the country. The result is that more than 500,000 restaurants remain in economic freefall, said Hudson Riehle, senior vice president of research at the National Restaurant Association (NRA).

"I think it's important to look at 2021 as a year of transition for the restaurant industry, and because the amount of the loss is so substantial, there's no way in a single year that it can be regained," he said.

Investments in off-premises capabilities will continue in 2021, Mr. Riehle predicted. This is especially true for full-service restaurants, which have had to invest more heavily to build delivery and takeout services during the pandemic.

Restaurants across segments have simplified menus to meet the surge in off-premises orders. Full-service restaurants were most likely to streamline menus, with 63% of fine dining restaurants and 53% of casual dining restaurants offering fewer menu items in 2020, compared to 35% of quick-service restaurants.

On the Border to-go margaritas. The ability to add alcoholic beverages to off-premises orders has been a lifeline for full-service restaurants.

CHAPTER FIVE

"Over half of millennial say it's more likely for them to choose a restaurant based on that option of having alcohol available," Mr. Riehle said. "There are certain municipalities and areas that will allow this to continue in the post pandemic environment."

Full-service restaurants also have upgraded their takeout and delivery packaging to preserve product integrity, while restaurants across segments have found new ways to repurpose shared dishes for individual consumption.

"You're seeing a big demand and increase for single-serve type packaging and single-serve type products," Mr. Russell said. "It provides not only safety during the pandemic, but convenience. People are becoming accustomed to that, they like the individual choice."

Going forward, restaurant operators will need to balance increased demand for single-serve items in off-premises orders with sustainability concerns.

"The communication point is almost more important than actually doing it," Mr. Riehle said. "The greater emphasis on off-premises has turned a spotlight on the inadequacy of certain packaging and delivery concepts in terms of the containers, and the re-engineering of these is already

CHAPTER FIVE

underway. Ordering from restaurant using mobile applications. There's little doubt that several years from now, the availability of the typical restaurant operator to have sustainable packaging, and eco-friendly practices on the off-premises market will definitely be enhanced."

While investments in digital technologies to support off-premises capabilities will be critical going forward, restaurants can expect consumers to return to dining rooms in the future.

"The pent-up demand for restaurant services remains quite elevated," Mr. Riehle said. "This is basically consumers saying they're not using restaurants as much as they would like in their daily lifestyle."

Sysco found restaurant sales improve almost immediately once local restrictions are rolled back.

"When a restriction in a local area changes and improves, there are people who have been waiting to celebrate those anniversaries, birthdays and other events," Mr. Russell said. "We see the data improve dramatically as soon as those restrictions are eased.

CHAPTER SIX

Politics and the Hospitality Sector in COVID Times

When the World Health Organization first called COVID-19 a pandemic on March 11, 2020, few people had any idea what the world was in for. The progression was swift: borders clamped shut, authorities issued stay-at-home orders, and public life ground to a near halt. Most of the world had no experience dealing with an infectious disease outbreak of this scale. The previously unknown virus, now called SARS-CoV-2, could spread through the air, often before (or, in some cases, possibly without ever) causing any symptoms. COVID—though mild for many people—struck down elderly and more vulnerable individuals (and

CHAPTER SIX

occasionally very healthy ones) with a vengeance, launching a wave of fear, suffering and death unlike any in recent memory.

"In the beginning, when this started a year ago, we knew that it was spreading. And we knew that it also was lethal in some percentage of people," says Stanley Perlman, a virologist at the University of Iowa, who is an expert on coronaviruses, a group that includes SARS-CoV-2. "But I don't think we had a full appreciation about how bad it was says Stanley Perlman, a virologist at the University of Iowa, who is an expert on coronaviruses, a group that includes SARS-CoV-2.

"Among the biggest shocks was that the U.S. fared worse than most other countries, with more than 29 million cases and nearly 530,000 deaths as of this writing. "We absolutely can't say that we had the most robust response to the pandemic, up till this point, because we have had a higher death rate per capita than so many other places," says Monica Gandhi, a professor of medicine at the University of California, San Francisco.

As the country raced to react to this new and terrifying scourge, mistakes were made that together cost hundreds of

CHAPTER SIX

thousands of lives. Yet the tireless efforts of health care workers, along with an unprecedented vaccine push, have saved countless others. Scientific American interviewed scientists and public health experts about the biggest mistakes in the U.S.'s response, some of the key successes and the lingering questions that still need to be answered.

Downplaying the danger and sidelining experts. During the pandemic's crucial early days and weeks, then President Donald Trump and other authority figures actively minimized the virus's threat. Trump dismissed it as no worse than the flu and said the pandemic would be over by Easter.

"One thing that shouldn't have been done is people downplaying the infection," says Stanley Perlman, a virologist at the University of Iowa, who is an expert on coronaviruses, a group that includes SARS-CoV-2. "That was a real big problem, because if you let the pandemic get out of control and don't take it seriously, it gets worse." The U.S. Centers for Disease Control and Prevention initially told the media that the threat to the American public was low. When a CDC spokesperson acknowledged in late February that disruptions to daily life could be "severe," the agency was quickly sidelined—and Trump himself became the government's main conduit for COVID updates through his daily briefings. "The Trump administration really tightly controlled what [the CDC] could put out," says Angela Rasmussen, a virologist at the Georgetown University Center for Global Health Science and Security. This muzzling of the CDC and top government health experts made it hard for them to communicate accurate and lifesaving scientific information to the public. Under President Joe Biden's administration, government

Science agencies and health officials have been given renewed respect and independence. But rebuilding public trust in these authorities will still take time.

Slow and flawed testing. The CDC developed its own test for the virus rather than employing a German-developed one used by the World Health Organization. But the CDC test was flawed, causing a deadly delay while scientists worked out the problem. The agency was not designed to produce tests at the scale needed to spot the infections as they silently spread through the population. Meanwhile the Food and Drug Administration was slow to approve tests

CHAPTER SIX

made by private companies, says Caitlin Rivers, an epidemiologist at the Johns Hopkins Center for Health Security. She also says the earliest criteria for getting a test were too stringent—one often had to have been hospitalized with severe symptoms and have recently traveled to a "high-risk" area.

As a result of these hurdles, the virus spread undetected for weeks. By the time testing became somewhat more available, community spread was already rampant in many places, making it difficult or impossible to do contact tracing and isolate people before they infected others. "In this pandemic, things moved so quickly that when you screwed up for two or three weeks, it made a difference," Perlman says.

Testing availability has improved but remains uneven: Some experts have argued for the use of widespread rapid antigen testing, a type that is cheap, does not require sophisticated laboratory processing and could be done at homes, schools or offices. But some scientists still have concerns about the accuracy of these tests, and the FDA has been slow to approve them.

CHAPTER SIX

Inadequate tracing, isolating and quarantines: The timeworn methods of combating an infectious disease—testing people who may be sick, tracing their contacts, and isolating or quarantining those who are positive or exposed—worked for COVID as well. The WHO repeatedly stressed the importance of these measures, and countries that followed this advice closely (such as Vietnam, Thailand, New Zealand and South Korea) succeeded in controlling their outbreaks. In addition to its test problems, the U.S. did not do an adequate job of isolating those who were known or suspected to be infected (or had recently traveled to a high-risk area), tracing their contacts or requiring quarantines for those who were exposed. China imposed extremely strict, city-wide quarantines. Other countries required those who may have been exposed to stay at a government-approved hotel or other facility for a quarantine ranging from a few days to a couple of weeks. Such policies would likely have been harder to implement in the U.S., a nation that prides itself on personal freedoms. But not doing so came at the expense of keeping the virus in check.

Confusing mask guidance: Although face masks are now widely considered a crucial part of stopping transmission,

CHAPTER SIX

U.S. and global health authorities were slow to recommend them for public use. Many countries in East and Southeast Asia, including China and Japan, had normalized mask wearing well before the pandemic—in part because of the SARS outbreak in 2002–2003. Unlike the SARS virus, however, scientists now know that SARS-CoV-2 often spreads before a carrier develops symptoms (and possibly even if they never do). In the early weeks and months of the COVID outbreak, the CDC and WHO stated that face masks were not necessary for the general public unless a person was experiencing symptoms or caring for someone who was. The agencies also initially urged people not to buy high-filtration N95 and surgical masks because they were needed for health care workers and were in short supply because of inadequate government stockpiles. Though perhaps well-meaning, the WHO's and CDC's guidance sent a mixed message about masks' effectiveness—and about who deserves protection. The CDC changed course and recommended cloth face coverings in April. The WHO did not do so until June, citing inadequate evidence of their efficacy before then. The CDC did not respond to a request for comment, and the WHO referred Scientific American to press briefings that

CHAPTER SIX

addressed these issues. In these briefings, experts pointed to a lack of high-quality evidence for mask use. The WHO's director general also stated that, in the absence of other public health measures, "masks alone will not protect you from COVID-19."

Even after health experts reached a consensus that masks were effective, Trump refused to set an example by wearing one in public. Instead he mocked people who wore them, and many of his supporters rejected masks as well. A study in Nature Medicine published online in October estimated that universal mask wearing could have saved nearly 130,000 lives during the fall and winter of 2020–2021. Most states did ultimately institute mask requirements, and Biden has made them mandatory in government buildings and on interstate transit. Yet several states, such as Texas and Mississippi, have just removed mask mandates and other restrictions entirely.

Airborne spread and "Hygiene Theater." early in the pandemic, U.S. health authorities believed the virus spread primarily by direct contact or relatively large droplets from a nearby cough or sneeze—not by far smaller droplets, called aerosols, that linger in the air. As a result, officials

CHAPTER SIX

placed a huge emphasis on washing one's hands and cleaning surfaces. Scientists now believe transmission from surfaces is not the main way the virus spreads and that aerosols play a much larger role. Ensuring proper ventilation and wearing well-fitted, high-quality masks are much more effective ways to reduce transmission than deep cleaning surfaces. Yet the latter—which critics have dubbed "hygiene theater"—continues to be a focus of many offices and businesses.

Structural racism fueled health inequities: The pandemic exposed and exacerbated deep-rooted racial and economic inequities in health and health care. Black and Hispanic individuals and other people of color were sickened with, and died of, COVID at disproportionately high rates. Many people in Black and brown communities had already long suffered from high rates of underlying conditions such as obesity and diabetes as a result of inadequate health care, lack of access to nutritious foods and outdoor space, and higher exposure to pollution. They also comprise a large percentage of essential workers in frontline industries with an inherently high risk of COVID exposure, such as nursing homes, meatpacking plants and restaurant kitchens. The uneven death toll is a wake-up call that far too many

CHAPTER SIX

people of color lack access to preventative health care, as well as protections such as paid sick leave or hazard pay. The public health experts have been tackling this problem for a long time, she notes, adding, "we need to draw on these lessons about underlying vulnerabilities from other disciplines that have such a deep understanding of how communities are affected and how to engage effectively with hard-to-reach communities."

Decentralized response: The U.S. government's structure meant that much of the pandemic response was left up to state and local leaders. In the absence of a strong national strategy, states implemented a patchwork of largely uncoordinated policies that did not effectively suppress the spread of the virus. This caused sudden, massive spikes of infections in many local outbreaks, placing enormous strain on health care systems and leaving no region untouched by the disease.. The Trump administration has been widely criticized for how the pandemic played out here.

The U.S. government's response to the novel coronavirus pandemic has been confusing, inconsistent, and counterproductive. Since February, the data from China, South Korea, and Italy have clearly shown that the virus

CHAPTER SIX

spreads rapidly in areas that do not practice social distancing—and that simple measures to keep people apart can significantly slow the rate of new infections. But the administration of U.S. President Donald Trump did not coordinate any social distancing. And even as acute cases overwhelmed Italy's hospitals, the administration made few efforts to shore up the U.S. health-care system, increase the number of ventilators in hospitals, or make testing widely available.

Many blame these failures on the president, who initially downplayed the severity of the crisis. As at March 4 2020, Trump insisted that COVID-19, the disease caused by the new coronavirus, was no worse than the flu. A week later he claimed that the U.S. health-care system was well prepared for the outbreak. For encouraging the nation to sleepwalk into a crisis, Trump does indeed deserve blame. But even more blameworthy has been the president's assault on U.S. institutions, which began long before the novel coronavirus appeared and will be felt long after it is gone.

By relentlessly attacking the norms of professionalism, independence, and technocratic expertise, and prioritizing

CHAPTER SIX

political loyalty above all else, Trump weakened the federal bureaucracy to such an extent that resembled a "Paper Leviathan," the term the political economist James Robinson use to describe autocratic states that offer little room for democratic input or criticism of government—and exhibit paper-thin policymaking competence as a result. Bureaucrats in these countries get accustomed to praising, agreeing with, and taking orders from the top rather than using their expertise to solve problems. The more American bureaucrats come to resemble autocratic yes men, the less society will trust them and the less effective they will be in moments of crisis like this one.

There was arguably no industry hit harder or faster by the coronavirus pandemic than restaurants. The urgent need for economic relief to keep small—and not-so-small—businesses afloat has turned restaurateurs, chefs, and servers into de facto activists for their own livelihoods.

So the November election was top of mind for owners and workers throughout the industry. While many were more concerned with staying afloat in the week ahead than with policy that won't take shape until January, members of the field were certainly keeping an eye on which

CHAPTER SIX

administration—and which local lawmakers—would be controlling their fates in four months' time.

From takeout-only storefronts to fine-dining establishments, the single universal requirement of eating at a restaurant—that, to consume your food, you need to remove your face mask—has made the industry's reopening during the coronavirus pandemic especially fraught. With restrictions on indoor dining capacity and colder weather in many parts of the country, soon to make outdoor dining thought to be a less likely setting for transmission of COVID-19—less appealing, getting these businesses through the upcoming months is more important to operators than ever.

These restaurant industry professionals—from Top Chef judge and restaurateur Tom Colicchio to the owner of a business shuttered by the coronavirus pandemic—told Fortune.com which issues were most important to them during the election cycle.

The top priority for many throughout the restaurant industry is the urgent need for economic relief. One in four unemployed workers since the beginning of the coronavirus pandemic in the United States have been restaurant

CHAPTER SIX

workers, according to the Independent Restaurant Coalition.

The group, formed to protect the interests of independent owners in the industry, is lobbying for the Restaurants Act, which would provide $120 billion in relief for the industry. Advocates are calling for that legislation in addition to the Paycheck Protection Program, which was available to all sorts of businesses.

The bill was endorsed by operators at all levels of the industry, from mom-and-pop shops up to representatives of national chain establishments. "We're comfortable asking for special treatment," says Sean Kennedy, executive vice president for public affairs for the National Restaurant Association, "because we are uniquely affected."

President Trump has heard from restaurant operators over the past several months, including through a May roundtable. "The Trump Administration had undertaken unprecedented actions to alleviate the burden coronavirus has imposed on the restaurant and hospitality industry," White House deputy press secretary Sarah Matthews said in a statement to Fortune. "From launching the Paycheck Protection Program to providing employers the option to

CHAPTER SIX

defer their payroll taxes, President Trump has been on the front lines providing flexibility and relief for America's restaurateurs throughout this pandemic."

As a candidate, rather than an officeholder, Democratic nominee Joe Biden has not as directly addressed the restaurant industry, but the Biden campaign points out that his proposals to aid small businesses would apply to much of the sector.

"Small businesses, especially restaurants, are the beating heart of our communities, but across the country they are struggling to keep their doors open," Biden campaign spokesperson Rosemary Boeglin said in a statement to Fortune. "The Trump Administration has left them out to dry, siding with big corporations and largely shutting minority-owned businesses out of COVID recovery funds. This translates to millions of jobs lost and far too many businesses permanently shuttered. Joe Biden has a restart plan for small businesses like restaurants to get back up and running and get workers back on payroll."

Economic relief includes not just saving these establishments, but also supporting workers who remain laid off as restaurants downsize or who don't feel safe

CHAPTER SIX

enough to return to work as their employers reopen. People throughout the restaurant industry say they are eager to see more federal relief in the form of unemployment funding.

And in an open letter published September 24, 150 restaurant owners and chefs endorsed Biden in the 2020 presidential election, arguing that Trump's COVID-19 response is what put the restaurant industry at risk.

"The perception of job security has been snatched from us," says Christy Perera, a former maître d' at a New York Michelin-starred restaurant who was laid off in March. Perera relied on the extra COVID-19 unemployment funding, which expired in July. Now she's continuing to look for jobs outside of the restaurant industry, translating her customer service experience to remote customer service positions.

Trump signed off on enhanced $600 weekly unemployment benefits at the beginning of the pandemic and Okayed a $300 weekly benefit following the lapse of the original agreement. Biden has a proposal to overhaul the unemployment system to create "employment insurance" that would place the cost of the program on the federal, not state, government.

CHAPTER SIX

Sean Kennedy, executive vice president for public affairs for the National Restaurant Association is eager to make clear that workers at some of the nation's chain restaurants face these same concerns. "If you're a franchise owner and you own just one restaurant, you face the same issues as any other independent," he says. "If you're an employee at a chain, it doesn't matter what logo is on your vest—your job is not assured."

The federal government, however, can't solve every problem the restaurant industry faces. While government relief would overwhelmingly help restaurants make it through this year, many have been forced to close, in part because of factors that are controlled by state and local lawmakers.

Many restaurateurs have cited struggles with their landlords as one reason why they couldn't remain open. Camilla Marcus, the owner of the restaurant west~bourne in New York's SoHo neighborhood, closed her business in early September after failing to negotiate a percentage-of-sales rent agreement with her landlord. She was forced to make a decision this month because of a personal guarantee that

CHAPTER SIX

would have kicked in, making her personally liable for any missed rent.

"Tenants are being leveraged as a backstop for a pandemic," she says. "Most closures are because tenants and landlords don't see the situation in the same way."

Marcus says she believes that city and state lawmakers should intervene to reform tax structures that incentivize landlords to have a vacant storefront rather than a struggling tenant. These kinds of regulations vary widely by city and by state. In New York City, where Marcus was forced to close her business, Mayor Bill de Blasio has proposed a vacancy tax that would tax building owners who leave storefronts empty for longer than six months. The proposal would require the support of New York's state government. New York's City Council is considering recovery measures that include making sidewalk dining permanent in a bid to boost business.

Deepti Sharma, the founder of the food tech startups FoodtoEat and Bikky, has come to a similar conclusion after working with restaurant owners. Sharma is running for City Council in New York and hopes to address city issues from increasing the minimum wage for tipped

CHAPTER SIX

workers to those landlord and tenant issues. "To me, what's important is, What do these lawmakers believe in? Do they believe in fair wages?" Sharma asks.

But the restaurant industry had political concerns long before the coronavirus pandemic hit. Tom Colicchio, the Top Chef judge and restaurateur, has been a leading voice calling for economic relief for the industry, but also in food policy; he launched a podcast about the subject earlier in 2020.

The top political concerns on the minds of many in the industry? Health care and childcare, Colicchio says. Restaurant owners—like most small-business owners—say they don't have good options for providing health care. Restaurant workers, in turn, often lack access to employer-sponsored plans. Trump has criticized the Affordable Care Act—and has said he has a replacement plan—but has not yet introduced any concrete proposals. Biden has pledged to protect the Affordable Care Act and supports creating a public health insurance option, the likes of which could be accessed by workers in the restaurant industry without employer-sponsored coverage.

CHAPTER SIX

When it comes to childcare, restaurant servers and cooks often work late at night, without reliable options for their children's supervision, Colicchio says. Neither presidential candidate has put forward proposals that would close that gap in care, but both have addressed childcare as an issue. Trump, during his presidency, increased the size of the tax code's childcare tax credit from $1,000 to $2,000. Biden supports an $8,000 tax credit and enhanced funding for after-school programs and community centers.

The other issues that most affect the industry? Immigration policy and climate policy. "It's no secret that a lot of immigrants work in the restaurant industry—most of them on the books, paying taxes," Colicchio says. "We need immigration policy to bring workers in where they have the same protections as anyone else in this country. We need a guest worker program that works."

Biden generally agrees with Colicchio's assessment of the shortcomings of these programs; his campaign's immigration platform notes that the U.S.'s current temporary worker program is "cumbersome, bureaucratic, and inflexible." He pledges to work with Congress to reform the temporary work visa system.

CHAPTER SIX

Trump's immigration policy generally runs counter to the kind of protections for immigrant restaurant and food industry workers that Colicchio describes. The President supports a wall at the U.S.-Mexico border and other restrictions on both authorized and unauthorized immigration. At the onset of the coronavirus pandemic, the White House moved to suspend programs for temporary foreign workers, citing high unemployment within the U.S.

"And it goes without saying that climate affects everything" from food supply to national security, Colicchio says. "If we're not going to have a planet, it doesn't matter what happens to restaurants." Trump's climate policies prioritize "balancing environmental protection with economic growth," and the administration has reversed or weakened several regulations intended to address climate change. Biden's climate proposal aims for the United States to achieve a "100% clean energy economy" and reach net-zero emissions by 2050.

These big-picture issues are hard for restaurateurs to think about when their immediate crisis is so urgent. But policies on health care, climate, and immigration are all on the table

CHAPTER SIX

in November alongside economic bailout proposals—and will be influencing the votes of the people in this industry.

Economic relief, still, remains an important first step. Says Perera: "Restaurants need an injection of capital so when you pull up Seamless in six months, you won't have just McDonald's and Burger King as your options."

Individual US states are in charge of their own public health policy, and despite President Biden urging caution, some are lifting restrictions.

The new President has emphasized the use of face coverings and social distancing until the vaccine rollout can change the nature of the virus, saying he hopes the US will be "closer to normal" by July.

More than 30 states still have a mask mandate in place, which generally requires people to wear a face covering inside private businesses and public buildings.

But in January and February 2021, several states removed their mask mandates, like North Dakota, Iowa and Montana.

Most states have limits on the number of people who can enter businesses such as shops, bars and restaurants, but

CHAPTER SIX

many of these limits are also being relaxed or removed altogether.

In Texas, the state-wide mask mandate and social distancing requirements are no longer in place, and all businesses were able to open at 100% capacity from 10 March.

Mississippi Governor Tate Reeves has also lifted that state's mask requirement, and has now allowed businesses to open at full capacity.

Arizona and West Virginia have lifted capacity limits at restaurants and bars, but are keeping face coverings and social distancing requirements in place. Connecticut will do the same from 19 March.

In Michigan, restaurants and bars are now allowed to operate at 50% capacity, up from 25%.

Louisiana has done the same - allowing 75% capacity up from 50%.

From 19 March, restaurants outside of New York City can operate at 75% capacity, up from 50%. Restaurants in New York City itself must continue to operate at 35%.

CHAPTER SIX

Governors have pointed to plummeting cases and hospital admissions in recent weeks as reasons for reopening.

Across the US, Covid cases have been dropping since the middle of January, but they have begun to level off recently.

New York was the only state to record more cases and California more deaths. Both of these states are maintaining restrictions, and mask wearing is enforced.

Some Pennsylvania restaurant owners say the increase from 25% to 50% indoor dining capacity might not even help all that much once it's too cold for outdoor dining.

They are still asking for the data behind the decisions and say as of today, they haven't seen anything concrete.

The President of the Pennsylvania Restaurant and Lodging Association, John Longstreet, says Governor Wolf's latest announcement about restaurant capacity is a step in the right direction.

"50% is probably sustainable for many; it's sustainable for a lot. That will definitely help the situation."

CHAPTER SIX

Under the current 25% indoor dining restrictions, it was estimated that about 7500 PA restaurants could close and 200,000 people would lose their jobs. Although Longstreet still believes there will be a significant number of restaurants that close permanently in Pennsylvania.

What he says is hard for the industry is that they haven't seen solid evidence that restaurants are contributing to the spread of COVID-19 in Pennsylvania.

"We went into this with the concept that science would drive the decisions and then that seems to have gotten abandoned along the way," said Longstreet.

A recent study by the CDC found adults who tested positive for COVID-19 were approximately twice as likely to have reported dining at a restaurant than were those with negative SARS-CoV-2 test results, likely because people can't wear a mask while eating or drinking.

That study looked at people in about 10 states, not including Pennsylvania.

Still, State Health Secretary Doctor Rachel Levine says the commonwealth does have enough data to make decisions.

CHAPTER SIX

"We had this evidence from our own qualitative and quantitative data, we also had evidence from other states, and we were also following specific recommendations from the white house task force," said Levine.

A look at the DOH data on restaurants

Between July 13th and September 5th, there were 44,830 new COVID-19 cases in Pennsylvania.

Through contact tracing, the PA Department of Health says a little less than half of those cases answered questions about what they did the 14 days before they tested positive.

Of the people who did answer, less than 6% said they went to a restaurant.

Longstreet said, "And it doesn't say they got it from the restaurant."

At this point, the DOH has not provided or confirmed any evidence to prove that's where those people actually contracted the virus.

However, a spokesperson said the decision for dining capacity is not based on just the contact tracing data.

CHAPTER SIX

"Public health isn't looking at one specific thing, but looking at the entire picture. We may have some limited data on specific restaurant and bar information, we also have quantitative data, the anecdotal information, the information that we've gotten from essentially areas that took this action compared to an area that didn't take this action and that scientific analysis to be able to look at what those case studies have shown and what those case studies can translate too," said April Hutcheson, Pennsylvania Department of Health Communications Director.

Longstreet said, it's frustrating for us and it's frustrating for organizations like yours that have been trying diligently to obtain the data too.

Even though a federal judge made a recent ruling that some of the Governor's COVID-19 mitigation plans were unconstitutional, the judge said the decision doesn't deal with the restaurant capacity. "The plaintiffs did not challenge Wolf's occupancy limits, and his ruling does not impact those orders. Nor did the lawsuit challenge the Wolf administration's order requiring people to wear masks in public."

CHAPTER SIX

Los Angeles County's health director acted "arbitrarily" and didn't prove the danger to the public when she banned outdoor dining at restaurants as coronavirus cases surged in November, a judge ruled in a case other businesses may use to try to overturn closures and restrictions.

The county failed to show that health benefits outweigh the negative economic effects before issuing the ban, Superior Court Judge James Chalfant wrote. He also said the county did not offer evidence that outdoor dining presented a greater risk of spreading the virus.

"By failing to weigh the benefits of an outdoor dining restriction against its costs, the county acted arbitrarily and its decision lacks a rational relationship to a legitimate end," the judge wrote.

Chalfant limited the outdoor dining ban to three weeks and said once it expires Dec. 16 the Department of Public Health must conduct a risk-benefit analysis before trying to extend it.

It was the first victory for California restaurants challenging health orders that have crippled their industry. But there was no immediate relief for LA county restaurant

CHAPTER SIX

owners because a more sweeping shutdown ordered by Gov. Gavin Newsom now is in effect.

The California Restaurant Association, which brought the lawsuit, had hoped the judge would lift the ban but still was pleased with the result.

"I do think that this is going to hold the county's feet to the fire when they decide to close down an entire sector of economy," association lawyer Richard Schwartz said. "You can't have a cure that's worse than the disease."

Chalfant's ruling clears the way for restaurants to return to operation when Newsom's order expires.

Coronavirus cases and hospitalizations have reached record levels in Los Angeles County and much of the rest of California. LA County is the state's largest with some 10 million residents and has a disproportionately large number of California's cases, hospitalizations and deaths.

More than 30,000 restaurants in Los Angeles County were closed to diners for months after a statewide shutdown order in March relegated them to offering takeout. They never fully recovered as they tried to navigate ever-changing regulations for reopening that eventually allowed

CHAPTER SIX

dining on patios and makeshift seating areas in alleys, parking lots, sidewalks and blocked-off streets.

Governor Greg Abbott has lifted all COVID-19 dining restrictions, including the statewide mask mandate, effective March 10.

Texas has lifted nearly all the restrictions on dining capacity and social distancing, meaning restaurants in North Texas can return to full capacity, and bars can reopen at 100 percent capacity, effective next Wednesday, March 10.

Gov. Greg Abbott made the announcement during a press conference on Tuesday, Texas Independence Day, nearly a year to the date that first coronavirus case was confirmed in Texas.

Touting the strength of the Texas economy even during the lockdown, Abbott told a group of diners and associates at Montelongo's, a Mexican restaurant in Lubbock, "It is now time to open Texas 100 percent. Everyone who wants to work should have that opportunity, and every business that wants to reopen should be open."

CHAPTER SIX

The new order effectively rescinds almost all of Abbott's COVID-related executive orders from the past year. It removes capacity restrictions from all business, including restaurants, as well as bars, which have been closed in Dallas County since June of 2020. It also removes the statewide mask mandate, an announcement that drew cheers from the crowd gathered at the restaurant.

The announcement leaves in place a policy implemented by Abbott in October that stated that in regions of Texas where COVID-19 cases rise above 15 percent of total hospitalizations over a seven-day period, local governments in that region can implement COVID mitigation strategies, such as requiring masks and enforcing decreased capacity limits. However, Abbott said, "Under no circumstance can a county judge jail anyone for not following COVID orders," and that no penalties can be imposed for failing to wear a face mask under those conditions.

In early December 2020, Dallas County restaurants were required to decrease indoor capacity to 50 percent as part of that plan. Those restrictions were finally lifted, bringing indoor capacity back to 75 percent, on February 17 2021.

CHAPTER SIX

Abbott stressed the importance of personal responsibility in continuing to combat the disease.

"COVID has not, like, suddenly disappeared," he said. "But it is clear that state mandates are no longer needed. Removing state mandates does not end personal responsibility. Personal vigilance is still needed to contain COVID."

Abbott also said private business are free to implement their own covid mitigation measures, such as requiring masks and reducing capacity, but that the state will no longer enforce these rules.

While coronavirus cases in the Dallas area have been slowly declining since the holiday season, although experts have warned against loosening statewide restrictions, especially with new, more contagious variations appearing in Texas.

In a February interview with Propublica, Caitlin Rivers, a computational epidemiologist at Johns Hopkins Center for Health Security, cautioned states against reopening measures.

CHAPTER SIX

"Now is not the time to relax," she said. "When you create the same conditions that allowed the last surge, you should expect the same results."

Texas does have a bigger population than most states, but even in per capita terms it has one of the highest case rates - with about 143 confirmed cases per 100,000 people over the week, according to the Centers for Disease Control (CDC).

There are hopes that fewer people who catch Covid will end up in hospital now vaccines are being rolled out, with the most vulnerable being protected.

The governors of Texas and Mississippi have highlighted their states' successful vaccine rollouts as a key factor in enabling them to fully reopen.

New mutations of the disease, many of which are more contagious that the original strain that infected Americans last year, is of particular concern right now. As of late February, only about 5 percent of Texans had been vaccinated, and it is not yet clear how effective the current vaccines are at preventing the new mutations. Texas still does not consider restaurant employees or other food

CHAPTER SIX

service workers a priority category for receiving the vaccine

The emergence of more contagious Covid variants is also a worry, with the CDC warning they pose a real threat to the country's progress .

The Republican governors of both states made clear that the economy was a major consideration, insisting that with cases dropping and vaccines rolling out, it was time to restore livelihoods and reopen 100%.

New coronavirus strains represent more than half of all current cases in New York City, Mayor Bill de Blasio and his team revealed on the 10th day of March 2021.

One strain, known as B.1.256, which was first identified late last year in the city, made up 39 percent of virus samples from the five boroughs over the past week, Dr Jay Varma, senior advisor for public health, said during the mayor's press conference. That is up from 31 per cent of samples a week earlier.

Over the same time period, the proportion of the B.1.1.7 strain, which was first identified late last year in the UK, had risen to 12 per cent of genomic samples, up from 8 per

CHAPTER SIX

cent a week ago, Varma said. There were no additional cases of strains that had been first identified in Brazil and South Africa.

Preliminary analysis indicated the B.1.256 strain was more infectious than the original coronavirus, but did not appear to cause more severe illness or reduce the effectiveness of vaccines, Varma said.

All other variants of interest have typically been regarded as more infectious than the original virus, while a study released earlier on Wednesday showed the B.1.1.7 strain may be more lethal than previously thought.

Late February 2021, Mayor Bill de Blasio and his team urged residents to remain calm following a media report that a more infectious variant of coronavirus – the B.1.256 – that is more resilient to vaccines was spreading rapidly in the city.

Late February 2021 also, New York Governor Andrew Cuomo allowed restaurants in New York City to increase indoor dining operations to 35 per cent of capacity from 25 per cent in order to match the threshold in New Jersey, which was experiencing an influx of diners crossing the

CHAPTER SIX

Hudson River in order to take advantage of the slightly looser limit.

Cuomo announced that restaurants across the rest of New York state would be allowed to expand indoor dining capacity to 75 per cent on March 19 2021 from the current level of 50 per cent.

"We feel confident in this step given the improving metrics we have seen over the last several weeks in both New Jersey and New York City, as well as the continued ramp up of our vaccination program," New Jersey Governor Phil Murphy said in a joint statement.

New York City and the neighboring state of New Jersey will allow restaurants to operate indoor dining at 50 per cent capacity from March 19.

Before the Governor of New York City made the announcement to increase indoor dinning to 50 percent capacity, major chains like McDonald's Corp. and Chipotle Mexican Grill Inc. opted to keep their tables cordoned off due to health and staffing concerns. Other restaurants said opening at New York's limit of 25% capacity won't yield enough sales to warrant the additional staffing, cleaning and operational costs.

CHAPTER SIX

"For us, 25% is four tables," said T.J. Steele, chef and co-owner of the Mexican restaurant Claro in Brooklyn. "Restaurants are already on such slim margins. Unless overhead was being reduced 75%, the numbers don't add up."

The city's restaurant owners were already struggling financially after being closed for more than five months during the initial Covid-19 outbreak. Allowed to reopen at limited capacity in September 2020, indoor dining lasted less than three months before being halted by Governor Andrew Cuomo to quell a post-holiday Covid surge. While cases declined from January highs, the seven-day average of new cases in the city remains higher than on Dec. 12, when Cuomo shut down indoor dining.

Cuomo's surprise announcement on Jan. 29 2021 to let restaurants host their customers indoors again in time for Valentine's Day provided establishments with little time to prepare. Indoor dining isn't as easy as just opening the doors -- restaurants have to clean, line up waiters and kitchen staff and restock pantries with booze and food. Still, the change will bring extra revenue to establishments

CHAPTER SIX

currently limited to delivery, takeout and outdoor dining in the midst of winter.

Steve Kanellos, co-owner of Court Square Diner in Long Island City, said he was hard-pressed to find eight more part-time workers to staff up ahead of Friday's reopening.

"It's a different type of business now," he said. "You got to make sure your plates are washed and everything is clean, so you have to give people a couple of days ahead of time."

He said indoor dining will bring in an additional $5,000 per week in sales, although costs, like paying additional workers, will also rise as a result. That will make it hard to earn a profit, especially on weekdays, since workers at nearby office buildings haven't returned.

Chipotle, which operates about 110 restaurants in the city, said it won't reopen dining room because it needed more time to prepare and notify employees. McDonald's also is opting not to resume indoor dining yet and will monitor the city's Covid positivity rates as it makes a decision when to allow customers to eat inside.

At Luthun, which serves American cuisine in the East Village, chef Nahid Ahmed is tweaking his menu because

CHAPTER SIX

he doesn't have time to source international ingredients. "We don't have that inventory to be ready on such short notice," he said. Instead of the sea bream and fresh wasabi he usually gets from Japan, he'll serve Gulf red snapper and mustard greens.

Daniel Boulud, whose dining empire includes the flagship Daniel on the Upper East Side, said he needs the same amount of staff no matter the closing time, so the earlier limit ends up being significant -- especially on a holiday like Valentine's Day.

"To stop reservations early, financially it's a disaster," he said.

Dan Kluger, chef and co-owner of Loring Place in Greenwich Village, said he'll be operating at a loss.

"It's not enough -- especially without proper financial assistance," he said, adding that looser restrictions just outside city limits provide unfair competition. "It doesn't make sense to keep the city's restaurants closed when you could go one block from Queens into Nassau county and restaurants are at 50%."

CHAPTER SIX

Neighboring New Jersey kept indoor dining open at 25% even when New York shut it down in December -- and the state recently expanded capacity to 35%. Nearby Westchester is operating at half capacity.

Kluger said more lenient restrictions elsewhere also drove restaurant employees out of the city. "A number of people have moved away because they couldn't afford to stay in New York with no real guarantee of work," he said.

Already more than 110,000 restaurants have closed permanently or for the long-term across the country, with New York City seeing more than 4,000 closures, according to the New York State Restaurant Association. Many of the city's restaurateurs, including celebrity chef Tom Colicchio, are lobbying Washington for $25 billion in federal aid for restaurants and small businesses.

In the meantime, restaurants are taking it day by day.

"I have stopped planning for my business because the change has happened so many times over the last year," said Roni Mazumdar, owner of three Indian restaurants including Adda Indian Canteen in Long Island City. His recommendation to changes mandated by the city: "Don't get too excited."

CHAPTER SIX

These variants represent more than half of current cases in New York City. These various strains of Covid could cause another set- back to reopening of restaurants if the government deem it necessary to initiate another lockdown restrictions.

CHAPTER SEVEN

Politicians and their Hypocrisy

Everybody hates a double standard. But leaders who don't follow their own rules may be doing so for reasons that make perfect sense to them.

In order to minimize the suffering caused by Covid-19, global leaders are asking everyone to make sacrifices. People around the world are giving up, for a period, many of the things they love doing: visiting friends and family, travelling, shopping, congregating with others. It's hard to do, but since governments are advising that this is the only responsible path to take, most people are taking it.

If there is one group of people whom you would expect to follow these new rules stringently, it would be the people

CHAPTER SEVEN

issuing them. Politicians and government officials are more intently aware of the gravity of this situation than anyone, and have the added responsibility of setting an example for the rest of us. Why is it, then, that so many of them fail to take their own advice?

Scotland's chief medical officer, Dr Catherine Calderwood, was forced to resign after the press discovered that during lockdown she had made two separate trips to her second home, an hour's drive from her family home in Edinburgh. In New Zealand, the health minister Dr David Clark was demoted after he broke national lockdown rules in order to take his family to the beach. In South Africa, a minister was suspended after being photographed having lunch with her friend.

A leader's authority depends on people perceiving them as a person of integrity; by acting in a hypocritical manner, leaders undermine their own positions

This is not a phenomenon limited to the current crisis, of course, or to governments. In 2019, the chief executive of McDonald's, Steve Easterbrook, was fired after it was disclosed that he was romantically involved with an employee. While there was no indication that the

CHAPTER SEVEN

relationship was anything but consensual, the relationship clearly violated the company's strict guidelines on workplace affairs – guidelines for which Easterbrook was ultimately responsible.

A leader's authority depends on people perceiving them as a person of integrity; by acting in a hypocritical manner, leaders undermine their own positions. And most leaders like to be liked, yet people are angered by double standards. Why, then, is this behavior so common – and what's behind it?

Daniel Effron, a social psychologist and associate professor at London Business School, studies hypocritical behavior. "People can be inconsistent without getting called hypocritical," he says. "If a drug addict tells people not to start taking drugs, few people would condemn them for it. But if someone is preaching virtue in public while practicing vice in private, people get angry because they think that person is claiming a moral benefit -- of appearing like a good person – which they don't deserve." It's unfairness, not inconsistency that really gets to us.

If leaders know that hypocrisy goes down badly, why do they give people reason to accuse them of it? The simplest

CHAPTER SEVEN

explanation is that they think they can get away with it. But although that may be true in some cases, Effron points out that most people like to see themselves as virtuous. A subtler reason is that they end up practicing one thing and preaching another in a bid to please different audiences.

A subtler reason is that they end up practicing one thing and preaching another in a bid to please different audiences

"In all sorts of organizations, people get caught between the conflicting demands of different stakeholders," says Effron. "One constituency wants X, the other wants not-X, and the leader tries to satisfy both: one with talk, the other with action, even though the talk and the action contradict each other."

Leaders, particularly during a crisis like the current one, are often working extremely hard for what they perceive to be the common good. They might be striving to keep people healthy in a pandemic or securing the future of their organization. Psychologically, they are amassing moral credits in the bank. That makes them likely to judge their own behavior more kindly than they would do otherwise, even when it verges on the unethical.

CHAPTER SEVEN

"We can always think of explanations for why 'I should be an exception'," Effron says. "And we're really good at convincing ourselves that those reasons are right."

Wearing a mask is important. For you and those around you. For elected officials? Not so much. Actually, all the COVID rules are for us, not them. COVID-19, and the accompanying lockdowns, have made it painfully clear: We plebes have to follow the rules; the elites do not.

The day before Thanksgiving, Denver Mayor Michael B. Hancock urged his constituents to remain in their households and refrain from travel during the holiday if they could.

That same day, he boarded a plane to join his wife and daughter in Mississippi.

The decision ignited calls of hypocrisy, and the mayor issued a public apology to those "angry and disappointed" in his decision. The decision ignited calls of hypocrisy, and the mayor issued a public apology to those "angry and disappointed" in his decision.

CHAPTER SEVEN

"I apologize to the residents of Denver who see my decision as conflicting with the guidance to stay at home for all but essential travel," he said

Hancock is one of several elected officials who faced criticism recently for not following their own health advice during the coronavirus pandemic -- in particular around Thanksgiving and other gatherings.

San Jose, California, mayor: 'I commit to do better'

On the 1st December 2020, the mayor of San Jose, California, issued a public apology for attending a Thanksgiving meal with more households than currently allowed under state regulations.

In a statement posted on social media, Mayor Sam Liccardo said the gathering at his parents' house consisted of eight people from five households. Restrictions issued Nov. 13 limit gatherings at a private household to three, he acknowledged.

"I apologize for my decision to gather contrary to state rules," he said. "I understand my obligation as a public official to provide exemplary compliance with the public health orders, and certainly not to ignore them.

CHAPTER SEVEN

Liccardo noted that he and his family took precautions such as wearing masks when not eating and sitting their own household at distanced tables on a backyard patio.

"I commit to do better," he added.

Austin, Texas, mayor: 'It was a lapse in judgment'

During a Facebook video message posted Nov. 9 2020, while he was in Mexico, the mayor of Austin, Texas, Steve Adler said, "We need to stay home if you can, do everything you can to try to keep the numbers down. This is not the time to relax."

Adler had traveled to Cabo San Lucas via private jet, according to the Austin-American Statesman, which first reported on the trip Wednesday. One Austin restaurant used that to lambast the mayor.

"Politicians be like 'Stay home unless you have a private jet," El Arroyo wrote on its restaurant signage .That evening, Adler apologized for his "confusing" behavior of traveling while urging others to be cautious.

"I want you to know that I regret that travel," Adler said during a Facebook Live update. He noted that the trip didn't

CHAPTER SEVEN

violate any state rules at the time, but that he feared "it could lead to some taking riskier behavior now."

"I recognize that my travel set a bad example," he said. "I know that in my position, I need to send a clearer message."

"I'm sorry I took that trip. It was a lapse in judgment," he added.

New York governor: 'It's hard to do'

The holidays are forcing many people to make difficult decisions -- politicians included. For weeks, Gov. Andrew Cuomo had implored New Yorkers to celebrate Thanksgiving with only their immediate households. So it came as a surprise to those following his daily briefings when he said during a Nov. 23 radio program that his mother and two daughters would travel to Albany for the holiday.

"His arrogance and hypocrisy knows no bounds," Republican New York Rep. Elise Stefanik said on Twitter. "Do as I say, not as I do."

CHAPTER SEVEN

At a press briefing the following day, Cuomo discussed a change in his Thanksgiving plans, saying his daughter in Chicago and his mother would no longer be coming.

"It's hard to do, and it's so much easier just to say, 'We'll do it the way we normally do it,'" he said during the briefing. "That's the easy way. 'Come over. We'll be careful.' It's a mistake."

"It's hard, but sometimes hard is smart," he added.

California governor: 'I made a bad mistake'

Dining has also been a source of controversy for leaders. California Gov. Gavin Newsom faced backlash following reports that the Democrat attended a large dinner at a restaurant in Napa Valley. The event was attended by several couples outside his household, said Newsom, who has urged constituents to avoid social gatherings that mix households.

In a statement, he said he and his family followed the restaurant's health protocols but added they "should have modeled better behavior and not joined the dinner."

"I made a bad mistake," Newsom said during a press briefing a few days later.

CHAPTER SEVEN

California Gov. Gavin Newsom, who groveled for forgiveness after being caught attending a large birthday dinner at The French Laundry restaurant in Napa Valley. When pictures from the event surfaced, the hypocrisy was glaring: The governor was seen with his wife at a large table full of lobbyists without mask, all sitting in close proximity.

But, hey: You're not the governor — so if you want to celebrate Thanksgiving in his state, remember: "No more than three households, including your own," at the gathering, and keep your distance.

Newsom isn't the only one to live it up while everyone suffers. Gov. Cuomo, for example, is rarely seen in a mask, yet his Twitter feed never stops harassing you to "mask up." (And, by the way, he's just thrilled with himself over his handling of the COVID-19 crisis, even though it resulted in more deaths than any other state and, according to The New York Times, seeded the virus throughout the country.)

The governor's daughter recently posted a picture of her dad, two of his daughters, one of "the boyfriends" and Cuomo's secretary all hanging out with no social distancing

CHAPTER SEVEN

or masks. Were all of them part of the same household? Doubtful.

Yet you, of course, have to avoid friends and family — you know, just in case.

One of Cuomo's most famous constituents similarly seems to think rules are for the little people. He actually broke quarantine after testing positive for the virus.

The constituent's wife posted pictures of herself working out indoors, without a mask, with a personal trainer, while gyms in the state remained closed. And he was recently photographed getting a haircut, without a mask, which would result in a $1,000 fine for the rest of us.

I'm referring, of course, to Gov. Cuomo's brother, CNN host Chris Cuomo, who gets a pass on all of his bad behavior because of his last name (and left-wing politics).

Politicians and their families are just not like the rest of us. Newsom sent his kids back to hybrid, in-person private school in Sacramento County while public schools there remain closed.

"The spirit of what I'm preaching all the time was contradicted, and I got to own that," he said during the apology. "I need to preach and practice, not just preach and not practice, and I've done my best to do that. We're all human. We all fall short sometimes."

On Nov. 24, the Los Angeles Board of Supervisors voted 3-2 to prohibit outdoor dining for three weeks, effective the next day. Following the vote, Supervisor Sheila Kuehl, who voted in favor of the ban, dined outdoors at a restaurant, her spokesperson confirmed with ABC News. FOX 11 in Los Angeles first reported on the meal.

"She ate there, taking appropriate precautions, and will not dine there again until our Public Health Orders permit," her spokesperson said in a statement.

During the board meeting, Kuehl said outdoor dining was "probably more dangerous in terms of contagion than any other kind of business," according to a report by Los Angeles ABC station KABC.

"The hypocrisy on display from Democrat elected officials all across the country is unreal," Republican National Committee Chair Ronna McDaniel said on Twitter following reports of Kuehl's meal.

CHAPTER SEVEN

The outdoor dining ban was in response to a surge in new COVID-19 cases in the county. Hospitalizations also doubled since Nov. 13, health officials said this week. A modified stay-at-home order went into effect on Monday, additionally prohibiting all public and private gatherings with those not in someone's household and closing playgrounds and card rooms.

Speaker Nancy Pelosi famously got a haircut at a salon in California, though salons were supposed to be closed there at the time.

Sen. Dianne Feinstein, who has called for nationwide mask mandates, was seen walking maskless through an airport in September and again in the hallway of the Capitol.

DC Mayor Muriel Bowser traveled to Delaware for a Biden victory party, but didn't follow her own quarantine protocols upon return. Celebrations, you see, are "essential" for your betters; they're too important to follow the rules they set for others.

Chicago Mayor Lori Lightfoot announced new lockdowns. "You must cancel the normal Thanksgiving plans," she said. The previous week, Lightfoot was whooping it up in the street, without mask and shouting through a bullhorn

CHAPTER SEVEN

(and perhaps blowtorching her spittle at the crowd) during a Biden victory party.

Sen. Chuck Schumer also partied for Biden without a mask. Apparently all these politicians seem to think if you're partying for a good cause, masks are unnecessary.

"Don't listen to politicians, listen to scientists," say their defenders! Yet that's not really how it works. Scientists give their perspective, and politicians enact rules based on that. But if they tell us to be concerned, to take precautions, to change everything about the way we live and to do so indefinitely — and then don't do it themselves — what are we supposed to think?

The message that comes through loud and clear: Wink, wink — COVID's not really that big a deal.

These hypocrites have to know their behavior undermines their credibility and helps spread the virus they say they want to fight. The only possible conclusion is that they just don't care.

CHAPTER EIGHT

CHAPTER EIGHT

COVID-19 and Civil Liberties

The government's broad powers to protect the public during declared emergencies are well-established, but this power is not unfettered. Emergency powers exist against a backdrop of individual rights and liberties, many of which, such as First Amendment rights to assemble and worship and 14th Amendment rights to be free from discrimination, are sacrosanct and should be abridged only after careful and cautious consideration — even in emergencies, like the coronavirus pandemic.

The courts have noted that an "inherent tension exists between the exercise" of personal freedoms and rights "and the government's need to maintain order during a period of social strife," as stated in the 1994 California appellate

CHAPTER EIGHT

court decision in the matter [In re Juan C [A person coming under the Juvenile Court Law]. The government's burden is to successfully navigate that tension by protecting the public health and safety, while preserving individual rights and liberties. "[T]he government must make every effort to avoid trammeling its citizens' constitutional rights. By the same token, those rights are not absolute. The Government's regulatory interest in community safety can, in appropriate circumstances, outweigh an individual's liberty interest,'" the court said. This tension was most recently manifest by U.S. Attorney General William Barr ordering all federal prosecutors to monitor coronavirus-related restrictions from state and local governments "that could be violating the constitutional rights and civil liberties of individual citizens."

Unfortunately for the government, there are no black-and-white answers to how much proscription of liberties and rights is too much. In fact, depending on the nature of the emergency, a justifiable short-term infringement may not be justified in the long-term. In general, courts are extremely deferential to governmental decision-making.

212

CHAPTER EIGHT

Here is a brief overview of key issues to spot and questions to ask as local government continues to respond to the novel coronavirus pandemic:

First Amendment Rights

Freedom of Assembly and Association

Protests: local agencies can regulate aspects of protests but must do so within the parameters of deferential constitutional and emergency powers case law.Does the local agency have an up-to-date, constitutional ordinance regulating protests and similar free speech gatherings?If there is no ordinance, is the proposed approach to regulating the event in line with case law?

Access to public spaces: limiting access to public spaces can violate rights to assemble and travel.

Do restrictions restrict public access more than necessary to protect the public's health and safety?

Do restrictions limit access only to residents? If so, such restrictions could violate rights to travel.

Freedom of Religion

CHAPTER EIGHT

Do bans on large gatherings that prohibit holding worship services contain exceptions for other activities that could render the emergency order hostile to religious exercise and constitutionally suspect?

Human Rights Abuses in the Enforcement of Coronavirus Security Measures

This virus is no respecter of persons. Coronavirus is a pandemic of global proportions which some have termed the third world war. Due to the pandemic, quarantine measures have been put in place across the globe. While typically restriction of movement of free people would fall under a human rights violation, there is an exception for threats to a nation that pandemics fall under. Nonetheless this exception does not cover the human rights violations in the enforcement of quarantine measures which have been brought to light around the globe. This abusive policing are not new, but the media coverage in most cases is. In response, the U.N. in a resolution about the Coronavirus pandemic should include recommendations that address these abuses.

Coronavirus has been around for almost a year now and has been contracted through person-to-person contact by people

CHAPTER EIGHT

in over 200 countries. By contrast, HIV/AIDS was found in 1983, can only be contracted through specific activities where body fluids are present, and incidents—after 37 years—have only been found in 142 countries (however, 32 million have died). The most recent Ebola crisis lasted from 2014–2016, was transmitted through direct contact with infected fluids, and spanned across just three African nations. When a pandemic, such as AIDS and Ebola have been deemed "a threat to international peace and security" the United Nations Security Council has been known to step in by adopting resolutions. The U.N. Security Council is mulling over some draft resolutions in response to Coronavirus, but without U.N. guidance countries have imposed quarantine and social distancing measures on their own. It is the enforcement of such quarantine measures that has concerning human rights implications.

Over one third of the world's 7.8 billion people are on lockdown. In fact, more people are under lockdown today than were even alive during WWII.

These quarantine measures on their face, restricting the movement of free people, are a violation of the U.N. Universal Declaration of Human Rights. The Declaration

CHAPTER EIGHT

was adopted in 1948 in "recognition of the inherent dignity and of the equal inalienable rights of all members of the human family." Some of the listed enumerated rights that are violated by quarantine orders are, the right to: liberty,[xiv] freedom of movement, freedom of religion in community with others, freedom of peaceful assembly and association, work and protection against unemployment,[xviii] education, and freely participate in community.

However, while quarantines may violate these rights the U.N. has said that in response to serious public health threats to the "life of a nation," human rights law allows for restrictions on some rights. Those restrictions, however, must be justified on a legal basis as strictly necessary. This "strictly necessary" standard must: be based on scientific evidence that is not arbitrary nor discriminatory, be set for a determinant amount of time, maintain respect for human dignity, be subject to review, and be proportionate to the objective sought to achieve. Putting quarantine measures in place from the worldwide medical communities' recommendations to stop the spread of a global pandemic seems to be exactly this type of situation, but the implementation is not without its own set of problems.

CHAPTER EIGHT

While social distancing has been lauded as the method to "flatten the curve" People in poor countries rely more heavily on daily hands on labor and informal sector employment to earn enough cash each day to feed their families, they live day-to-day and cannot afford to stockpile food and necessities, and they frequently do not have easy access to clean water. In impoverished places social distancing cuts off access to wages, food, and water that is not supplemented in any other way.

Article 5 of the Universal Declaration of Human Rights says, "no one shall be subject to torture or to cruel, inhumane, or degrading treatment or punishment." As reported above there are some articles of this declaration that can be suspended when "strictly necessary" for "the life of a nation," however, Article 5 is not one of them. What follows is a survey of enforcement abuses taken from news articles documenting how the quarantine measures have been enforced around the world.

Filipino president Duterte told the country in a public address that lockdown violators could be shot. While there have not been any reports of anyone being shot, reports have alleged that police have put people in public animal cages, and subjected others to physical punishments which the police video and then post online to shame the violators.

In Brazil, people found on the streets without a reason had their feet bound in the public square. This is occurring while the Brazilian president publicly criticizes the stay at home orders and actively contradicts the directions of Mayors and governors. Because of the inconsistent quarantine measures some criminal gangs have imposed their own "coronavirus curfew," posting signs and using megaphones to tell citizens to stay at home "or else." Police are also using helicopters to create sand storms to drive people off of the beaches.

The South African police rounded up 1,000 homeless men and crammed them into a soccer stadium where they were assigned ten to a tent. Adequate social distancing would have required no more than two per a tent. The homeless men interviewed said that the virus would spread like wildfire among this group, they would be safer "social distancing" by themselves on the street, and they were terrified they were sent there to die. South African police

CHAPTER EIGHT

also used physical punishments, water cannons, and rubber bullets on people violating restrictions.

Amnesty International reported that in Iran possibly 36 prisoners were killed who were protesting in fear of their risk of contracting coronavirus. These protests sprung up in multiple prisons that had promised to release certain categories of prisoners due to the pandemic and then went back on their promise.

There are other instances that disproportionately affect the poor but perhaps do not rise to the level of an Article 5 human rights violation. A Chinese-Australian working in Beijing was fired from her job and deported for going for a run. The United Arab Emirates, Australia, Singapore, Austria, Hong Kong, and Britain have imposed fines exceeding $3K for violations. India, Britain, Mexico, Singapore, Hong Kong, and Russia have threatened and imposed prison time for violators.

Just as the Locust Effect points out it is countries with police forces set up to maintain the control of the ruling class from colonial times that have the most widespread reports of police abuses during this time of quarantine enforcement. Tellingly, it is not the police tactics that have

CHAPTER EIGHT

changed in these places, only the international spotlight on them that this pandemic has created. However, it is precisely because of this spotlight that the U.N. should use the extra latitude afforded in times of crisis to speak out against the abuses and call for their end. Member states recognize that interference in their private internal affairs can be overridden times where international security and peace are threatened, and this is just a time as that.

The tension between private liberty and public health in the United States is hardly new. Americans have demanded the latter in times of plague and prioritized the former in times of well-being since at least the Colonial Era. Politicians and business leaders have alternately manipulated and deferred to that tension for about as long.

In 1701, members of the Massachusetts Bay Colony fought a yearlong political battle to enact the nation's first quarantine laws against opponents who said such measures were too severe. In 1918, during the flu pandemic, the mayor of Pittsburgh brought a ban on public gatherings to a swift — and premature — conclusion over concerns about a coming election.

CHAPTER EIGHT

In 2020, the same tension is back with a vengeance. The nation is under siege from the worst pandemic in a century, and the United States is on track to suffer more deaths than any other industrialized country from SARS-CoV-2, the medical name for the novel coronavirus.

Attorney General William Barr ordered Justice Department lawyers to "be on the lookout for state and local directives that could be violating the constitutional rights and civil liberties of individual citizens." He was talking about state and local orders closing businesses and requiring people to shelter in place to help combat the spread of the virus. "The Constitution is not suspended in times of crisis," Mr. Barr said in an April 27 memo.

Yet the same Mr. Barr, early in the outbreak, was seemingly so concerned about its impact that he proposed letting the government pause court proceedings and detain people indefinitely without trial during emergencies effectively suspending the core constitutional right of habeas corpus.

Temporary limitations on some liberties don't seem to concern most Americans at this moment. Polls show that 70 percent to 90 percent of the public support measures to

CHAPTER EIGHT

slow the spread of the virus, even if those measures require temporarily yielding certain freedoms and allowing the economy to suffer in the short run.

Civil liberties may feel to some like a second-order problem when thousands of Americans are dying of a disease with no known treatment or vaccine in he early days of the virus. Yet while unprecedented emergencies may demand unprecedented responses, those responses can easily tip into misuse and abuse, or can become part of our daily lives even after the immediate threat has passed. For examples, Americans need look no further than the excesses of the post-Sept. 11 Patriot Act.

As the nation starts looking ahead to the next phase of its battle against the coronavirus, we need to have a more honest conversation about the extent to which governments may impose restrictions on their citizens that would not — and should not — be tolerated under normal conditions.

Consider the rights to free speech, association and religious exercise under the First Amendment: These freedoms are central to our self-definition, and yet they have all been infringed on to varying degrees across the country, as states ban gatherings where the virus can spread quickly and

CHAPTER EIGHT

easily. In Maryland and Iowa, for example, all types of large events and gatherings, including church services, have been prohibited. (Many other states have exempted religious services from their bans, which raises the separate question of whether the government is impermissibly favoring religion.)

Bans like these are legal, as long as they are neutral and applicable to everyone. A state may not shut down only certain types of events, or prohibit speakers expressing only certain viewpoints.

But even if all these bans are legal on their face, what happens as the 2020 election approaches? Speech and association rights are at their peak in the political context, and Americans will be especially wary of any incursions on those rights in the months or weeks before Election Day. What if a state lifts some restrictions on large gatherings, then reimposes them in the days before an election? That may be necessary if there is another wave of the virus, and yet in a highly polarized political environment, citizens might well distrust official motivations behind a crackdown, and that could generate public unrest.

CHAPTER EIGHT

This is why it's so important for the authorities to build that trust now, and to rely openly on scientific consensus when imposing — and lifting — bans on gatherings and other events.

Another area of concern is the government's ability to know where we are and whom we're with. In normal times, the authorities generally have to obtain a warrant to search your personal property, like a cell-phone, or to retrieve its data to find your location.

Cell-phones are particularly useful at this moment, when it's crucial to know where infected people have been, and whom they've been close to. Several countries around the world, as well as some American states, have rolled out apps that either encourage or require their citizens to check in regularly and report their locations.

But giving the government access to all that data carries huge risks. There were already far too many examples of law-enforcement officials abusing their access to cell-phone data in the pre-Covid era, taking advantage of revolutions in technology to track people in ways that no one would imaginably consent to. Even if people give their consent to be tracked during the pandemic, governments

CHAPTER EIGHT

have a very poor track record of relinquishing new powers once they have them.

The question then becomes: Can cell-phone data be used in a way that helps stem the spread of the coronavirus while also being kept out of the hands of the government to avoid abuse, now or down the road?

Apple and Google are in the process of producing an app that would use secret codes to track people through their phones, while leaving the location data on those phones. People who test positive would be given the choice of putting their phone on a list. Other people's phones could automatically check that list, and if any were within range of the infected person, those people would be notified that they could be at risk.

Fine, in theory. But for a system like this to work, the public needs to buy into it. Enough people have to use these apps to make them effective — at least 60 percent of cell-phone users, by some estimates — and no city or country is anywhere close to that level of adoption. In Norway, only 30 percent of people have downloaded this type of location app.

CHAPTER EIGHT

Another hurdle is that the big technology companies have a poor record of protecting their users' private information.

In the end, contact tracing — a central feature of any comprehensive public-health response — will need to be a cooperative endeavor, involving not only downloadable apps but perhaps hundreds of thousands of human beings, all doing the hard work of direct outreach to find those people at the highest risk of infection.

It would be one thing if the calls to "reopen" America from the former President Trump and his allies were part of a coordinated pandemic response strategy by a federal government that had taken strong and science-based measures from the start. But the White House failed to do that at virtually every turn, which makes the current protests ring hollow.

It's possible that at least some of the current lockdowns could have been avoided had the Trump administration led the way back in January when we still had time to take advantage of the information coming out of China and prepare the United States for what lay ahead. In that sense, these devastating shutdowns represent a catastrophic failure of timely government action. Even today, top officials are

CHAPTER EIGHT

refusing to take the most basic safety measures. Vice President Mike Pence toured the Mayo Clinic but refused to follow the clinic's requirement to wear a mask. What message does he think that sends to the American people? (On Thursday Mr. Pence visited a plant producing ventilators in his home state, Indiana, and wore a mask.)

In a large self-governing society, civil liberties exist as part of a delicate balance. That balance is being sorely tested right now, and there is often no good solution that does not infringe on at least some liberty. At the same time, the coronavirus provides Americans with an opportunity to re-imagine the scope and nature of our civil liberties and our social contract.

Across the U.S., elected officials from Pennsylvania to Oklahoma suspicious of big government and outraged with orders to close churches, gun stores and other businesses deemed non-essential insist that the public health response is being used as an excuse to trample constitutional rights.

The shutdowns reinforced long-held beliefs by some that governments would eventually use a national emergency to limit civil liberties and the vitriol is particularly strong across the pine forests of eastern Washington state where

CHAPTER EIGHT

conservative Rep. Matt Shea is a co-founder of the Coalition of Western States, a loose federation of politicians suspicious of big government, plus militia supporters.

Its goal is to "stop unconstitutional actions against United States citizens," according to a December report into Matt Shea's activities paid for by the Washington state House issued just before his own caucus exiled him.

After Washington State Gov. Jay Inslee issued the earliest U.S. mandatory closing of schools and businesses, Shea questioned whether Inslee would use the state's National Guard to enforce his orders and if he would force inoculation of residents after a coronavirus vaccine becomes available.

"Quarantine is only supposed to be for sick people not mandatory for healthy law abiding people," Shea wrote on Facebook. "Otherwise constitutionally and legally that starts creeping into martial law territory."

Joining Shea in the vast expanse of eastern Washington, hundreds of miles and political light years away from ultra liberal Seattle, was Republican gubernatorial candidate Loren Culp, who wants to deny Inslee a third term. Culp is

CHAPTER EIGHT

the police chief of the town of Republic and author of the book "American Cop: Upholding the Constitution and Defending Your Right to Bear Arms," praised by rocker Ted Nugent.

"If I choose to peacefully assemble, go to Church, go to a gun shop, take my family fishing, open my business, enjoy the outdoors, or exercise any of my constitutional rights, I should not be restricted from doing so by a would-be dictator," Culp told supporters during a recent conference call.

Shea's efforts were lambasted by the Southern Poverty Law Center, which said in a statement that he was promoting fear mongering and providing "legitimacy for a network of extremists" in western U.S. states "at a time when hundreds of Washingtonians, and thousands more Americans, are dying from coronavirus"

The lockdown order criticism isn't limited to states led by Democrats. From northern Idaho, where suspicion of government also runs deep, Bonner County Sheriff Daryl Wheeler demanded in a letter that Republican Gov. Brad Little reconsider his statewide stay-home decree.

CHAPTER EIGHT

Wheeler's letter questioned the reliability of World Health Organization coronavirus information and said "now it is time to reinstate our Constitution."

"You can request those that are sick to stay home, but, at the same time, you must release the rest of us to go on with our normal business," Wheeler wrote.

Little allowed restaurants to continue drive-through services and deliveries, but that didn't appease arch-conservative members of his party, like State Rep. Heather Scott, also from northern Idaho.

She called the governmental response to the virus "a way to chip away at the foundations of our Constitution to push a global, socialistic agenda while in the midst of a national emergency."

The criticism has stretched to Pennsylvania, where Republican State Rep. Daryl Metcalfe blasted Democratic Gov. Tom Wolf for his stay-home order and business closures.

"You were not elected to be our master or dictator but a servant leader in the executive branch," Metcalfe wrote.

CHAPTER EIGHT

"You have no authority to imprison any citizen in their home."

North Dakota's closure of businesses and schools ordered by Republican Gov. Doug Burgum even managed to draw ire from a doctor-politician, Republican Assemblyman Rick Becker.

"Government itself is going to be causing far more damage to America by its reaction to coronavirus than the coronavirus itself," Becker told the conservative One America News Network.

Politicians angry with lockdown orders had a meaningful impact on policy after Republican state lawmakers overturned Democratic Gov. Laura Kelly's executive order limiting the size of religious gatherings to 10 people. Kelly challenged the action, and the Kansas Supreme Court reinstated her order on technical grounds.

The COVID-19 pandemic has challenged faith communities, especially as physical distancing measures complicate religious gatherings. In the United States, the restriction of gatherings varies on a state-by-state basis. According to Pew Research Center data, most states granted some form of religious exemption to the pandemic

CHAPTER EIGHT

rules, but 10 prevent any form of in-person religious meetings. In response, many faith leaders canceled in-person services or moved to virtual platforms, but others continue to hold services in defiance of state orders. The widespread stay-at-home orders are emerging as a new battleground for debates on religious freedom. Some faith communities are suing in federal court, claiming the mandates infringe on their First Amendment right to free exercise of religion. Religious freedom will remain a key concern as the coronavirus crisis continues to change the tone and tenor of everyday life.

Ongoing debates over religious freedom in the COVID-19 pandemic often pit personal liberties against public health response, leading to polarization of the issue. The American public is roughly split along partisan lines when it comes to restricting religious gatherings during the pandemic. In this sense, religious freedom can be said to be part and parcel of the broader coronavirus culture wars, where it is difficult to find common ground on how society should respond to the pandemic. Especially since the exact end of the pandemic remains unclear, it is imperative to find solutions that respect both religious freedom and public health concerns.

CHAPTER EIGHT

The US Supreme Court has temporarily blocked New York from enforcing attendance limits at places of worship in areas hit hard by coronavirus.

In a 5-4 vote, the court ruled that the state's congregational cap violated rights to religious freedom.

In an unsigned order, it said the rules "single[d] out houses of worship for especially harsh treatment."

This was one of the first consequential rulings since conservative Justice Amy Coney Barrett was appointed.

President Donald Trump appointed her to replace liberal predecessor Ruth Bader Ginsburg, who died in September.

Justice Barrett voted in the majority, along with other Trump appointees Neil Gorsuch and Brett Kavanaugh.

The three liberal justices dissented, as did conservative Chief Justice John Roberts.

Earlier this year, before Justice Ginsburg's death, the court voted to leave similar restrictions in place in California and Nevada.

The Supreme Court's decision was a major victory for the Roman Catholic Diocese of Brooklyn and Agudath Israel,

CHAPTER EIGHT

an Orthodox Jewish congregation, which had challenged the restrictions imposed by New York's Governor Andrew Cuomo.

On 6 October 2020, Governor Cuomo shut down non-essential businesses in targeted areas where coronavirus infections had spiked, as part of efforts to control infection rates. Places of worship were also limited to gatherings of 10 in "red" zones, and 25 in "orange" ones.

In court, the Catholic Diocese of Brooklyn said the restrictions unfairly singled out places of worship. Agudath Israel of America also argued that its members were subject to "discriminatory targeting."

New York argued in response that it had been the epicentre of the US coronavirus outbreak in the spring. It also said religious gatherings were being treated less stringently than secular gatherings like concerts, which were banned entirely.

But the Supreme Court's unsigned majority ruled that "even in a pandemic, the Constitution cannot be put away and forgotten. The restrictions at issue here... strike at the very heart of the First Amendment's guarantee of religious liberty."

CHAPTER EIGHT

The court's action will not have an immediate impact since the groups that sued are no longer subject to the restrictions they fought against

Even mostly liberal California saw a rebellious sign, when angry anglers disrupted a teleconference with state regulators who had planned to discuss a potential limited ban on freshwater sport-fishing in several rural countries. Many callers mistakenly thought a statewide ban might be imposed.

Officials ended up canceling the Fish and Game Commission meeting to decide whether emergency powers should be granted to a governor's Department of Fish and Wildlife appointee because local officials feared visiting anglers could spread the virus.

More than 500 participants jammed the teleconference after a group of conservative politicians, sheriffs and media outlets told social media followers that the administration of Gov. Gavin Newsom, a Democrat, was planning the statewide ban, the Sacramento Bee reported.

After the teleconference, Republican California U.S. Rep. Doug LaMalfa wrote on Facebook that "using this quarantine period to advance government control that

CHAPTER EIGHT

would never sell otherwise is a breach of trust," the Bee reported.

The developments across the U.S. worry Eric Ward, executive director of the Portland, Oregon-based Western States Center progressive civil rights group.

He accused the politicians of "performative drama and exaggeration that puts their constituents at more risk.

Commenting on the human rights implications of restrictions on people's lives due to the COVID-19 pandemic, Equality and Human Rights Commission Chief Executive, Rebecca Hilsenrath, said:

"We are walking a tightrope. We need to find the balance between saving lives from coronavirus, and allowing people the hard won freedoms that are the framework for those lives - such as a right to a private and family life, to freedom of assembly, and to an education. This must go hand in hand with an economic recovery that provides everyone with an adequate standard of living.

"At the same time, we must protect those many other lives which will be put at risk without access to appropriate health and social care, such as older and disabled people,

CHAPTER EIGHT

patients with cancer or with mental health challenges - or risked through the rising rates of domestic violence.

"In lockdown we heard how those in residential care were being protected as much as possible from the virus, but we also heard how people were deprived of family when they needed them most. Staying at home to protect the NHS was a simple message but it may have stopped screening and the right to health care for those with other conditions such as cancer. Blanket approaches may well have other consequences. The virus isn't going anywhere anytime soon and we have to make sure that our efforts to live free from coronavirus don't come at too high a price.

"As more restrictions are considered, we're calling on the Government to make sure that protections are proportionate, measured, and rooted in science and the law. Any changes that restrict our rights must be flexible, with review and end points, and remain open to challenge. If we want to protect public health and save lives, then changes need to complement or enhance our human rights, not treat them as optional.

CHAPTER NINE

Food & Culture

There are many things that set mankind apart from the animal world - our minds have allowed us to develop civilization, create incredible technology, and literally change the face of our planet.

With all the advances of the human race, we often forget that our uniqueness in the animal kingdom goes back even further and deeper, back to the very roots of our existence and to one of our most basic needs - food.

The human relationship with food is truly unique - from our ancestor's first cooking food to today where we are literally changing food on a molecular level.

Beyond the technological relationship we have with food, humans are also unique in our emotional connection with

CHAPTER NINE

food. In the rest of the animal kingdom, food is by and large simply a matter of providing nutrients to one's body. Animals eat out of instinct.

Humans, on the other hand, see food as so much more than just a nutritional need. In fact, we often use food in a destructive way - overeating and eating unhealthy foods - which negatively impacts our bodies instead.

For humans, food seems to sit on an emotional level first before being an instinctive need.

The answer lies in humankind's deep connection with food. It is not just about mindless eating - it is about preparing, creating, discovering, exploring, inventing, and changing our food and food landscape. The role of food in human culture truly does separate us from our animal relatives.

Part of our connection with food does come from our primitive animal brain. Having a strong desire and connection with food makes seeking it out a priority. Food is, of course, a necessity and anyone who has given a dog a treat understands that animals too get satisfaction and joy out of eating.

For humans though, it goes further.

CHAPTER NINE

Food is Love

We don't just use food to satisfy our own needs but to show an emotional connection with others. From mother's first milk to our grandmother's homemade stew, food is a way we connect and show love for others.

You know a relationship is getting serious when your partner invites you over for a home-cooked meal. When a neighbor or friend suffers a loss, we bring them casseroles and soups. When a best friend is dumped, we rush over with ice cream and cookies.

Preparing and sharing food with people you love solidifies the connection you have.

Food is Memory

Because we apply so much emotional importance to food in the moment, it only makes sense that it would also become an important part of our memories.

Studies have shown that humans recall memories more easily and clearly when they are attached to a physical sensation as well as an emotional experience. From the sounds of war to the feeling of first touching snow, when

CHAPTER NINE

we use our five physical senses we create stronger memories.

No wonder so many memories are attached to food then.

Perhaps it is a memory of a great meal shared with close friends or just recalling the delicious crepe you ate while walking the streets of Paris on your honeymoon.

Food has the ability to activate multiple senses - smell, sight, and of course taste - to help us remember some of life's most meaningful and magical moments, whether large or small.

Food is Identity

The human species has always placed strong importance on cultural identity. In the beginning, being able to identify someone as belonging to one group or another was an issue of safety and security. The question of "are they a friend or a foe" did not rely on an individual person but rather their identity as part of a group.

Food, in turn, became a way of quickly identifying people.

Today, food is a way to connect to our heritage and to our own cultural identity, whether that means a bowl of ramen

CHAPTER NINE

for a young Japanese boy in Tokyo or a new immigrant family in the United States making tamales for Christmas dinner.

Whether people stay home and learn the recipes of their ancestors - making old family recipes with their grandmothers - or move halfway around the world and still keep their cherished recipes "from the home country," food is a way to identify who you are, where you come from, and the history of your people.

Food is Connection

When you think about it, in the history of mankind, eating alone was never something truly normal. Perhaps a hunter would snack while out alone in the forest but meals were always something shared. Families and friends would gather together to eat. All major social events seemed to include food, from weddings to funerals.

Today, with the way technology and work culture creates physical isolation, eating alone is much more common but even so, people seek out others to enjoy a meal with - to connect with.

CHAPTER NINE

While food is often used to separate us into different groups, it can also be used to connect us.

When you go on a first date, what is the most likely situation? Dinner, right? Or if not that at least a cup of coffee at a cafe. The picturesque image of the happy family always seems to show them sitting around a dinner table. Even in the business world, connections are made over coffee or a business meeting lunch.

Connection and inclusion is an important human need - isolation is one of the top causes of depression. Combining that need for connection with another basic human need - food - ensures not only our physical health but our emotional health as well.

Food means Understanding

As the famous cookbook author James Beard said, "Food is our common ground, a universal experience."

It doesn't matter if you are Black, White, or Brown - you eat. It doesn't matter if you are Christian, Buddhist, or Muslim - you eat. The foods we eat around the world are vastly different but the connection we have with food and the act of eating is something we can all relate to.

CHAPTER NINE

This universality allows food to create a true opportunity for universal understanding.

When you realize that a father halfway around the world just wants to provide and feed his children like any other good father, you can connect with him on a deeper level. You see this across cultures - the use of food to solidify an understanding between people. We literally speak of peace being created with the "breaking of bread."

When people come together over food, they can better relate to each other, whether that means a family trying to form better bonds of understanding or enemies trying to forge a new peace.

Food is Creation

There is a beauty in old family recipes. Passed down from generation to generation, these pieces of the past connect us with our heritage.

At the same time though, food for mankind has always represented progress, change, and invention. From the first days of agriculture to the molecular gastronomy trends of today's top restaurants, food has always shown the true ability of the human imagination.

CHAPTER NINE

Think about it - what would Italian food be without tomatoes? And yet, this crucial ingredient was only introduced to Europe a few hundred years ago.

The success of the human species relied on our ability to adapt, change, and create, especially when it came to food sources.

Food is both nutrients and art.

Today we continue to stretch our minds and abilities from the creation of new hit street foods to fine dining restaurants pushing the realm of what is food further and further to the future.

Food is Joy

This goes back to that primitive animal brain. Enjoying food makes sense - if we didn't have a strong drive to eat, we wouldn't have survived as a species. And yet, the joy humans get out of their food is so much more than an evolutionary trick of survival.

Throughout history, the wealthiest of society would display their wealth through great banquets and feasts. In the same way art and music would signify "the good life," so would food. Food was about living well and enjoying life. In

CHAPTER NINE

reality though, the cost of the feast or the rarity of the ingredients mattered little.

Anyone who has enjoyed the sweet taste of a fresh peach or a hot bowl of delicious soup on a cold day knows the simple, peaceful joy food can bring. When you eat something that just tastes so perfect that it literally reminds you to stop and appreciate all you have in your life - that is the unique joy and magic of good food.

Food and food culture quite obviously makes up an important part of who we are, how we connect, what we value, and how we express ourselves as human beings.

As our world becomes more and more interconnected, as people move across the globe, and as Western culture becomes more and more dominate, the food and food culture landscapes of our world will continue to change and evolve.

Change is inevitable but it is important to honor and acknowledge the ways we have all personally grown and been shaped by our own unique food cultures.

Perhaps it is time to learn to make your grandmother's famous pie or to write down the story of the first

CHAPTER NINE

homemade meal you cooked for your spouse, even if it did involve burnt garlic bread or spilled red wine.

Just as we honor our past with stories and literature, let us preserve our food cultures with the memories they evoke and the recipes that bring them back to life.

Food culture (by definition) refers to the practices, attitudes, and beliefs as well as the networks and institutions surrounding the production, distribution, and consumption of food.

That's a mouth full so let's break it down — food culture is the connection, beliefs, and experience we have with food and our food system. It incorporates our cultural heritage and ethnicity, but is not limited to it.

Our food culture is as much about our ethnic cultural heritage, as it is about our environmental culture and the way our surrounding impact the foods we eat and the way we experience them.

There are many different food cultures of the world, some more distinctive and globally famous than others, and some which very rarely leave their regional environment but are

CHAPTER NINE

still just as significant to the local community they influence.

Different food cultures around the world are influenced by many factors, but the most noticeable is arguably the way in which different food cultures utilize specific ingredients and spices to evoke unique flavor profiles that define their food culture.

This is why food cultures often vary regionally even within one country depending on the landscape, weather, and history that each region uniquely experienced. While the United States is not known for having the most positive food culture, this is something that is very apparent as local cuisines in the United States vary drastically depending on what region you live in. The same holds true for Italian food culture, which varies drastically from North to South.

But regardless of what ingredients, flavors, or traditions exist between the different food cultures of the world there are two things that act as connected threads woven throughout them all — community and pleasure. There isn't a food culture in the world that does not include these two parts of our food experience, even though they are often highly overlooked and undervalued in the American interpretation of food culture.

What this means is that we were meant to enjoy our food (it is why we experience pleasure when we eat it), and we were meant to enjoy our food with friends and family. Food cultures were founded on the way in which food was used to celebrate religious holidays, community events, and family gatherings. In other words food was celebrated and respected as an essential part of what makes humans human.

To break it down even further food cultures, no matter where in the world, all encompass a few key components:

They involve sharing food with community and family

They value the needs of the land over the convenience driven desires of people

They use food to celebrate religious and community events

They focus on local and seasonal ingredients, and use them to create unique and distinguishable flavors

They value their food experiences and then move on with their day

CHAPTER NINE

Food is not something to be manipulated, it is meant to be shared and celebrated

This is where we begin to be able to clearly see how our food is meant to support the land it is grown on, nourishing both our bodies and our environment, as well as something that we are meant to live in balance with, not control.

For these reasons it is easy to see how food and culture conflict significantly with the Western diet culture that exists today to separate ourselves from our food culture, and instead turn our food into something to be controlled and measured.

But what does food culture have to do with one's health? Well — everything.

Without a strong food culture food becomes something that we manipulate for personal gain. It stops being something that we respect, and instead becomes something that we aim to control, and the more we aim to control our food the less we truly value and experience it.

Because food cultures are deeply rooted parts of our natural history that have evolved and developed overtime, they are essential parts of how we support our overall health and

CHAPTER NINE

nourish our bodies. However, over the past half century within the United States especially, commercially processed foods and the insurgence of supermarkets and marketed diet culture have disconnected many Americans with their traditional food culture to the point where they may not even recognize it anymore.

For so many Americans the phrase food culture doesn't mean much. Food is something that comes packaged, that is counted and manipulated, and overall disconnected from any real meaning. At some point we decided to remove the culture from our food and our health began to suffer.

All you have to do is take a look at the blue zones of the world (the areas of the world researched to have the happiest and longest lifespan) to understand that our food culture is as much a part of our personal and societal well-being, as our food is itself.

The good news is that every single person is capable of creating a strong food culture for themselves, and their family. You don't need to grow up in an environment with a strong food heritage in order to incorporate some of the building blocks that make up a strong and unwavering food

CHAPTER NINE

culture. All you need to do is focus on bringing the culture back into food culture.

Think about the real foods that make you happy. The ones your grandmother may have made you, or a dish you had abroad that you couldn't stop thinking about. Then start to get to know what foods grow in your own local environment. How do the seasons and growing periods change? What foods and flavors do you find yourself cravings during different parts of the year? Lean into those questions and allow your mind and your body to bring enjoyment and curiosity back into your food.

You do not need to identify with one particular country or food heritage in order to develop a strong food culture. Your food culture can be anything you want it to be, and can incorporate many ethnic flavors, dishes, and traditions so long as your food culture is based in the values I detailed above.

There are no rules when it comes to developing a strong food culture. Some people may have grown up with one, while others develop one later in life. Regardless, the most important thing to me is that more people (especially here in the USA) start to change the way they view their food,

CHAPTER NINE

and more importantly the way in which they experience and value it.

The way brands connect with consumers has changed drastically over the years.

It used to be that companies would develop their brand positioning largely through introspection—by identifying what they saw as the defining attributes and benefits of their brand, then pushing that version on to the market. They operated as though they were in complete control.

Now, the idea of building brands in such an insular manner feels archaic. Today, brands need to look more actively and purposefully at the culture buzzing around them—in entertainment, in fashion, in news, on social media—and use that awareness to inform how they should best position and integrate themselves into the world.

This is a more powerful form of branding, because by engaging with culture more directly, brands in effect can become a part of that culture, thereby deepening their relevance and connection with customers. And that has never been more prescient or necessary.

Here's why.

CHAPTER NINE

Both brands and culture are shaped by stories.

Humans build culture—and, by extension, brands—primarily through telling stories.

That's how we make sense of the world and of ourselves: storytelling. It's innate. Cavemen told stories to make sense of the stars. Tribes and nations tell stories to create community. And since the dawn of capitalism, we've been telling stories to sell ourselves and our brands, too.

This is important to understand because it's in this way that culture and brands are inextricably linked. The best brands are defined by and establish themselves through great stories and storytelling.

But the way brands tell stories to impact culture has changed—by necessity.

Brands today live in a more transparent and accessible world—one in which it's possible, through mechanisms like social media, to interact with consumers more directly.

Now, if companies develop brands in a silo and ignore what's going on around them, they come off as out of touch. Consumers no longer want to be told what their culture looks like, nor what stories define it—they want to

CHAPTER NINE

take part in that development. Your brand must be a part of the culture, because consumers are a part of that culture.

The goal for brands today, then, is this: tell stories that ingratiate your brand in the culture so you become a part of it, too.

To accomplish this, the most successful brands integrate aspects of the culture into their core message, and/or connect their brand to recent events or moments that reflect what they want to stand for.

The Aunt Jemima brand of syrup and pancake mix will get a new name and image, Quaker Oats announced, saying the company recognizes that "Aunt Jemima's origins are based on a racial stereotype."

The 130-year-old brand features a Black woman named Aunt Jemima, who was originally dressed as a minstrel character.

The picture has changed over time, and in recent years Quaker removed the "mammy" kerchief from the character to blunt growing criticism that the brand perpetuated a racist stereotype that dated to the days of slavery. Quaker, a subsidiary of PepsiCo, said removing the image and name

CHAPTER NINE

is part of an effort by the company "to make progress toward racial equality."

"We recognize Aunt Jemima's origins are based on a racial stereotype," Kristin Kroepfl, vice president and chief marketing officer of Quaker Foods North America, said in a news release. "As we work to make progress toward racial equality through several initiatives, we also must take a hard look at the portfolio of our brands and ensure they reflect our values and meet our consumers' expectations."

Kroepfl said that the company has worked to "update" the brand to be "appropriate and respectful" but that it realized the changes were insufficient.

Aunt Jemima has come under renewed criticism recently amid protests across the nation and around the world sparked by the death of George Floyd in Minneapolis police custody.

People on social media called out the brand for continuing to use the image and discussed its racist history, with the topic trending on Twitter.

In a viral TikTok, a singer named KIRBY discussed the history of the brand in a video titled "How To Make A Non

CHAPTER NINE

Racist Breakfast." She concludes the post, which has racked up hundreds of thousands of views across platforms, by saying, "Black lives matter, people, even over breakfast

In a statement to NBC News, KIRBY said she felt "a sense of relief knowing that my future children will not grow up in a world where their ancestors' oppression is insensitively used as a marketing tool on a box."

"I hope that other brands swiftly follow suit," she added.

Hours after the Aunt Jemima announcement Wednesday, Mars Inc., which owns Uncle Ben's a parboiled rice product that features a Black man on its packaging, which has been similarly criticized as racist announced that "now is the right time to evolve the Uncle Ben's brand."

"We don't yet know what the exact changes or timing will be, but we are evaluating all possibilities," the company said.

Retiring Aunt Jemima matters because the logo is "a retrograde image of Black womanhood on store shelves," Riché Richardson, an associate professor of African American literature at Cornell University, told the "TODAY" show. "It's an image that hearkens back to the

CHAPTER NINE

antebellum plantation. ... Aunt Jemima is that kind of stereotype that is premised on this idea of Black inferiority and otherness."

"It is urgent to expunge our public spaces of a lot of these symbols that for some people are triggering and represent terror and abuse," Richardson said.

In a 2015 piece for The New York Times, Richardson wrote that the inspiration for the brand's name came from a minstrel song, "Old Aunt Jemima," in which white actors in blackface mocked and derided Black people.

The logo, Richardson wrote, was grounded in the stereotype of the "mammy ... a devoted and submissive servant who eagerly nurtured the children of her white master and mistress while neglecting her own."

The company's own timeline says Aunt Jemima was first "brought to life" by Nancy Green, a Black woman who was formerly enslaved and became the face of the product in 1890.

In 2015, a judge dismissed a lawsuit against the company by two men who claimed to be descendants of Anna Harrington, a Black woman who began portraying Jemima

CHAPTER NINE

in the 1930s, saying the company hadn't properly compensated her estate with royalties.

Quaker said that the new packaging will begin to appear in the fall and that a new name will be announced later.

The company also announced that it will donate at least $5 million over the next five years "to create meaningful, ongoing support and engagement in the Black community."

Daina Ramey Berry, a professor of history at the University of Texas, said the decision to drop the name and the image of Aunt Jemima is significant because the brand normalized a racist depiction of Black women.

Aunt Jemima, she said, "kept Black woman in the space of domestic service," associating them with serving food under a "plantation mentality."

Berry also said it would be misguided to lament the change by Quaker as a loss of representation for Black women.

The criticism of Aunt Jemima's image, she said, "is about the representation — the stereotypical and traumatic and abusive ways in which we are represented."

CHAPTER NINE

Land O'Lakes also quietly gets rid of iconic Indian maiden mascot

Land O'Lakes released new packaging without an Indian maiden for the first time in nearly a century in February 2020.

For nearly a century, the Land O'Lakes Indian maiden has kneeled by the side of a blue lake holding out an offering of a 4-stick box of butter.

No more. The Minnesota-based farmer cooperative has redesigned its packaging to focus on celebrating farmers ahead of its 100th anniversary next year.

"We need packaging that reflects the foundation and heart of our company culture — and nothing does that better than our farmer-owners whose milk is used to produce Land O'Lakes' dairy products," President and CEO Beth Ford said in a statement in February 2020.

The new packaging looks much like the old packaging — blue lake, green pine trees, yellow horizon — just minus Mia, the name of the Indian maiden.

The release made no mention of why the company decided to remove the character from their packaging. The entire

CHAPTER NINE

Land O'Lakes website seems to have been scrubbed of any mention of the iconic mascot.

For Native Americans who have long criticized the use of Indian mascots, the change is a welcome one.

"It's a great move," said Adrienne Keene, a professor at Brown University, author of the popular Native Appropriations blog and citizen of the Cherokee Nation. "It makes me really happy to think that there's now going to be an entire generation of folks that are growing up without having to see that every time they walk in the grocery store."

But Keene thinks the company missed an important opportunity in not explaining why they removed the image of the Indian maiden from their brand.

"It could have been a very strong and positive message to have publicly said, 'We realized after a hundred years that our image was harmful and so we decided to remove it,'" Keene said. "In our current cultural moment, that's something people would really respond to."

The Indian maiden first appeared on Land O'Lakes packaging in 1928, 320 farmers in St. Paul as it was first

CHAPTER NINE

called — founded seven years after the Minnesota Cooperative Creameries Association —.

Arthur C. Hanson, an illustrator for the ad firm Brown and Bigelow, came up with the original design evoking rural Minnesota with a blue lake, green pine trees and a Native woman center stage in a buckskin dress and feather headdress.

It imbued the Land O'Lakes brand with a sense of naturalness, nostalgia and American authenticity, a tactic used by thousands of companies to sell everything from butter to cigarettes to motorcycles, as a recent exhibition at the Smithsonian shows. Keene noted in one blog post that she could create an entire breakfast menu plus snacks using ingredients with Native mascots.

The packaging was redesigned in the 1950s by Patrick DesJarlait, a highly-successful Ojibwe artist from Red Lake. He said he was interested in "fostering a sense of Indian pride" across the Midwest.

"Today is a very different time than the 1950s. The 1950s was the termination era, and there were a lot of real threats to Native people's existence," Keene said, referring to the federal campaign to dissolve treaties, dismantle tribal

CHAPTER NINE

governments and eliminate reservations. "During that time there might have been some power to being able to associate with a major brand like Land O'Lakes and to have a role in shaping the representation."

Robert DesJarlait, the artist's son, says he's glad Land O'Lakes removed the Indian maiden his father helped create but also continues to be proud of his father's legacy, which includes creating the Hamm's Beer bear and being one of the first Native modernist painters.

"It was a source of pride for people to have a Native artist doing that kind of work," said DesJarlait, who's also an artist. "He was breaking a lot of barriers . . .Back in the 50s, nobody even thought about stereotypical imagery. Today it's a stereotype, but it's also a source of cultural pride. It's a paradox in that way."

DesJarlait and Keene said people have come to better understand the impact of these representations.

"The conversation has shifted so much. We have scientific, psychological research that shows the harms of these types of representations," she said.

CHAPTER NINE

The American Psychological Association in 2005 called for all American Indian mascots to be retired, citing a large body of social science research showing how racial stereotypes and inaccurate representations harm Native young people's self-esteem and social identity.

Keene says the Indian maiden stereotype is deeply entrenched in American culture, presenting Native women as being pure, sexually available and something to be conquered like nature.

"It's not a benign image," Keene said.

Then there's the "boob trick" in which you can make the packaging even more disrespectful by turning Mia's knees into her boobs. "Something lots of dads teach their kids," one YouTuber noted.

Months after pausing production while rethinking Eskimo Pie's over 100-year-old branding, accused of being derogatory toward the native people of the Arctic, parent company Dreyer's Grand Ice Cream made public its rebrand as Edy's Pie, a name inspired by one of the company's founders, Oct. 2.

CHAPTER NINE

The same day, the parent companies for Mrs. Butterworth's pancake syrup and Cream of Wheat cereal also vowed to revisit their packaging accused of being rooted in racist stereotypes or imagery, though the companies have released no further updates on what will change.

Colgate said June 18 2020 that it would "review and evolve" top-selling Chinese toothpaste brand Darlie, which once featured a smiling man in blackface and whose name (originally Darkie) translates to "black person toothpaste."

Nestlé said on June 22 2020 that it will stop selling under its Colombian Beso de Negra brand cookies and that it is rebranding its Australian-based Red Skins and Chicos sweets, describing their controversial names, which have prompted several years of complaints, as "out of step" with the company's values.

Dixie Beer, New Orleans' oldest brewery, announced on June 26 that it would change its name to shed any connotations of slavery, and has since asked for the public's help in picking a new name.

In July, the Indian subsidiary of Unilever revealed the new name for popular skin-lightening brand "Fair & Lovely" would be "Glow and Lovely," a move met with backlash

CHAPTER NINE

from critics who characterized it as merely a cosmetic change for a product that promotes harmful beauty standards.

Mars announced September 23 that Uncle Ben's will become Ben's Original and that the logo of an elderly African American man in a bow tie will be removed following criticism of the term "uncle" as derogatory and the brand's imagery as being reminiscent of servitude.

Racial stereotyping in products branding and imaging is not always negative, but is considered harmful in that the repetition of a stereotype naturalizes it and makes it appear normal. They are mental ideologies that the consumers' assigns meaning to base on their membership in a social category in order to process information as such stereotyping does not by definition carry negative or positive values. Because of this we see many different outcomes; racial stereotyping can be positive for the producers as well as the consumers in instances where specific demographics are being targeted. However it can be perceived negatively in instances where the stereotyping begins causing offence. Manufacturers and advertisers should be aware of the potential to cause serious or

CHAPTER NINE

widespread offence when referring to different races, cultures, nationalities or ethnic groups.

CHAPTER TEN

Concept of Free Enterprise

Free enterprise is widely acclaimed in the United States. Politicians, generally, declare in favor of it; editorialists frequently laud it; Chambers of Commerce have writing contests about it; even automobile stickers praise its virtues. Yet much of our enterprise is restrained, restricted, hampered, regulated, controlled, or prohibited. As an old saying has it, "What you do speak so loud I can't hear what

CHAPTER TEN

you are saying." By our practice, we say that we believe in free enterprise—except for public utilities, for the railroad, mail delivery, medical services, housing, financing, and real estate transactions, large corporations, except for education, interest rates, farmers, small business, industrial workers. In short, a case could be made that Americans believe in free enterprise except in whatever activities they happen to be considering.

It may be helpful, then, to consider free enterprise in terms of itself, minus all the partisan exceptions. The approach here will be to pose five questions: What is free enterprise? What are the objections to free enterprise? How may the objections be answered? What are the practical advantages of free enterprise? Is free enterprise necessary to freedom? The answers to these should provide some perspective on free enterprise.

Free enterprise, also known as free market or capitalism, is an economic system driven by supply and demand. Private businesses and consumers control the marketplace with little to no interference from the government. In this type of system, the government does not have a central plan for the nation's economy.

CHAPTER TEN

Free enterprise is a way of going about meeting our needs and wants by providing for ourselves or by freely entering into transactions with others. The opposite of free enterprise is hampered, restricted, controlled, or prohibited enterprise. The enterprise itself must be conducted in an orderly fashion within the framework of rules, but if the rules inhibit entry or hamper activity they become restrictions on enterprise. It is clear enough, for example, that traffic at an intersection must be regulated in its flow but that reasonable rules promote rather than inhibit the effective use of the street. On the other hand, if a city made a rule that taxicabs were to be limited to those presently in operation it would be equally clear that enterprise was being hampered. In a similar fashion, if a city adopted a rule forbidding any taxi to use the streets within its boundaries, that type of enterprise would be prohibited. Thus, government may be an adjunct or an obstacle to enterprise.

The components of free enterprise include:

Freedom to choose which business to open and how it operates.

Right to own private property.

CHAPTER TEN

Driven by the desire to maximize profits.

Competition among the producers of goods and services.

Right of consumers to spend their money freely.

In a free enterprise system, consumers are the people who pay for products and services. Ultimately, it is their self-interest that helps drive this type of economic system. Consumers decide what they want to spend their money on and which businesses they want to purchase goods and services from. They shop around for the best possible goods at the lowest prices.

One of the biggest components of free enterprise is that people are free to choose. This also extends to workers, who have the freedom to choose the type of employment they wish to have. They not only get to choose which field they want to work in, but also which employers they wish to work for.

Businesses are the producers in a free market system. It is the businesses that are responsible for producing the highest quality goods and services at prices that maximize profits. Businesses respond to what consumers want and what consumers are spending their money on. While free enterprise allows entrepreneurs to open any kind of business they choose, it offers no guarantees that the business will succeed.

Free enterprise promotes economic growth by encouraging entrepreneurs to start new businesses. Multiple businesses offering the same or similar goods and services leads to competition, which is good for the consumer. When businesses compete with each other to produce better products at better prices, the consumer reaps the benefits. Likewise, competition can lead to innovation as businesses strive to come up with new ways to maximize their profits.

In free enterprise, there are three types of markets: resource, product and financial. Resource markets are marketplaces where businesses can obtain labor, raw materials and capital. Businesses tap into the resource market when they need to find new employees to work for their company. Product markets are the marketplaces where businesses sell their finished goods and services. This does not include the sale of raw materials or other intermediate goods needed to produce the final product. Financial markets are marketplaces where buyers and sellers exchange assets such as stocks, bonds, securities, currencies and more.

Whereas a free enterprise system has very little government interference, a socialist economic system comes with heavy government regulations. In between free enterprise and socialist economies are mixed economies. The United States has a mixed economy. While it is largely a free market, it is not unregulated. The government does impose some regulations to protect consumers and workers without infringing on the freedoms awarded to businesses in a free enterprise economic system.

Government has become involved in the American free enterprise system because its citizens want it that way.

• Government passes laws to help protect citizens from false advertising, unsafe food and drugs, environmental hazards, and unsafe products.

• All levels of government provide goods and services for citizens

• Education, highways, public welfare, and many others.

• Government regulates economic activity to help preserve competition in the marketplace.

CHAPTER TEN

- Government spends more than all private businesses combined, so it has become a huge consumer in the marketplace

Most free enterprise systems consist of four components: households, businesses, markets and governments.

Households — the Owners. In a free enterprise system, households — not the government — own most of the country's economic resources and decide how to use them. One of the resources that households possess is their labor, which they sell to existing firms or use to form new businesses.

In addition to selling their resources where they can get the highest price or largest profit, households also act as consumers. The wages and salaries of households purchase about two-thirds of all the production in the United States.

Consumers vote with their dollars, thereby directing production toward the goods and services they want businesses to provide. This is called consumer sovereignty.

Businesses — the Organizers. Businesses organize economic resources to produce a good or service. The people who start businesses are called entrepreneurs. They

CHAPTER TEN

are the organizers and innovators, constantly discovering new and better ways to bring resources together in the hopes of making a profit. Profit fuels the engine of business.

Entrepreneurs, lured by the potential for profits, create new businesses to satisfy consumers' needs and desires. The inability to make profits signals businesses to close or to reorganize their resources more efficiently. Efficiency means that resources are being used to produce the goods and services that society most desires at the lowest economic cost.

In a competitive industry, the presence or absence of profits sends an important signal about the industry's economic efficiency.

Markets — the Brokers. How and where do buying and selling activities take place? The answer is, in markets. Although markets are not necessarily people, they act as agents — something like a stockbroker or a real estate agent — to bring buyers and sellers together. Over time, markets have become increasingly complex.

Now, buying and selling can occur 24 hours a day from anywhere in the world via the Internet. A market is any place or any way that buyers and sellers can exchange goods, services, resources or money.

Free markets are an extension of personal freedom. The premise of a market system is that people benefit from their own purposeful actions. Football fans stand in line for Dallas Cowboys tickets because they believe they will be better off if they can purchase tickets and go to the game. The team owner also benefits because the team must make a profit to remain in business. Both the owner and the fans are better off when tickets are sold.

That's what free enterprise is all about — cooperation and mutual benefit. No one is forced to buy football tickets, no one is forced to sell football tickets, and no one is forced to play football.

Another basic institution for free enterprise is private property. For enterprise to be free, those who engage in it must be free; that entails having property in themselves and what they produce. Enterprisers must have title to their goods in order either to consume them or trade with others. Real property in land and buildings is essential to have a place to produce and to market goods and services. Private property not only supplies opportunities for the individual

CHAPTER TEN

to provide for himself but it also places inherent limits on his activity. He can only rightfully sell and convey to another what is his in the first place. Private property also sets bounds to enterprise by restricting the owner to the use of what is his own or to that which the rightful owner authorizes others to use.

A free enterprise system promotes the freedom of individuals, whether they are part of the majority or a minority. For example, when people buy pencils, they don't ask about the race of the lumberjacks who chopped the wood, the religious preference of the miners who dug up the graphite or the political Probably our most important competitive advantage in the world market today is our high level of technology and our ability to affiliation of the workers who molded the aluminum casing for the eraser.

Instead, they ask, Is this a good price for the product?

In a free market system, a business that expresses prejudice and discriminates in its decisions will face higher costs than firms that do not discriminate. This is because the discriminating firm will have a smaller pool of workers and other resources to choose from. Such unprofitable attitudes

CHAPTER TEN

will put them at a competitive disadvantage, and the market will tend to drive them

out. Although it is true that prejudicial attitudes still persist in a free enterprise society, it is also true that a free enterprise system does a better job than any other to make such attitudes unprofitable.

In a free enterprise system, entrepreneurs, or risk-takers, have a strong incentive to pay attention to the votes consumers register with their dollars. This is because entrepreneurs profit by meeting consumers' wants and needs.

The motor of free enterprise, indeed, of all enterprise, is individual initiative. Individuals provide the energy for the making of goods and providing of services. They conceive, invent, design, engineer, produce, and market goods through their endeavor. The great spur to produce is the increase of one's goods or the profit he may make by selling them. Here again, the importance of private property and free access to the market may be seen. If men cannot keep as property what they produce, if they cannot market it, their incentive to produce is lessened or removed.

CHAPTER TEN

Entrepreneurs continually strive to improve established products and discover new ones. In the end, both the producers and the consumers benefit. Producers can earn a profit, and consumers can obtain the goods and services they want. Free markets do not cater solely to the majority. They also provide products and services that appeal to individual tastes.

Societies in which one group of leaders makes all the economic decisions probably do not produce the things that groups with special interests would like to have. For example, it is doubtful that one central authority would think to produce both rap music and classical music, Super Mario Brothers and Trivial Pursuit, pizza and sushi, and Bran Flakes and Cap'n Crunch. But free markets provide all these things and much, much more.

Free markets provide a vehicle for serving the individual needs of an entire spectrum of interests, whether they represent the majority or only a small percentage of people.

Adam Smith, in The Wealth of Nations, showed us more than 200 years ago that people pursuing their own self-interests in a free enterprise economy, as if led by some "invisible hand," end up promoting the public interest. But

CHAPTER TEN

with all these people looking out for themselves, how does free enterprise result in such beneficial outcomes for society? That's where competition enters the picture.

For example, when computers first came on the market, they had great value but were extremely costly to produce. Relatively few businesses could afford them. But the lure of profits prompted other companies to start producing computers.

This added competition had two results. It prompted computer companies to cut costs in order to compete, and it led them to look harder and faster for innovations that could give their computers an edge over the others. Now, computers are much less expensive, more powerful and much more user-friendly than they used to be.

The great regulator of free enterprise is competition. Competition among sellers keeps prices down and tends to assure that the customer will be served. Competition among buyers provides a market in which those goods that are wanted can be sold at a profit. Prices are the result of this competition. Although any owner may offer his wares at a price acceptable to him, he can only sell when he has found a buyer willing to pay his price.

CHAPTER TEN

Competition and the lure of profits, combined with ingenuity, continue to drive the market forward.

The benefits of competition and free enterprise are not limited to one country. If free enterprise between people in Texas and California makes those individuals better off, then free enterprise between people in Texas and Mexico must make those individuals better off as well.

The larger the marketplace, the greater the choices available and the greater the competition. Competition results in greater efficiency and lower prices, whether it is between two companies in the same country or two companies on opposite sides of the globe.

Let us examine some reasons why we should support an American free enterprise system:

1. Jobs—free enterprise is the only system that can create the 20 million that we'll need in the next decade.

2. Opportunity— Regardless of wealth, status, or background, you have a chance to rise as high as your talent and hard work can take you.

CHAPTER TEN

3. Freedom of Choice— You are free to choose your own path. No one picks your profession or limits what you can do or become.

4. Innovation—Free enterprise encourages it, fosters it, embraces it, and rewards it. Free enterprise excels in the solutions business.

5. Small Business— Almost anyone in America can start a business if he or she really wants to. The barriers are low, the opportunities are endless, and if you fail, and many do, you can get up off the floor and try again.

6. Social Mobility— No other society offers so many avenues for individuals, families, and succeeding generations to move up the ladder of success.

7. Quality of Life— Free enterprise supports a quality of life that previous generations could only dream of. We are living longer and enjoying an unsurpassed level of material comforts because of free enterprise.

8. A Progressive Society— A strong economy, powered by free enterprise, generates the revenues to educate our children, care for the sick and elderly, provide

CHAPTER TEN

compassionate support for the less fortunate, and clean our environment.

9. A Better World— The size and success of our free enterprise economy have given the United States and its citizens an unmatched capacity to address global problems and improve the state of the world.

10. The American Dream— It could not exist without free enterprise, for it is our economic freedom that enables us to achieve our dreams. It is free enterprise that breathes life into the promise of America, which is that a better life is always within our grasp and our country's best days are yet to come.

Free enterprise is doing more to ensure human flourishing and improve the lives of people around the globe than any other system or program devised by man. Though rooted in the historical developments of American culture, free enterprise has spread globally because it expresses the universal human desire for flourishing and building a better future.

When allowed to grow, free enterprise creates equal opportunity for all members of society to leave poverty, create value and achieve goals, become economically

CHAPTER TEN

mobile, and build a more peaceful and secure future. Yet, in all of this discussion of market access and competition, a foundational concept is often left out.

When discussions of innovation and free enterprise take place, the common view is of trendy food trucks and Uber, tech companies and new storefronts. What is often lost in the conversation is the very human impact free enterprise has made on the world. The purpose of free enterprise is not merely to create economic growth or wealth. In fact, economic growth and wealth are merely a means to an end: greater human flourishing.

Our free enterprise system is valuable not just because it creates wealth, but because it empowers all people to live better lives. Between 1981 and 2001, free trade and foreign investment lifted 400 million Chinese citizens out of abject poverty. Entrepreneurship training programs in the United States assisted prisoners in rebuilding their lives upon release, and reduced their likelihood of recidivism. Entrepreneurship and economic opportunity empowers disadvantaged groups around the globe, helping them build up both financial and social capital. Global poverty is it an

CHAPTER TEN

all-time low, thanks in large part to the expansion of free enterprise. It is an idea worth fighting for.

One major obstacle to free enterprise is the persistence of overregulation. Some level of regulation is needed to ensure health and public safety, yet many regulations become burdensome and counterproductive. The European Commission, along with several U.S. scholars, point to difficulties in accessing financial capital and markets, transferring or setting up business entities, and burdensome administrative procedures as major challenges to entrepreneurs. These policies, no matter how well intentioned, have the unintended effect of limiting economic opportunity.

Despite the 2013 efforts under the European Commission's Entrepreneurship Action Plan and proposed legislative reforms in the United States, entrepreneurs face an uphill battle in turning their ideas into reality. Nevertheless, free enterprise advocates in Europe and America are working tirelessly to better manage the administrative and regulatory burdens that hold back innovation. The goal is broad, better trade relationships among major players is needed at the macro level, while at the same time it is

CHAPTER TEN

imperative to improve opportunities for small businesses, local innovators, and to fight against the growth of unnecessary restrictions.

Transatlantic cooperation would aid in the battle to cut the red tape. Efforts to reduce regulatory burdens that do not serve the public good are moving forward, but this process is complex. From opening access to both human and financial capital and greater access to markets to the use of technology to cross pollinate innovators and exchange ideas, America and other countries can work together to foster innovation. The healthy competition from the emerging European effort to take on Silicon Valley will only result in better products and services, and the creation of wealth and economic opportunity for more people. Efforts to reduce administrative burdens in the U.S will allow for greater economic growth and future international partnerships.

The foundation of healthy transatlantic partnerships is rooted in free enterprise, and in the shared desire to grow economic opportunity for all, all of which will build a more peaceful and prosperous world. America has an obligation to find ways to expand free enterprise, and empower more

CHAPTER TEN

of their citizens, and the world's citizens, to take part in the greatest economic revolution in human history. Working together, America can lead the way in building a more prosperous future for all.

CHAPTER ELEVEN

The Widespread Impact of the Restaurant Industry Shutdowns

Many communities have been experiencing a growing restaurant scene over the last few years. In fact, recent years have been considered the "golden age" for restaurants. For now, that restaurant scene is virtually non-existent, and it looks nothing like it did six months ago because of the novel coronavirus. Restaurants have lost nearly three times more jobs than any other industry since the beginning of the COVID-19 pandemic. While some restaurants are trying to keep their employees employed and their doors open with take-out only concepts, many have temporarily closed their doors.

CHAPTER ELEVEN

Restaurants are already fragile businesses, not known for lucrative revenue, but instead known for surviving on tight margins. As the industry reopens to the "new normal," will restaurants be serving at full capacity? What extra expenses will restaurants have to endure to reopen? Will people want to dine in? Will restaurants survive with increased expenses and government-imposed capacity limits? And, if they don't, what other businesses that support restaurants could fail with them?

The restaurant industry contributes an estimated 4% of the United States' gross domestic product — or roughly one trillion dollars. As an industry, it is the nation's largest private employer and the third-largest employer overall. Since the end of March 2020, 3% of restaurants have permanently closed as a result of COVID-19, according to the National Restaurant Association, the main trade association for the industry. For the other 97%, governments at the local, state and federal levels have put some protections in place over the last few months, which have likely prevented more restaurants from permanently closing.

CHAPTER ELEVEN

Some businesses are getting Paycheck Protection Program (PPP) loans, or other state or local funding; employees are getting stimulus checks and unemployment checks (and in some cases in an amount in excess of what they would be getting if they were working because of the short term federal increase); there are moratoriums in place on collections, foreclosures, garnishments and evictions in many jurisdictions. What happens, however, when these protections no longer exist? The National Restaurant Association has predicted that 11% of restaurants will close as a result of the pandemic. It is likely that this number will increase, especially if there is another wave of COVID-19 infections, as predicted. The financial loss by the end of 2020 for the restaurant industry is predicted to be $240 billion.

In the initial reopening of dining in options, restaurants will likely experience decreases in clientele and revenue, either because of government restrictions, customers' fears of dining in close spaces, or both. Further, restaurants, already running on thin margins, will have to incur new, unexpected costs, such as facemasks, disposable menus, disposable silverware, extra cleaning supplies, hand washing stations and other previously unforeseen business expenses, which may or may not be government-mandated depending on where the restaurant is located. Can smaller operations, which have been closed and have startup costs from those closures, take the strain of less revenue and more expenses and remain open for an extended period of time? Most restaurants that have been closed will need $25,000 or more to reopen their doors.

Further compounding the industry's problem are unknown answers to the questions of how long restrictions on public gatherings may last; how long it will take people to feel comfortable eating at a crowded restaurant; and how long restaurants will need to incur additional expenses. Lack of public confidence may be related, in part, to inadequate COVID-19 testing in many areas and the predicted 12- to 18-month time frame for a vaccine to be available.

In some jurisdictions, governments are allowing dining rooms to re-open, but at a mere 25% capacity. In such locales, restaurants that normally serve 100 customers may now serve only 25 at a time. In smaller restaurants that normally serve 40 customers at a time, they can now only serve 10 people at a time. While a PPP loan may allow (and in fact require) the restaurant to employ its employees as it

CHAPTER ELEVEN

did pre-COVID-19, how long can the restaurant industry realistically run on 25% of its prior capacity while maintaining pre-COVID-19 employment? Not long, think some restaurant owners.

Pre-COVID, successful restaurants usually make a 10% profit with a full restaurant. With these government-mandated restrictions, it is likely that this 10% profit will be gone, and most restaurants will be operating at a loss, at least in the short term, in reopening in the new COVID-era.

By embracing digital resources like virtual discovery days, restaurant brands can find new opportunities for growth in an era of social distancing.

Drive-thru, delivery and pick-up services are no longer optional.

Few industries have been hit harder by the COVID-19 pandemic than foodservice, and as the crisis persists, it is becoming increasingly clear that consumer behavior is unlikely to snap back to "normal" anytime soon. Fortunately, a "new normal" that offers its own opportunities for growth is already unfolding, and some restaurant brands are making strategic pivots to make the most of those opportunities.

CHAPTER ELEVEN

Chances are, this isn't the first time you've read the word pivot in relation to restaurant operations over the past few months. To stay afloat while dining rooms were ordered closed across the country, restaurant brands have had to adjust their operations to find new ways of engaging with customers through digital channels and off-premise services. And in many cases, those pivots have not only staved off the worst effects of the crisis, they have also helped brands find new customers and forced restaurants to find new, more cost-effective methods of service.

Now, restaurant brands need to begin applying those same strategies to business development.

That begins with the discovery process. Historically, once a franchise candidate is in the pipeline, restaurant brands kick off the mutual discovery process with a series of phone calls and advisory meetings before inviting them to headquarters for an in-person discovery day. Now that in-person anything is a risky proposition, brands should make the effort to personalize the experience upfront with video conferences in conjunction with phone calls. By having face-to-face virtual interaction earlier in the process, brands can get a better sense of their candidates, determining who

CHAPTER ELEVEN

meets or does not meet the qualifications, or align with the brand's core values. It will also provide a more intimate and engaging experience for candidates, allowing them to make a personal connection with the brand.

Then there's discovery day itself, which for most brands will remain a virtual occurrence for the near future. Executive team members can conduct one-one-one meetings and even provide facility tours through a growing number of video-conferencing platforms i.e. WebEx, Zoom, etc. Informational pamphlets and booklets can be sent to the prospective franchisee ahead of time to provide context and supplementary information for the experience.

Of course, an effective discovery process relies on an attractive business opportunity, and video-conferencing or not, prospective candidates aren't going to sign onto a brand that is not embracing growth and changes in the marketplace, which brings us back to those store-level operational pivots.

Drive-thru, delivery and pick-up services are no longer optional. Off-premises services are required. The question every restaurant brand needs to ask itself is not if, but how to implement those services. Whether by partnering with

CHAPTER ELEVEN

third-party services or building out your own off-site operation, you'll need to operationalize those services quickly, safely and show prospective franchise owners how and why your strategy is primed for profitability.

Restaurant brands should also consider reevaluating their payment systems and processes. Bringing all orders under one single point-of-sale system and implementing "safety first" measures such as Plexiglas barriers, face coverings, and gloves will create a safer and more uniform customer experience. Streamlining operations and integrating a contactless experience not only makes life easier for multi-unit franchisees and employees but it enhances the bottom-line in the new consumer landscape.

Change is difficult yet inevitable. Traditional development professionals might lament the loss of long-established industry practices, but restaurant brands that embrace and cultivate the new environment we've found ourselves in will find no shortage of opportunities for growth.

The COVID-19 pandemic has wreaked havoc on the restaurant industry, but it hasn't ended it. Thanks to quick reactions and a willingness to adjust. Establishments of all sizes, locations and niches have managed to stay afloat.

CHAPTER ELEVEN

With more restaurants reopening, it's become clear that some of these changes will last.

Amid the chaos of COVID-19, restaurants adapted because they had to. As 110,000 establishments closed permanently, the industry quickly learned that it must adapt to survive. Now that the sector's lived with these adjustments for some time, their long-term potential is more apparent.

Many of these changes will linger after the pandemic fades. Restaurants have learned their lesson and will shift to prevent or weather future crises. The industry will emerge from the pandemic an entirely different animal, and here's what that will look like.

The most obvious change to come to reopening restaurants is a renewed stress on health and safety. During the pandemic, increased health measures are a government-mandated necessity in some areas. After the pandemic, they'll be an optional but critical part of preventing future risks.

Some measures, like wearing masks and mandating a six-foot distance between seats, will likely fade with the virus. Others, like frequent hand washing, hand sanitizer stations for guests and regular disinfection, will persist. Overall, the

CHAPTER ELEVEN

industry will take cleanliness more seriously, going beyond meeting FDA regulations and taking a proactive approach to disease prevention.

Restaurant health and safety protocols may reach a scientific level. Some operators may look into metallic nano-particle coatings to sterilize and disinfect kitchen equipment.

Technology has proven an indispensable resource for restaurants amid the pandemic. From QR code-based menus to app-based reservations and ordering, technology has sustained the industry throughout the past year. These tools can continue to help restaurants outside of the pandemic, too, so the industry will grow increasingly tech-centric.

Technology like digital menus don't just make restaurants safer, but more efficient. As more restaurants start reopening and customers flood back in, these efficiency gains will be crucial. Even lower-volume establishments will streamline dining through technology, as it creates a more gratifying customer experience.

After some time, the industry will move past digital services and embrace automation. Robots are already

CHAPTER ELEVEN

crucial in food packaging plants, but they could see service in restaurants too. Robotic cashiers, cleaners and even cooks will augment the human workforce, helping businesses serve more guests, and do so faster.

Ghost kitchens — restaurants that deal exclusively in carry-out and delivery — predate the pandemic, but are now far more enticing. Online delivery orders alone generated $45 billion in 2020, and it will likely take a while before in-house dining regains its place of dominance. Ghost kitchens capitalize on this trend, so they'll remain valuable long after the pandemic subsides.

Even as restaurants reopen, the public may not feel safe dining in. Online ordering has also made getting take-out or delivery easier than ever before, which will carry this trend further. Dine-in establishments can't meet this consumer segment's needs as efficiently or effectively as ghost kitchens.

It's also impossible to ignore the economic benefits of the ghost kitchen model. Since it typically requires less space and fewer furnishings, it reduces overhead expenses. Experts warn that full-service restaurants may not recover

CHAPTER ELEVEN

until 2025, so many businesses may turn to ghost kitchens to recover faster.

Technology has had a positive impact within every facet of our society. From improving how we go about our everyday lives to specifically how we grow, process, and buy our food. What's more it has ultimately answered our insatiable demand for convenience.

CHAPTER TWELVE

Input of Technology in the Restaurant Industry

Order ahead apps have definitely changed the customer dining experience and provide the ultimate in customer convenience. These mobile tools allow consumers to view a restaurant's menu anywhere and place an order so that it's ready when they arrive.

And this technology has benefitted restaurant owners, too - giving them more time to prepare food and the ability to increase table turnover. Also, since most pre-order apps have online payment features, restaurant owners can sell

CHAPTER TWELVE

their meals in advance. All these result in better customer experience, and of course, improved business operations.

According to Stephen Dutton, a foodservice analyst at Euromonitor International, today's technology is transforming a restaurant's concept of customer service. "Technology is replacing the service elements that defined more traditional restaurants," he says. "Many new restaurant concepts feel they must leverage technology to remain relevant to younger consumers who have grown up in a more tech-enabled environment."

As revealed in Toast's 2017 Restaurant Technology Industry Report, 95% of restaurant owners agree that technology really does improve their business efficiency. Most of them now believe that technology tools like POS systems, ordering and payments platform, mobile applications can streamline their processes and simplify their work lives.

Delivery apps such as Foodora, UberEats, and Deliveroo are becoming more and more popular now as consumers lead busier lifestyles. This type of technology has provided them with ultimate convenience enabling them to order food anytime and anywhere, and have it delivered straight to their door.

Robotics is on the rise, too, when it comes to home delivery. In the US, Domino's Robotic Units can deliver hot pizzas directly to your home. The restaurant chain introduced them just last year to improve convenience for their customers and are leading the way on food delivery powered by technology.

"With our growth plans over the next five to 10 years, we simply won't have enough delivery drivers if we do not look to add to our fleet through initiatives such as this," says Domino's Group CEO and Managing Director, Don Meij.

"Robotic delivery units will complement our existing delivery methods, including cars, scooters and e-bikes."

Technology has had a positive impact within every facet of our society. From improving how we go about our everyday lives to specifically how we grow, process, and buy our food. What's more it has ultimately answered our insatiable demand for convenience.

CHAPTER TWELVE

So, what are the ways that tech is elevating the Food and Beverage industry specifically?

Just like other industries, the food and beverage sector is not perfect. There are many serious issues that need to be addressed such as high food waste and the lack of access to locally grown produce. However the sector has definitely embraced a number of technology innovations to solve these problems.

Vertical farming, precision agriculture, and drones are just some of these tech innovations that are helping to increase farming efficiency and output. It is estimated that by the year 2050, the earth's population will grow to 10.5 billion which means produce will need to be doubled to be able to meet the market's demand.

There's no doubt that technology is changing the food and beverage industry for the better. It's providing consumers with the ultimate convenience they're looking for and is helping the restaurateurs take their business to the next level. As we move further into the digital age, we're certain that more technology innovations will emerge to help shape the industry's future.

CHAPTER TWELVE

There are now dozens of ways to get food delivered to your home. While delivery has long been associated with pizza, now you can order everything from Mexican to Malaysian to McDonald's, all without even lifting yourself off the couch.

The traditional method of calling up your favourite restaurant and placing your order directly is increasingly being replaced by food delivery apps such as SkipTheDishes, UberEats and Foodora.

These apps enable food lovers to order a meal from the comfort of their home with just a tap on their phone. For customers, this method promises convenience and fast delivery. And for restaurants, the apps claim to increase profit by broadening customer reach, and reducing marketing costs.

However, these apps have their fair share of critics. In fact, a New Yorker article in February argued that not only are food delivery apps hurting restaurants' bottom lines, they may even force them out of business.

In an industry known for its slim profit margins, are food delivery apps actually good for the restaurant business?

CHAPTER TWELVE

Are they under duress?

Given the promise of more customers and greater profit, some restaurateurs feel like they have no choice but to submit to this new reality.

The main issue is the service charge. Most apps work by charging a fee for each delivery, usually a percentage of the total cost of the sale, covered by the restaurant (the customer pays a separate service charge). The charge to restaurants can be steep: UberEats currently takes a 35 per cent cut from each order. This is a significant chuck out of a restaurant's profits.

Restaurant owners have likened food delivery apps to a drug addiction: businesses build up a dependence on these kinds of food orders, even though in the long run they know it might not be financially healthy for them. One Toronto restaurateur was recently quoted as saying "If it wasn't for the massive amount of people who use Uber and Foodora for takeout, I would love to drop them."

As delivery becomes the more preferred option for food lovers, some restaurants have reported a decrease in patrons physically coming in to dine at their restaurant. While this is not surprising, for many businesses dine-in customers are their bread and butter, and are considered to be more profitable than having a third party order and pick up the food.

While many restaurants have reported a marked increase in customers and profit, the issues above can mean that food delivery apps are not a perfect fit for every business.

IP issues

Restaurant owners have found that some food delivery apps have included details of their business on the app, including their logo and menu items, without seeking permission. Most delivery app companies reach out to prospective restaurants before adding them to the app, but some do not.

A recent CBC article found that DoorDash has added a number of Ottawa restaurants without asking for approval. One restauranteur believes that for DoorDash it is "a relationship between themselves and their customers, the people ordering food. They don't see the restaurants as part of that equation".

This can have intellectual property repercussions if a third party is including your restaurant's name, logo and menu details on their app. For example, if your restaurant name

CHAPTER TWELVE

has been trademarked, then an individual or company needs to seek permission from you in order to use that name.

In addition, third-party food delivery can affect a restaurant's brand. Drivers working on behalf of these apps may not be vigilant at ensuring the food remains in good shape and at a suitable temperature while in transit. Customers who receive poor quality food due to the delivery methods may think twice before ordering from that restaurant again. Indeed, some restaurants won't even deal with food delivery apps anymore, as they see it as so damaging to their brand.

Over the last couple of years, there has been a growth in reliance on food delivery apps. This is due to how as people get busier with their everyday lives, they tend to prioritize convenience. With the current global pandemic, food delivery apps have been a vital part of most peoples' quarantine agenda. It's also the primary way that restaurants continue to generate sales amidst the mandatory restaurant and bar shutdowns put in place by the government. As a result, the digital food delivery sector is amongst the few businesses flourishing in the current crisis. The total

CHAPTER TWELVE

number of users for food delivery apps has also increased by 9.8% in 2020.

In addition to the companies benefiting, food delivery also acts as a source of income for many individuals. With over 14.7% of the US population currently being unemployed (2), food delivery acts as a viable source of income. Although many questions the safety involved with doing such a job, delivery apps have publicly committed to ensuring the safety of their drivers. This involves the option of 'contact-free delivery' which limits handling in transferring the food thus reducing the risk of the virus spreading. Several other mandatory safety measures are being implemented by restaurants as well. Many delivery apps are also working to provide restaurants with CDC issued guidelines in order to ensure that the food are handled safely.

Chef Ashish Alfred owns several restaurants in Maryland. He said he's never had a problem with delivery apps — he just saw them as bringing in extra business. Then the COVID-19 pandemic hit. Alfred now relies solely on delivery. And, he said, with apps like Seamless and Grubhub that charge as much as 40% in fees, "It's a huge,

CHAPTER TWELVE

huge chunk of our money. Especially because people are just, for the most part, using this money to pay their staffs."

According to the website Yelp, food delivery orders have doubled since the outbreak began. Many restaurants are closed. Business is now almost entirely delivery. And tension is growing between the restaurant owners and the delivery apps.

A class action lawsuit was filed that companies like Grubhub, Uber Eats and Postmates charge restaurants exorbitant fees, which, in turn, force restaurants to hike prices up for people who dine in.

Now Alfred is one of many restaurateurs asking customers to delete those apps.

"Look up your favorite restaurant, give them a call, see if they will deliver to you, and if they don't deliver and you can't leave the house, then do what you need to do."

Professor Douglas Miller of Cornell University understands some of the difficulties small restaurants are having right now but, he said, they have bigger problems than app fees.

CHAPTER TWELVE

"For most independent restaurants, [it's] very small margins," he said. "So I think them being closed is a bigger issue than using apps."

Still, Rutgers University associate professor Rebecca Givan said this crisis might shake up the entire food app industry.

"We're at a critical juncture where one of the questions is whether these companies will be able to continue essentially ignoring all regulations, whether we're talking about monopolies and price gouging or whether we're talking about how workers are treated," she said.

This week, San Francisco enacted an emergency cap of 15% on delivery apps. Several New York City lawmakers are pushing for a 10% cap.

"The mayor and the governor have the power to shut down in-house operations of bars and restaurants during an emergency, so they should be able to use those same powers to institute a cap on those delivery apps," said Justin Brannan , a New York City councilman.

Plenty of restaurants won't make it through this economic crisis. Brennan said there's no need to squeeze them even harder.

CHAPTER TWELVE

GrubHub announced in early March that they would offer "deferred commission fees" on products from independent restaurants (not including any big chains) that normally make up roughly 80% of their sales revenue. They have also taken the initiative to use its "Donate the Change" program to assist drivers and restaurants negatively impacted by the Coronavirus.

UberEats, additionally, has announced that it will be waiving its delivery fee when individuals order from an independent restaurant. UberEats has also declared the option for restaurants to receive daily payments instead of their conventional weekly payments to reduce the financial burden on restaurant owners. Additionally, they have committed to assisting drivers and delivery men who currently can't work due to exposure to the coronavirus. Postmates has also set up its "Postmates Fleet Relief Fund" which aims to cover COVID-19 related medical expenses for its employees, and are also looking into omitting commission fees for new restaurants that join the app during this period.

However, there remains growing backlash against delivery apps, as many claims that they are exploiting the current

CHAPTER TWELVE

pandemic to their economic benefit. GrubHub faced severe criticism when it announced that they made a whopping $363 million in sales revenue from January to March and continue to charge extremely high delivery fees especially when restaurants are struggling to stay open. This is a claim that has been made by restaurant owners for years now. Because these delivery apps are aware of how much business they bring to restaurants, they charge extremely high fees and are able to get away with it. This complaint has been amplified in the current economic condition. Many claim that because people primarily rely on delivery apps to ensure convenience and safety (as they don't have to leave their homes and expose themselves to any risks), those delivery apps have utilized this to their advantage by increasing food delivery fees. This is shown by the 16.3% increase in delivery fees between March 12 to March 18, compared to the first week of February- caused by the surge in demand for home delivery.

According to an online website LAist: For more than 60 years, Casa Vega, an old school Mexican restaurant in Sherman Oaks, had never bothered with delivery. It didn't need to. "We were always very busy," said owner Christy

CHAPTER TWELVE

Vega, whose grandparents started the business when they immigrated to Los Angeles from Tijuana in the late 1930s.

Before coronavirus, fans came to Vega's restaurant as much for the atmosphere as for the food, lingering over margaritas in the red, leather booths. In mid-March, when L.A. County ordered all restaurants to close their dining rooms, Vega realized the lack of delivery options was going to be a major problem. She and her team were, she admits, "completely unprepared" to reinvent the wheel.

In late April, after Casa Vega had been closed for more than a month, she reluctantly started contacting delivery apps. Although she had never cared for their business model — apps commonly take between 15% and 30% commission on every order — these were desperate times.

"We opened with a great demand, more than we ever anticipated. We were completely overwhelmed with orders, much more than we could possibly handle. I looked at everybody that night and said, 'Thank God we didn't do those delivery apps.' It kind of saved us," Vega says.

Casa Vega is one of a growing number of restaurants that have chosen to ditch delivery apps because of high commission rates, safety concerns or both. Although

CHAPTER TWELVE

restaurants had complained about delivery apps long before coronavirus, the pandemic has intensified their issues, especially in L.A. County, where 80% of restaurant jobs vanished almost overnight due to COVID-19.

Vega compares food delivery apps to piranhas, cannibalizing the industry they are supposed to serve. "It's not right," she says. "They take too much money. The fees are ridiculous."

Every restaurant in the United States negotiates its own contract with whatever app or apps they choose to use. If restaurants decide to use multiple services, apps often charge them higher commissions but if they sign an exclusive agreement with one app, rates will typically go down. Postmates for example, is the only app that offers delivery from L.A. hot spots Moon Juice and Howlin' Rays, whose ordering pages feature an #onlyonpostmates hashtag.

Those contracts often include non-disclosure sections that prohibit restaurants from publicly disclosing the apps' commission rates, making an already opaque process even less transparent.

CHAPTER TWELVE

According to LAist a popular local blog that covers local news, politics, restaurants and sports :

UberEats: A company rep said commissions vary based on the package a restaurant chooses. For restaurants that use the app only for ordering, meaning they have their own drivers and/or vehicles, the commission rates are about 15% on average. To use the UberEats platform and the UberEats delivery fleet, commissions range from 15% to 30%, according to the company.

Doordash/Caviar: In August 2019, Doordash acquired high-end delivery app Caviar for $410 million in cash. Since they're a private company, a spokesperson from Doordash declined to tell us their average commission fee or give us an average range of fees, saying the rates are confidential and vary by restaurant.

Grubhub: A spokesperson from Grubhub said their platform is "free," but if restaurants want the company to provide delivery drivers, it will cost them 10% of the total order. If restaurants want to use the app for "marketing" purposes, meaning their menus appear or are featured on the app when users in the area search for available delivery and pick-up options, that costs them another 15%. Two

CHAPTER TWELVE

restaurateurs told LAist that forgoing the marketing fee isn't realistic. They say that if you do, its unlikely users will be able to find your restaurant, let alone order from it. That would mean using Grubhub, on average, costs restaurants approximately 25% commission on each order.

Postmates: When we asked, "What is your average commission fee?," a Postmates spokesperson said they took issue with the word "fee.""Commissions are not 'fees,'" the representative wrote via email, "they are the main source of revenue for our company and they are how we pay for the services that we provide to businesses and our customers." The spokesperson said that the commission rates are decided privately with each restaurant and that "arbitrarily setting on-demand delivery prices has real consequences that undermine our ability to operate... and kills the whole industry's ability to provide the services restaurants need to stay open." They did not provide any numbers. (As of June 2020, Postmates is the most used food ordering app in LA, trailed closely by DoorDash, according to the Second Measure analysis).

When the coronavirus pandemic forced restaurants to stop dine-in service, delivery apps released statements of

CHAPTER TWELVE

concern and support for local businesses. But most of them did not significantly lower their commissions or fees.

DoorDash and Caviar made some temporary changes to relieve local restaurants during the shutdown. On April 10, both apps offered half-off their commissions through the end of May, and zero commission fees for new restaurants during their first 30 days with the service. Those relief programs ended on May 31, a DoorDash spokesperson told us.

In July, DoorDash and Caviar launched "Main Street Strong," an initiative that allows restaurants to set up a digital "storefront" on their own website, so they can sell directly to customers without a commission. That service is being rolled out slowly and there's already a waitlist to sign-up. The DoorDash spokesperson said although the program does not have traditional commission fees, it does have set-up, subscription and delivery fees. She declined to share those figures with us.

UberEats told LAist that at the start of the pandemic, they announced they would waive all commissions on pick-up orders made through the end of 2020 via the app. (Yes, most delivery apps also take commissions for pick-up

CHAPTER TWELVE

orders.) The company also says that between March 15 and the end of April, they waived "eater-facing" delivery fees at "independent restaurants." It was a good deal for consumers, temporarily reducing their delivery charges, but it didn't reduce the cut that restaurants paid to UberEats.

Grubhub, for its part, offered consumers a $10 off promo around the time stay-at-home orders were first issued. Restaurants who opted into the "Supper for Support" promotion received a $10 credit for the first 25 orders. After that, they could decide if they wanted to continue running the promotion at their own expense while still paying commission on the full, pre-discount cost of the order.

Joseph Badaro, who owns Hummus Labs in Pasadena, told LAist that the company repeatedly asked him to sign up for the promotion: "They're like, 'We're here to help you,' but it doesn't do anything to help the restaurant — other than sell food that eventually will lose 30% commission."

Meanwhile, food delivery apps were flooded with so many new restaurants itching to sign up, they couldn't keep up with the demand.

CHAPTER TWELVE

UberEats told LAist that since the coronavirus pandemic hit the U.S., they've seen self-sign ups decuple (i.e. increase tenfold; we had to look that up). If you're wondering how much money that is, in 2019, UberEats made an estimated $337 million in adjusted net revenue. Now, multiply that by ten.

Restaurants prepare and sell a physical product that can quickly spoil. Most of them, unless they're part of a chain, are small businesses operating on thin margins — about 6%, according to one financial statement analysis.

Food delivery apps, by comparison, are larger, more centralized tech companies that benefit from economies of scale. When a bunch of their clients go out of business, so what? New restaurants will open to meet consumer demand. If delivery apps don't care about the survival of individual restaurants, it's because they don't have to.

During her negotiations with delivery apps, Vega said the lowest fee she received was from UberEats, which pitched her a commission of 22%.

"I was just shocked, ethically and morally, that they weren't lowering the rates for restaurants [during the pandemic], yet they had so much business they didn't even have the

CHAPTER TWELVE

hardware to sign us up," Vega says. "We're not going to give 30% to companies that show no compassion for our industry at this time. It's just crazy. We're in a fight for our lives right now."

Vega is far from the only restaurateur who's fed up with delivery apps. Burgers Never Say Die, in Silver Lake, recently started charging extra on every order placed via Caviar to make up for the commission taken by the app. If you order one of their regular cheeseburgers in the restaurant or by phone, it'll cost you $7.50 (before tax). Order it on Caviar, and it'll cost you $9.50.

"Why are our delivery app prices so much higher than our in store prices? Well, it's because we're being charged 21% on every order, which means we're barely making any money on delivery app orders," owner Shawn Nee wrote in an Instagram post.

"Every time a delivery app service contacts us, I respond with the following: 'If you can give me [a] 10% [commission deal] on every order, we can continue this conversation,'" Nee told LAist. "We either never hear back from them, or we get some spiel about 'corporate' and how they won't let us go that low."

CHAPTER TWELVE

Burgers Never Say Die still offers delivery via Caviar but Nee told LAist that he encourages customers to place their orders directly by calling or walking up to the restaurant.

Wirt Morton, co-owner of Tito's Tacos in Culver City, told LAist that his restaurant's profit margin, despite its cult following and 60-year track record, is about 3% to 4%. But the lowest commission the delivery app companies offered him was 17%.

"We would lose money on every delivery. It just didn't make sense," Morton said.

Instead, he and his wife, who co-owns the business, decided to start offering delivery, something they've never done during their six decades in business. They chose local courier service StreetSmart Messengers, which requires its delivery drivers to complete the National Restaurant Association's food safety program. They deliver all items in "tamper-proof" packaging, according to Morton, so "no one puts their grubby hands on the food."

It doesn't come cheap. Customers who order delivery from Tito's Tacos have to pay a $10 fee for delivery within a 5-mile radius of the restaurant and there's an extra $2 to $3 per mile charge for customers who live farther away.

CHAPTER TWELVE

Morton knows the steep figure means he'll lose some customers, but he says it's worth it to know his patrons won't catch COVID-19 from one of his delivery orders.

Tito's is lucky to have a legion of hardcore fans, many of whom are willing to pay extra for their favorite hard-shell gringo tacos. "When it was announced that we were going to start delivery, we had people in Texas, Colorado, Connecticut and even overseas saying, 'Can you deliver here?,'" Morton says. (Sadly, he can't.) Restaurateurs who lack that kind of name recognition aren't so lucky.

May Matsuo-Rose, who grew up in Orange County, started Don Don Curry, a Japanese deli business, in 2016 in New York City. She started by selling Japanese comfort food such as curry, chicken katsu and egg sandwiches at farmers markets and pop-up events. When she moved to L.A., she rented space in a commercial kitchen near Exposition Park, planning to expand to food delivery and catering.

Of course, after COVID-19 hit, catering was out of the question. Delivery was the only way Matsuo-Rose could make a living, so she signed up with four of the apps. She also shared details about commission rates with LAist. (Although Postmates and UberEats had confidentiality

CHAPTER TWELVE

clauses in their contracts, since she has ended those contracts, she spoke freely.)

Here's what each app was charging her:

Postmates: 25%

UberEats: 30%

DoorDash: 30% (cut to 15% when the pandemic hit)

Grubhub: 33% (30% commission plus a 3% "processing fee")

At the end of May, Matsuo-Rose closed Don Don Curry. Relying solely on delivery apps to distribute food, she and her partner couldn't make enough money to pay the rent on their kitchen space and keep the business afloat.

"It's been really difficult because they take so much commission. It's not a sustainable way to do business. You're losing money feeding people," Matsuo-Rose said to LAist.

For restaurants that have been open for years and built a dedicated client base, Matsuo-Rose says she could see their delivery business thriving, even with the apps' commission fees. But for a new business, she says it's nearly impossible.

CHAPTER TWELVE

When thousands of restaurants joined delivery platforms during the COVID-19 pandemic, the competition was so intense it was nearly impossible to find newbies like Don Don on these apps. If restaurant owners couldn't pay the extra marketing fees, like the ones Grubhub charges, Matsuo-Rose says their businesses got buried by a glut of more established restaurants.

"Our rep at the kitchen even encouraged us to order from ourselves on these apps so we could trick the algorithm to make it seem like our restaurant is busier and more popular than it is," Matsuo-Rose says.

At the same time, trying to make a go of it without delivery apps, especially as a new restaurant, means you might not be able to attract any customers at all.

"If you're a brand new business, you have to market yourself just to let people know you exist." The apps, she said, "are a necessary evil."

Kevin Mok, who runs Mr. Obanyaki, a dessert shop in Monterey Park that sells milk tea, frozen yogurt and Tawainese wheel cakes, echoed those same sentiments as Matsuo-Rose.

CHAPTER TWELVE

"Postmates charges us 30%. Grubhub charges us 27%. It's a huge amount but there's nothing we can really do about it because we need the service," Mok says, adding that he has no other choice because he can't afford to hire his own driver.

Mok says on a $10 dollar order, for example, he pays about $3 in commission, $1 in sales tax and at least $2 on ingredients. After paying his rent and labor costs, he says, "I'm probably making $2 or $2.50 on that order."

"Right now, I'm able to survive," Mok says, "but the future is pretty uncertain. I don't know how much longer I can last." In April, he started a GoFundMe to raise extra money to keep his business alive.

Matsuo-Rose said restaurant owners who lack the English language skills to negotiate a better contract or the technical wherewithal to optimize their presence on apps are at an even greater disadvantage.

"It's hard because a lot of small restaurant owners are immigrants," Matsuo-Rose says. "Some are older and don't have the tech savvy to partner with these apps successfully. I'm in several Facebook groups where they're just like, 'I

CHAPTER TWELVE

can't even navigate this dashboard to set up the menu and then take the pictures.'"

On June 8, the L.A. City Council unanimously approved a motion temporarily capping third-party delivery app fees at 15% and limiting marketing fees to 5%. In the original motion, council member Mitch O'Farrell called these fees "exorbitant" and argued they made it harder for restaurants to survive during the ongoing "international emergency."

It wasn't an original idea. Several cities including San Francisco, New York, Chicago, Seattle, Washington D.C. and Jersey City had already capped delivery app fees in an attempt to dull the pandemic's blow to their respective dining scenes.

L.A.'s ordinance, which is set to expire 90 days after in-person dining is allowed to resume (this time, hopefully for good), also requires food delivery apps to provide an itemized rundown of all costs to customers. That includes the price of the food, the delivery fee charged to the restaurant, any other commissions or fees associated with the delivery and the tip.

All of the major delivery apps insist they are abiding by L.A.'s ordinance but in early July 2020, two local restaurant

CHAPTER TWELVE

owners told Eater LA that some delivery apps were still charging them between 25% and 30% commission on orders. The owners said when they asked Grubhub, DoorDash and Postmates about the new law; the companies either sent them generic statements, confusing messages or nothing at all.

A spokesperson for councilmember O'Farrell said, via email, that the city is currently surveying restaurants to gauge whether or not the ordinance is being followed.

"It is my understanding that restaurants can file a written report justifying when the ordinance was violated on the delivery application," the spokesperson told LAist. "The delivery app has 15 days from the written notice to make the necessary changes."

If the app doesn't make those changes, "civil action may be taken." The spokesperson said the City Attorney's office is "working on a plan" for what that might look like.

Even with a cap on commissions and fees, some restaurant owners are still ditching third-party apps. Morton says the city council's efforts sound good, but a 15% to 20% commission is still way too high for him. At those rates, he believes Tito's Tacos wouldn't be able to stay in business.

CHAPTER TWELVE

Other businesses aren't waiting for politicians or local ordinances to save them. They're looking for alternatives to the well-known delivery apps.

At the onset of the pandemic, Tock, a restaurant reservation system serving several cities across the country, has recast itself as a take-out (and, in some cases, delivery) platform. The company has less name recognition than Grubhub or DoorDash but its platform, which includes a website and an app, has become the go-to option for many of L.A.'s upscale restaurants.

Tock's Director of Marketing, Kyle Welter, told LAist that Los Angeles is "by far and away" one of their largest growing markets. More than 100 local restaurants now use the platform. Many of them, especially the ones that used to book reservations weeks in advance, are now offering prix fixe dinners or special menu items only on Tock. Bestia has a six-course "Bestia at home" menu that changes every three days while Republique offers family-style dinners, Bar Henry makes five-person craft cocktails and n/naka creates elaborate, two-tier bento boxes, all for pick-up. Wolfgang Puck told the Los Angeles Times that Tock helped him make take-out at Chinois worth it.

CHAPTER TWELVE

The site isn't as easy to navigate as the Big Four apps, likely because it wasn't originally designed to be an online ordering system. But Tock has a major upside for restaurants — its most basic plan charges restaurants a $199 monthly fee plus a 2% commission on prepaid reservations. If a restaurant doesn't want or need the reservation feature, the commission increases to 3%, with no subscription fee. For Tock's core clientele of high-end and midscale restaurants, where a dinner tab for two easily runs between $75 and $150 (without alcohol), this fee structure is likely a bargain compared to the steep per-order commissions most third-party apps charge.

"We are passionate about helping restaurants, and as a restaurant owner, I know how it works," Tock CEO Nick Kokonas told LAist via email. He owns four restaurants and two bars in Chicago.

Kokonas told LAist that since March, Tock has added about 60 restaurants a day, in 28 countries, but it isn't the only option for food businesses.

Joseph Badaro, owner of Hummus Labs in Pasadena, went a different route. He had spent months planning the opening of his Mediterranean restaurant, but when the

CHAPTER TWELVE

pandemic hit, his landlord wouldn't let him cancel his lease. So he figured he'd try to make it work, at least for a month, and opened in April

Badaro signed up for Grubhub, which kept him afloat for a while but he realized he was making nearly 70% of his profit through the app — and the app was taking 30% of it back. He started looking for options and decided to try ChowNow.

"What they do is just put an order platform on your site, and the customer is the only one that pays a delivery fee," Badaro says.

Instead of paying a commission, restaurants pay ChowNow a set fee. Badaro says for him, it's $150 a month. Although he still uses Grubhub for pickup (at a 15% commission), he stopped using the app for delivery in July and hasn't looked back.

"It was just simple math. My sales have been increasing, like week over week. I've literally talked to every single restaurant in my building about signing up with them," Badaro says.

CHAPTER TWELVE

That flat fee is part of ChowNow's ethos. "We are anti-commission," CEO Christopher Webb told LAist via email, adding that since March, the company has added more than 8,000 new restaurants to its platform. "Every restaurant in the country wants to, and needs to, move off predatory marketplaces like Grubhub if they want to survive the pandemic," Webb says.

San Francisco-based coffee roasting company Sightglass is using Toast, a tablet-based, point-of-sale system, to process takeout orders.

Unlike many third-party apps, Toast is transparent about its prices. The company generally charges restaurants $50 to $100 per month to use its system for orders and sales, both online and in-person. Aside from that, restaurants pay no other fees to the company. The ordering system is usually embedded into the restaurant's website.

After opening on March 14, the day before L.A. Mayor Eric Garcetti issued a stay-at-home order, Sightglass's first sit-down restaurant, located near La Brea and Melrose, had to close ite dining room.

For Stanley Morris, director of operations for Sightglass, the decision to use Toast rather than any of the Big Four

CHAPTER TWELVE

delivery apps was a no-brainer. "With delivery companies, unless you're doing a huge volume of orders, it's expensive. And I didn't see any consistent behaviors around sanitation and how they were handling everything," Morris said.

Sightglass had spent more than a year planning the debut of its first L.A. outpost, a 13,000-square-foot roasting plant with a 150-seat restaurant and a to-go coffee window near La Brea and Melrose. Opening day, on March 14, was a success. The next afternoon, Mayor Eric Garcetti issued a stay-at-home order. The restaurant had to pivot; it became Sightglass Provisions, a boutique provider of high-end prepared foods, farmer's market produce and, of course, locally roasted coffee.

When it did, Morris was able to quickly train his seven-person staff on Toast. Aside from that, all he had to do was create a menu for pick-ups and pre-orders and voila, the digital marketplace was born. Toast allows him to fill orders without paying steep commissions or using outside delivery drivers. For health and safety reasons, he prefers only Sightglass employees handle the restaurant's food. Everyone who enters the premises gets their temperature checked, all items are carefully sanitized and pick-ups are

CHAPTER TWELVE

entirely contactless. It's all part of the carefully choreographed quality-control system Morris has implemented to prevent COVID-19 transmission.

But even with the speedy reorganization, Morris says Sightglass is probably making less than 20% of its projected profit. "We're just trying to get through this. In the meantime, we're going to be the best business we can be, under the circumstances. Everyone's making this up as they go along," he says.

For food businesses that don't have the capacity to hire a delivery staff or create complicated ordering systems, solving the food delivery issue can be like a high school group project — sometimes it's better to just do it yourself.

Sara Valdes runs Sara's Market, in City Terrace, with her husband, Steven. The shop is a neighborhood convenience store with a bit of a glow-up. Alongside the usual bags of M&Ms and bottles of Tabasco, you'll find Kernel of Truth organic tortillas, bottles of natural wine, craft beer and oat milk.

The store didn't start making deliveries until May, when Sara and Steven outfitted a truck and started bringing their goods directly to a set location two days a week.

CHAPTER TWELVE

"People have expressed to us that they are still a bit hesitant to come into the store, so we give them the option to pick up from the truck," Steven Valdes told LAist in August 2020.

The Sara's Market truck isn't like a typical food truck. You don't order at the window and wait until your number is called. Instead, you place and pay for your order in advance via Toast. For Sara Valdes, the best part is that she doesn't have to pay any commissions or rely on third-party apps.

"It's always been a family-owned business, so whatever we do, we can do it ourselves," she said.

They charge a $5 delivery fee per order, a number they can keep low since they don't have to pay steep commissions. Valdes says they also use the truck to help generate revenue for other businesses in East L.A. Their pickups usually occur at local businesses such as George's Burger Stand on Cesar Chavez, where their patrons might be tempted to grab a pastrami burger or some chili cheese fries. Valdez wants to share the wealth with neighborhood restaurants that might not have the resources to deal with delivery apps or online ordering platforms.

CHAPTER TWELVE

At the start of the coronavirus pandemic, Valdes said business was slow. Now, the shop is generating about the same revenue as it did pre-pandemic — not something you hear often from people in the food industry.

"We are getting big support from the community, which we really, really appreciate," Valdes says. If you want to support your local restaurants, bars, convenience stores and markets but aren't sure how, she has a piece of advice: Call them and ask.

"Just straight ask them, 'What is the best way I can order that would benefit you the most?'" Valdes said. "I always tell everyone to shop local, support local, even if it's just a gallon of milk. That's still a sale for that person and that's still income coming in. I feel like everybody's in the same boat right now, struggling in one way or another. But I think as long as each community sticks together, we will all actually get through this."

As more restaurants close for good — pour one out for Dong Il Jang, Broken Spanish, Baco Mercat, Jun Won, Swingers, Here's Looking At You, Trois Mec along with the countless small establishments that will never see their names mentioned in a media outlet — and the timeline for

CHAPTER TWELVE

a full reopening remains murky, many restaurant owners realize that if they want to survive, they'll have to re-imagine their businesses for the long haul.

"We're not going back to what we thought the restaurant business was, maybe ever," said Morris, of Sightglass. "You can't make it on a few tables on the sidewalk or with just takeout. It's sad and it hurts and it's painful, but it's reality."

At Casa Vega, Christy Vega knows she won't be able to rely on the same business model she's used for more than half-a-century but she's not sure what comes next.

"The future of the restaurant industry is completely up in the air," Vega said. "Sadly, I think the landscape will look much different in 2021. That said, restaurateurs by nature have amazing heart and passion. Resilience in times of chaos is second nature for us. So I still have hope."

Clearly food delivery apps have the potential to increase patronage for restaurants, and many businesses can testify to the positive difference that these apps have made.

However, restaurant owners should be vigilant at making sure the information on these apps, such as menu items and

CHAPTER TWELVE

logo, is correct. And at any time you wish to opt out, you can usually do so by contacting the delivery company directly.

If you are having serious issues dealing with these food delivery apps, consider consulting a lawyer. After all, brand protection is incredibly important to a business, and once that brand has been damaged, there can be a long recovery time.

According to an online story by Vivian McCall, Allison June Palmer is the kind of cool, tattooed bartender who loves her job.

She's lucky to be working at Chef's Special Cocktail Bar in Bucktown, she said, where they've shut down indoor dining until she and all her colleagues are vaccinated.

While Palmer feels valued, she said many of her industry friends aren't so fortunate. She knows many servers and restaurant staffers who work long hours, for little pay and, for much of the past 11 months, exposure to COVID-19.

"We're dealing with more people unmasked and eating than any other industry," Palmer said recently from her home in Logan Square. "For once in the hospitality

CHAPTER TWELVE

industry, we need to stop trying to please everybody and start taking care of ourselves."

With millions of residents in Chicago to vaccinate, the city has prioritized restaurant workers in the so-called group 1c — which Chicago officials estimate won't start getting vaccinated until March 29.

Meanwhile, indoor dining is accelerating. Restaurants can now seat 40% of their total capacity or up to 50 people, whichever is fewer.

Officials say they may soon allow 50% capacity if COVID-19 cases and hospitalizations continue to decline. As at February, the rolling 7-day average test positivity in Chicago was 3%.

Restaurant workers who talked to WBEZ a radio station in Illinois Chicago said they agree some of the groups ahead of them ,which include health care workers, the elderly, and frontline workers like teachers and grocery store workers should be a priority.

But, they're frustrated that indoor dining keeps getting expanded, increasing their risk to COVID-19 before they can be vaccinated.

CHAPTER TWELVE

Palmer pointed out that her husband, who works in a brewery, which is considered a manufacturing job, got his first dose — even though he only comes face-to-face with his masked coworkers. She doesn't think its right for most restaurants to open up before workers have a chance to protect themselves.

"I'm angry at both the city and the bigger restaurant corporations because it seems like they are the ones pushing to be open, even without vaccines, and the city is allowing that," she said. "I'm in the service industry, not the servant industry."

To be sure, many restaurants are facing their own untenable dilemma — stay open to keep some money flowing, to keep some jobs for their employees. Shut down and you're putting people out of work — and may not open again.

And many aren't. In Chicago, restaurants big and small have shuttered. According to the National Restaurant Association, 17% of all restaurants and bars nationwide — a total of 110,000 — have either closed temporarily or for good.

The weight of the long wait for a vaccine

CHAPTER TWELVE

Theresa Martinez has worked at a north side cafe since the start of the pandemic. She was grateful for the recent snow storms because it meant fewer customers.

For workers like her, the months of waiting and exposure have been exhausting and demoralizing. Panic attacks and crying fits have become an everyday part of her life, she said, sometimes behind the bar, with people watching. She can't pretend for customers anymore. Seeing them walk through the door is terrifying, she said.

"Every time somebody comes in, they'll ask you 'Hi, how are you?' I've just stopped answering that and if they push the question, I'll actually answer: 'I don't know. I can't answer that for you, at least not in the way you want me to,'" Martinez said, choking back tears.

"Having to put on a smile to be like, 'How can I help you? What can I do for you? How can I make your life easier?' Having to set aside my own feelings has been a lot," she said.

Martinez said people who dine out are trying to forget about the pandemic, and it feels like they're dragging workers like her into that fantasy.

CHAPTER TWELVE

She's even gotten bad reviews for breaking the illusion. One man left a Yelp review mocking her nervousness. It wasn't the first or last time. People sometimes wrote the company email about her.

After she spoke with WBEZ, Martinez was fired for those reviews. She's not happy about losing the job, but is also relieved it's over. Her dream is for workers to walk off the job or form a union.

"Anything that would help put us, not even at the forefront, not even ahead, just help us feel like we mattered," she said. "It's just really hard because I feel like I've invested all my life skills in one industry and now I can't get out."

Living with fear, unable to quit

Many restaurant workers say they find themselves in this position — unable to quit, unable to find better or safer employment — because of their background, economic status, or age.

Take undocumented restaurant veteran Sabrina, who said she started working under the table for $5 an hour at a pizza joint when she was 15. (WBEZ did not use her real name to protect her identity as an undocumented person).

CHAPTER TWELVE

She says the industry is full of people who — like her — don't have many options.

She thinks the pandemic has revealed a divide among her customers as well. The nice ones stay home and order to-go. The most difficult customers sit in, bickering about masks, because they don't believe COVID-19 is serious, she said.

"It [comes from] a place of privilege for people to say, like, you could just work somewhere else," she said. "Would they ever take that position? No. You have to serve these a**holes who are like, 'Don't worry, I've got antibodies.' It's super insulting. We don't want to be here and you want to act like that to us?"

Sabrina is trying to get out — and works a second job from home. She barely sleeps and it's exhausting, but she won't stop now, even without a vaccine.

She's too afraid to lose her place in the industry she's always relied on even if she and others feel its taking advantage of them.

Also according to Jaime Wilson who works in a restaurant said, since August, I have been an "essential" employee.

CHAPTER TWELVE

This label is supposed to be a badge of honor, a testament to the necessity of my work, and an acknowledgement of the risks I take in public each day. What it really means is that I ride on a crowded bus to a café where I interact with countless strangers. It means that I work in fear, and constantly worry about exposure and risk, since I do not have the luxury of deciding who walks through our doors.

Some of my co-workers and many of my peers have held this title even longer, since March, unable to apply for the unemployment benefits that kept so many people safe at home, and instead forced to overwork, and expected to volunteer their safety for the sake of economic and cultural survival.

There was an implied promise made when we were first called "essential," which is that, as restaurant workers, we were understood to be vital to the overall welfare of the public. But now that the vaccine is here, we have once again been shrugged off, left to navigate bureaucratic opacity, and to wonder if anyone will finally help us.

Frustration with the vaccine rollout in New York is not unique to hospitality workers, with dangerously low supplies, booked appointments, and inconsistent messaging

CHAPTER TWELVE

testing everyone's patience. This is also not a way of arguing that we deserve priority over health-care workers and other vulnerable populations. Instead, my colleagues and I think that, after almost a year of risking our own health in the name of some greater good, we simply deserve an answer to the question: When will we be able to receive the vaccine? After days of sifting through government announcements, Twitter feeds, and online applications, the answer is that no one really knows.

A long-awaited update came on January 11 2021, but it only created further confusion as new groups of "essential frontline workers" became eligible, part of the "1b" phase. According to the vast majority of government announcements, this includes grocery, education, and public-transit workers. "Other essential workers" are slated for later phases, without any specified timeline. Meanwhile, fluctuating, subjective terms like "public-facing," "frontline," and "essential" continue to circulate, though it remains largely unclear who actually creates these collective definitions and assignments of worth.

While statewide guidance specifies that this current phase will only include grocery workers, one city website lists

CHAPTER TWELVE

"food and grocery-store workers" as eligible. What this means is unclear, and the inconsistencies do not stop here. Another city appointment portal merely requires that its users be "public-facing essential employees," and it is unclear whether this is a way of expanding the definition, or merely offers an unintentional loophole.

Taken together, the information seems to indicate that "grocery workers" can try to sign up for an appointment, while "restaurant workers" must wait. But even then, the definitions are hazy. Is a cashier at a bakery, say, a restaurant worker, or a grocery worker? Furthermore, as restaurants have increasingly been forced to adopt market models, with so many businesses shifting to sell pantry items, prepared foods, or CSA subscriptions, the line between what qualifies as "restaurant" work versus "grocery" work is practically nonexistent. For example, wine stores qualify under the "grocery" umbrella, but that definition fails to incorporate the countless restaurants that have converted into wine shops to avoid going out of business during the pandemic.

Instead of clear guidelines, food-service workers are caught in a troubling limbo, again. Yet the only thing that's

CHAPTER TWELVE

changed since dining curfews went into effect and restaurants first began converting to takeout-only menus is that the number of cases, and the risk of dealing with the public, has continued to increase. It has never been more dangerous to work in restaurants than it is right now — and we're still being given no assurance that anyone will prioritize our safety.

We did not choose to be "essential," and in fact many of us would prefer not to be labeled as such. This assignment of value comes from other people, the same groups who flip-flop between keeping restaurants opened, or closed, or something in-between where we must pay rent but cannot actually serve customers inside.

The reality is that we never should have been "essential" in the first place. We should not have been expected to go out in the streets in the earliest weeks of the pandemic, or when hospitalizations steadily increased this fall. We should not have been sacrificed for the greater cause of perceived normalcy and stability. We should have instead been enabled both financially and politically to close our doors, clear out our walk-ins, and stay home.

CHAPTER TWELVE

The Centers for Disease Control and Prevention (CDC) has recommended that the food service workers be included in round 1c of the coronavirus vaccination distribution under the "other essential workers" designation according to a release made in December 2020. The CDC however didn't provide an expected vaccine deployment timeline. The National Restaurant Association urged the United States government in July 2020 to prioritize food supply chain workers and restaurant workers to help us maintain a safe and secure supply chain from farm to table. But essential worker prioritization for the vaccine is determined by the governments, so the vaccine's impact on the restaurant industry will likely differ across the country.

CHAPTER THIRTEEN

CHAPTER THIRTEEN

The New Normal

The COVID-19 pandemic has changed life as we know it. As the rate of infections begins to slow down in some hard-hit areas, early signs of recovery are appearing. Some towns, cities and states are starting to slowly reopen businesses, public areas and more.

What will "the new normal" mean for you? Lisa Maragakis, senior director of infection prevention, discusses things to consider, possible next steps and how you can continue to keep yourself healthy.

CHAPTER THIRTEEN

How can I protect myself from the coronavirus as cities and states start to reopen?

The protective practices you learned and followed in March and April of 2020 can continue to protect you and your family while slowing the spread of the coronavirus:

Social and physical distancing. Staying at least 6 feet away from anyone not living in your household can help you prevent infection.

Handwashing. Washing your hands for at least 20 seconds frequently throughout the day, or using hand sanitizer, is an effective way to avoid getting sick with the coronavirus or other germs.

Wearing a face mask protects others from illness if you're carrying the virus and don't know it.

Practice safe grocery shopping and food handling.

Continue to practice mindfulness and stress relief, as you did during stay-at-home orders. Mental and emotional well-being is a key aspect of health.

Staying informed about coronavirus can also help you:

CHAPTER THIRTEEN

Know what to do if you think you have the coronavirus: whom to call, where to go.

Understand what to expect if you're diagnosed with COVID-19.

Look out for signs of the coronavirus in babies and kids. Although the majority of children who contract COVID-19 have mild symptoms, a small percentage of patients under age 18 have experienced severe disease, including a rare inflammatory condition.

Understand who's more at risk. Older people and those living with heart disease, diabetes and other chronic illnesses have a greater chance of dying from COVID-19

Even with a vaccine, what will our new normal be?

There's only one thing certain – our new normal will keep changing, and it will change very quickly.

You may have to wear a face mask outside all the time.

Even if the Government does not mandate it, you will still feel better psychologically when you wear a face mask.

Your employer may ask you to work from home and do virtual meetings a lot more than before.

CHAPTER THIRTEEN

Schools may reduce the size of their classes and do a lot of virtual teaching.

You may cook a lot more at home, or have food delivered a lot more often than before.

E-businesses like online food ordering, online shopping and video on demand, will thrive.

Restaurants may no longer be able to seat the same number of people, due to social distancing requirements.

There will be increased sanitation and cleaning everywhere.

You will try to keep a 2m distance from everyone. Polite personal space will have a wider circumference.

Temperature checks will be conducted everywhere.

Cinemas and airlines will mandate spaced out seating, as will public transport like buses and trains.

They may also charge you double the price to cover their operations.

Same for live concerts and sports, or alternatively, those may be cancelled indefinitely or only performed or played for broadcast.

CHAPTER THIRTEEN

There will be a lot more requests for video on demand.

You may also be required to install contact tracing apps on your phone.

What comes next: How leaders can cope with America's 'new normal'

In a time where anxiety and optimism are neck and neck, here's what's ahead for business, the economy, and the fight against COVID-19.

In a time where anxiety and optimism are neck and neck, here's what's ahead for business, the economy, and the fight against COVID-19.

In Fortune's February/March 2021 issue, they explored "What Comes Next": what's ahead for business, for the economy, and for the battle against COVID-19. Read the four features that make up that package—on the economy, cybersecurity, banking, and America's heartland.

You've heard the phrase roughly 10,000 times by now. There's no doubt the expression has been popping up in your inbox regularly. It's very likely, in fact, that you've said it yourself more than once: "The New Normal."

CHAPTER THIRTEEN

Sure, it's catchy and alliterative. And it taps into the sense of dislocation that we all feel after a year of uncommon upheaval, sacrifice, and, for many, forced isolation. But what, exactly, does it mean?

"There is this almost religious fervor with which we talk about the new normal," says Amy Webb, the founder and CEO of the Future Today Institute, a management consulting firm. "And I've been curious for a while now: What is driving us to seek that out? And I don't actually think the answer is that people want to know what the future is so they can plan for it. I think, instead, that desire to know the new normal is really our collective desire to have things stop changing so much."

The psychological imperative to slow down and normalize the path forward is a perfectly understandable response to the jarring turbulence of the past year. Most disruptive of all, of course, has been the SARS-CoV-2 virus, which has already infected some 100 million people around the world and taken the lives of more than 2.1 million. The pandemic has exacted an enormous economic toll, but it has also accelerated the development of new technologies and

CHAPTER THIRTEEN

transformed the dynamics of how we work and live, introducing variables that are hard to predict long term.

As much as we might like to hit "pause," however, it's not really an option. If anything, the need to understand what comes next—for business, the economy, and our collective battle against COVID-19—is more urgent than ever. And the key to understanding may lie in this insight: After the turmoil of the past 12 months, some things are now permanently new; some things are still Normal; and the challenge is to recognize and navigate between the two.

For a case in point, look no further than the election of President Joe Biden. He's a lifelong centrist, a self-consciously traditional politician who might as well have "Normal" silk-screened on his hygienic face masks. But the fact that the Democrats now have narrow control of both houses of Congress for at least the next two years is undoubtedly New: It's a power shift with ramifications for Wall Street, global trade, and our relationship with China. That it follows the most contentious election in contemporary times, marked by the outgoing President's desperate attempt, through misinformation, to reverse the

CHAPTER THIRTEEN

results of an election he lost definitively, only adds to our anxiety about this New moment.

The reboot in Washington is absolutely top of mind for Ian Bremmer's clients. The founder and president of the Eurasia Group, a political risk consulting firm, says that every customer wants to know, "How different is Biden? How much can he govern? Is the U.S. actually facing some structural challenges that are deeper than we thought?"

Wall Street appears to be betting that life under Biden will be the best kind of Normal. From Election Day through Biden's inauguration on Jan. 20, the S&P 500 rose 14.3%. In fact, the Biden boost was more than twice as strong as the Trump bump from four years ago, when the S&P rose 6.2% in the same span. For now, it seems the market is shrugging off any concerns about onerous new regulation or tax increases. Meanwhile, it almost appears as if the big banks are competing to issue the most bullish GDP forecast: JPMorgan Chase predicts the U.S. economy will grow 5.8% in 2021. Morgan Stanley sees 6.4%. And Goldman Sachs is forecasting 6.6%. That's a lot of pent-up demand, a belief that consumers will get Normal with a vengeance.

CHAPTER THIRTEEN

Much of the confidence, of course, stems from the early rollout of highly effective vaccines—developed, in a new way, at record speed—to counter COVID-19. After a bumpy start, the vaccination distribution effort in the U.S. is picking up speed, even as the virus mutates and becomes more infectious. President Biden first announced a goal of distributing 100 million doses of vaccine in his first 100 days in office; by late January, he was pledging the U.S. would have enough doses for 300 million Americans by the end of summer.

In international relations, the New Normal may in fact resemble the Old Normal. The Biden administration will move quickly to smooth over ruffled relationships with key allies. A return to a less disruptive style of diplomacy in trade negotiations and the restoration of a globalist mindset in the White House add up to a predictability that business can embrace.

Still, there are stiff challenges ahead: The pandemic has only deepened and highlighted the problem of income inequality in the U.S. And it has further disrupted the ecosystem of business, as thousands of small enterprises have closed even as corporate behemoths, particularly the

CHAPTER THIRTEEN

tech giants on which we're increasingly dependent, have surged.

Technology has been our salvation as we've muddled our way through the pandemic. During lockdowns, it has allowed us to Zoom with colleagues, to binge-watch, to shop our looks online, and to socialize in isolation. But to many, this New doesn't feel Normal. Regulators, elected officials of both parties, and consumers are getting a little uncomfortable with Big Tech's heft and sway. In January, a Fortune and SurveyMonkey poll found that 64% of U.S. adults would like to see the federal government investigate at least one large tech company for antitrust violations. (Google and Facebook are already on the docket.)

Bremmer believes that the actions of the social media companies to "deplatform" President Trump in his final, dark days in office add an unexpected dynamic to the debate. In the eyes of Republicans, he says, tech regulation is now a partisan battle. "The tech companies are suddenly all in on the Democratic side, whether they like it or not," says Bremmer. "I can't remember a time when the most important companies in the U.S. economy were going to be

CHAPTER THIRTEEN

in such a partisan battle with one political party." It may not be Normal, but it's definitely new.

CHAPTER FOURTEEN

An Act of Bio Terrorism

Two theories on the origins of COVID-19 have been widely circulating in China and the West respectively, one blaming the United States and the other a highest-level biocontainment laboratory in Wuhan, the initial epicenter of the pandemic. Both theories make claims of biological warfare attempts.

However, like the episodes of biological warfare during the mid-twentieth century, the spread of these present-day theories reflects a series of longstanding and damaging trends in the international scene which include deep mistrust, animosities, the power of ideologies such as nationalism, and the sacrifice of truth in propaganda

CHAPTER FOURTEEN

campaigns. Also, the threats associated with biological warfare, bioterrorism, and the accidental leakages of deadly viruses from labs are real and growing. Thus, developing a better global governance of biosafety and biosecurity than exists at present is an urgent imperative for the international community in the broader context of a looming Cold War II. For such governance, an ethical framework is proposed based upon the triple ethical values of transparency, trust, and the common good of humanity.

The devastating consequences of the COVID-19 pandemic for individuals, families, communities, countries, and the world as a whole offers vivid proof that microbes could be just as destructive and terrifying—if not more so—than the use of nuclear weapons. And it is much less difficult to forge biological weapons than nuclear ones. As a result, driven by their hunger for power and dominion, states and terrorist groups may feel increasingly tempted to access and exercise such super-biological means of destruction. Furthermore, the safety of the scientific laboratories where the most dangerous pathogens are researched (and sometimes created) has long been a sword of Damocles hanging over humankind.

CHAPTER FOURTEEN

In recent years, China has been investing heavily in strategically important sectors in science, technology, and biomedicine. A plan exists to establish half a dozen labs of the highest level of biocontainment, biosafety level-4 (BSL-4) or P4 (pathogen or protection level 4), in several cities. As a fruit of international cooperation primarily with France, the first BSL-4 lab was built at the Wuhan Institute of Virology (WIV) of the Chinese Academy of Science in 2017. When it became fully operational in 2018, authorities and scientists enthusiastically celebrated the lab as another landmark in science achieved by China, that is, in the typical spirit of patriotism or nationalism (Xinhua News 2018). However, overseas experts were raising questions about the safety and even the necessity of such labs.

Their concerns included the possible leakage of pathogens as well as the potential development of biological weapons (Cyranoski 2017). In 2018, U.S. intelligence also warned about the safety risks of the lab (Rogin 2020). A few days after the lockdown of Wuhan in late January 2020, a U.S. newspaper linked the origins of severe acute respiratory syndrome coronavirus2(SARS-Cov-2,then called 2019-nCoV) to China's covert biological weapons programme, citing an Israeli biological warfare expert (Gertz 2020).

CHAPTER FOURTEEN

More sensationally, scientists from the Indian Institute of Technology published a preprint scientific paper where they reported their findings on four unique inserts of key structural proteins of HIV-1in 2019-nCoV, a result which was "unlikely to be fortuitous in nature"(Pradhanetal.2020).In other words, the novel coronavirus had been genetically engineered. Soon afterwards, the researchers withdrew their paper, citing a need for "re-analyzing of the data." Many Chinese also suspected a connection between the virus and the WIV. As a response, Shi Zhengli, an internationally known virologist at the WIV who discovered that the SARS virus originated in bats, posted on Twitter-like Chinese social media platform Weibo— a post which was reported in many media outlets:

"The 2019-nCov is nature's punishment on the human race for uncivilized behavior [i.e., eating wild animals]. I swear on my own life that the virus has no connection with the laboratory. To those people who believe in and are spreading the rumors perpetrated by third-rate media outlets ,as well as believing in the unreliable "academic analysis" of Indian scholars, I would like to give this advice: Shut your dirty mouths!"

CHAPTER FOURTEEN

Not surprisingly, this response has hardly helped to scotch the theory that the release of covid 19 was not an act of bio terrorism, however understandable.

Shi's indignation may have been. Scientific truth can never be guaranteed by swearing on one's own or anyone else's life but must be grounded on objective evidence. Asking people to "shut their mouths" can only be counterproductive when it comes to convincing them with sound theories and establishing trust and trustworthiness. Ideally, the final say on the issue should come from an independent party—in this case, Shi herself and the WIV itself have an obvious conflict of interest. Mainstream scientific research and the more reputable mass media denounced the theory that the novel coronavirus had been genetically engineered or was a bioweapon (e.g., Andersen et al. 2020; Barclay 2020). Yet, the fact that the virus is not human-made does not necessarily excludes the possibility that the virus escaped the lab by accident (Field 2020; Guterl et al. 2020).

This remains an open question; without independent and transparent investigations, it may never be either proven or disproven. The leakage of dangerous pathogens had already

CHAPTER FOURTEEN

occurred more than once in other labs. China's official reaction has added fuel to the fires of suspicion. In mid-February, Chen Wei, a major general in the People's Liberation Army and a leading biological weapons expert at the Academy of Military Science, was appointed to take the helm at the WIV.

In late December 2019 Dr. Li Wenliang, an ophthalmologist at Wuhan Central Hospital, sent a WeChat message to his medical school alumni group telling them that seven people with severe respiratory and flu-like symptoms had recently been admitted to the hospital. One thing they had in common, besides their symptoms, was that they'd all visited a local wet market at some point in the previous week.

The illness bore an uncanny resemblance to SARS, but with a novel aspect as well; could it be an outbreak of a new disease? If so, what should be done?

But before any of the doctors could take action or alert local media outlets, the chat thread was shut down by the Wuhan police and Li was accused of spreading rumors. Mind you, the chat wasn't in a public forum; it was a closed group exchange. But the Chinese Communist Party

CHAPTER FOURTEEN

(CCP) is able to monitor, intercept, and censor any and all activity on WeChat; for the Chinese people, there's no such thing as a private conversation.

The police gave Li an affidavit stating he'd spread false information and disturbed public order. He was instructed to sign this document retracting his warning about the virus and to stop telling people it existed, otherwise he'd be put in jail.

So he did. A little over a month later, on February 7, Li died of the novel coronavirus in the same hospital where he'd worked—he'd been infected with the virus while trying to treat sick patients, who'd continued pouring into the hospital throughout the month of January.

By this time the CCP had leapt into action, unable to deny the existence of the virus as hundreds then thousands of people started getting sick. Travel restrictions and quarantines went into effect—but it was already far too late. As of this writing, the virus has spread to 168 countries and killed almost 21,000 people. Schools and businesses are closed. We're in lockdown mode in our homes. And the economy is taking a massive hit that could lead to a depression.

CHAPTER FOURTEEN

How different might our current situation be if the CCP had heeded Li's warning instead of silencing it—or if the virus had first been discovered in a country with a free press?

"People are arguing that China has done a good job of handling the virus. I disagree," said Alex Gladstein, chief strategy officer at the Human Rights Foundation. "The reason we have this global pandemic right now is because of Chinese censorship and the government's totalitarian nature."

Dr. Boyle who drafted the Biological Weapons Act and a Professor of International Law at the University of Illinois College of Law discusses the coronavirus outbreak in Wuhan, China and the Biosafety Level 4 Laboratory (BSL- from which he believes the infectious disease escaped. He believes the virus is potentially lethal and an offensive biological warfare weapon or dual-use biowarfare weapons agent genetically modified with gain of function properties, which is why the Chinese government originally tried to cover it up and is now taking drastic measures to contain it.

The Wuhan BSL-4 lab is also a specially designated World Health Organization (WHO) research lab and Dr. Boyle contends that the WHO knows full well what is occurring.

CHAPTER FOURTEEN

Dr. Boyle also touches upon GreatGameIndia's exclusive report Coronavirus Bioweapon - where it was reported in detail how Chinese Biowarfare agents working at the Canadian lab in Winnipeg were involved in the smuggling of Coronavirus to Wuhan's lab from where it is believed to have been leaked.

Dr. Boyle's position is in stark contrast to the mainstream media's narrative of the virus being originated from the seafood market, which increasingly was questioned by many experts .

American Senator Tom Cotton of Arkansas also dismantled the mainstream media's claim that pinned the coronavirus outbreak on a market selling dead and live animals.

In a video accompanying his post, Cotton explained that the Wuhan wet market (which Cotton incorrectly referred to as a seafood market) has been shown by experts to not be the source of the deadly contagion.

Cotton referenced a Lancet study which showed that many of the first cases of the novel coronavirus, including patient zero, had no connection to the wet market - devastatingly undermining mainstream media's claim.

CHAPTER FOURTEEN

"As one epidemiologist said: 'That virus went into the seafood market before it came out of the seafood market.' We still don't know where it originated," Cotton said.

"I would note that Wuhan also has China's only bio-safety level four super laboratory that works with the world's most deadly pathogens to include, yes, coronavirus."

Such concerns have also been raised by J.R. Nyquist, the well known author of the books "Origins of the Fourth World War" and "The Fool and His Enemy," as well as co-author of "The New Tactics of Global War". In his insightful article he published secret speeches given to high-level Communist Party cadres by Chinese Defense Minister Gen. Chi Haotian explaining a long-range plan for ensuring a Chinese national renaissance - the catalyst for which would be China's secret plan to weaponize viruses.

Nyquist gave three different data points for making his case in analyzing Coronavirus. He writes: The third data point worth considering: the journal GreatGameIndia has published a piece titled "Coronavirus Bioweapon – How China Stole Coronavirus From Canada And Weaponized It .

CHAPTER FOURTEEN

The authors were clever enough to put Khan's Virology Journal article together with news of a security breach by Chinese nationals at the Canadian (P4) National Microbiology Lab in Winnipeg, where the novel coronavirus was allegedly stored with other lethal organisms. May 2019, the Royal Canadian Mounted Police were called in to investigate; by late July the Chinese were kicked out of the facility. The chief Chinese scientist (Dr. Xiangguo Qiu) was allegedly making trips between Winnipeg and Wuhan.

Here we have a plausible theory of the NCoV organism's travels: first discovered in Saudi Arabia, then studied in Canada from whence it was stolen by a Chinese scientist and brought to Wuhan. Like the statement of Taiwan's intelligence chief in 2008, the GreatGameIndia story has come under intensive attack. Whatever the truth, the fact of proximity and the unlikelihood of mutation must figure into our calculations.

It's highly probable that the 2019-nCoV organism is a weaponized version of the NCoV discovered by Saudi doctors in 2012.

As the author J.R. Nyquist puts it:

CHAPTER FOURTEEN

We must have an investigation of the outbreak in Wuhan. The Chinese must grant the world total transparency. The truth must come out. If Chinese officials are innocent, they have nothing to hide. If they are guilty, they will refuse to cooperate.

The real concern here is whether the rest of the world has the courage to demand a real and thorough investigation. We need to be fearless in this demand and not allow "economic interests" to play a coy and dishonest game of denial. We need an honest inquiry. We need it now.

The corrupt establishment will do anything to suppress critical sites like the Burning Platform, etc., from revealing the truth. The corporate media does this by demonetizing sites like mine by blackballing the site from advertising revenue.

The COVID-19 Pandemic has almost certainly been the restaurant industry's greatest challenge to date. Never before have so many restaurants been forced to cease operations – some never reopen. Early indications, from China and other countries where the pandemic seems to be more under control, suggest that guest demand likely will not immediately rebound when restrictions are lifted.

CHAPTER FOURTEEN

However, restaurants that have adapted during the crisis and plan ahead to innovate further and apply what they learned optimizing their restaurant model for the "next normal" will be much better positioned to bring sales back to pre-crisis levels. As I always tell my teams "luck favors the prepared."

As we boldly wade into 2021, we do so with guarded optimism, we can see a light at the end of the tunnel and we are hopeful it is not the train. We are hopeful and optimistic because one thing is certain...at some point, dining in restaurants will once again be a pleasure that people across the country can enjoy.

The actions that savvy restaurant operators take now will go a long way toward preserving their business through the crisis and equipping their restaurants to serve guests, not just during—but also long after—the recovery. Here are three glimmers of hope that we can grasp onto within the restaurant industry.

CHAPTER FIFTEEN

Now and Beyond

Online ordering, curbside pickup and third-party delivery have never been so hot. At the onset of the pandemic, DoorDash sales went up 110% from the start of 2020. Nearly half of Americans began ordering delivery or pickup from restaurants one to two times a week. Digital services such as delivery apps have been able to keep the industry alive during the darkest of times.

Now that many customers are well adjusted to online ordering, curbside pickup and third-party delivery, these means of interacting with customers are not going away any time soon. Businesses should continue to emphasize and put marketing dollars toward these channels, especially

CHAPTER FIFTEEN

to captivate younger generations. Who doesn't want food delivered to them in the comfort of their own home?

The Marion County Public Health Department has stepped up in numerous ways to help during the pandemic. Particularly, its team has done an amazing job working with restaurants to keep customers safe. As it enforces safety precautions, it protects guests and provides resources and information to help businesses pass the "Smell Test." Think about the last time you walked into a restaurant – did you look around?

During the COVID-era, customers will often look around with a mental checklist to decide if a business, restaurant or venue is successfully enforcing the rules that will keep them safe. Does the restaurant or business have the Centers for Disease Control and Prevention's recommendations clearly visible? Are other customers social distancing? Are all the staff members and customers wearing masks? These are a few of the check boxes that can be crossed off during the Smell Test.

The Marion County Public Health Department is helping to keep people safe and businesses to reopen safely, while enforcing safety, and even increasing safety measures

CHAPTER FIFTEEN

during times of heightened concern. No longer should individuals fear the health department, as it should be praised for its tremendous work!

Fall back, spring forward!

As we approach the one-year mark of the onset of the pandemic, the world has learned how to adjust to the "new normal." With spring upon us and warmer weather in Indianapolis, local eateries can attempt to breathe a (masked) sigh of relief. Outdoor dining during the warmer weather is a welcome alternative to off-premises only. Though the prospect of full-capacity indoor dining in the coming months is unlikely, restaurants can look forward to filling more outdoor seats than ever before once we hit spring. After every storm there is often a rainbow.

The restaurant industry is not the only one with glimmers of hope for 2021. Looking ahead, shopping malls, movie theaters and other small businesses can see the light at the end of the tunnel. Businesses – whether restaurants or not – should continue to move forward with and put an emphasis on delivery or curbside pickup initiatives. These innovations allow customers with varying comfort levels to be reached and provide business. All industries should

CHAPTER FIFTEEN

continue to listen to the Marion County Public Health Department and enforce safety measures. As we reach warmer weather and the vaccine rollout continues, foot traffic will increase. Business owners will begin to see more and more customers enter their stores seeking the quality services and products they know and love.

With a new president comes new perspectives that can manifest new ideas on the current COVID-19 pandemic. Before COVID-19, labor—namely rising wages and the ever-evolving state of regulations—represented the firmest storyline among independents and large chains alike. Naturally, it took a backseat to coronavirus. Will it jump back in? Is it there already? How will vaccines impact everything? Or will labor simply join a host of other rotating challenges?

Regardless of where operators turn, they'll find a shifting industry that won't feel the same state-by-state, market-to-market and from one segment to another. If anything, that will be COVID-19's signature and one that will be felt for years to come—the divergence of sectors, blurring of models, and shattered or accelerated trends that had no choice but to gain speed in the wake of dine-in restrictions.

CHAPTER FIFTEEN

One thing about mid-March's COVID-19 introduction is that the floor fell out across the map. Food-away-from-home spending collapsed as consumers started hoarding groceries and other essentials. Buying paper towels became a treasure hunt.

Simon-Kucher & Partners, a global strategy and marketing consulting firm, released data back in May that teased a seismic deviation. Pre-COVID-19, 67 percent of meals were consumed away from home. During the crisis, it shifted to 45 percent. The company's survey data said after the pandemic (six to 12 months) this would slide to 37 percent home-cooked, and 63 percent away from home. While a 4 percent difference doesn't seem massive, if you go off the National Restaurant Association's 2020 projected figure of $898 billion sales for 2020 (before COVID-19), it's roughly a $50 billion annual sales opportunity gone for restaurants.

BTIG analyst Peter Saleh said restaurants, in essentially every state, felt the brunt of pantry-stuffing behavior until May/June. Since then, large states, including Texas and Florida, reopened for indoor dining, increasing capacity along the way. However, the West Coast and Northeast

CHAPTER FIFTEEN

oscillated between opening with limited capacity to closing entirely for in-person dining (New York City being the latest), never breaching 50 percent capacity. The result is these markets significantly lagged the national average on the pace of sales recovery.

Saleh believes this divergence sets up an uneven recovery for the coming year as those lagging geographies will see an outsized comeback, reversing regional dynamics of the past nine months.

We're talking more about comparable recovery and, in particular, for those publicly traded companies that are going to bounce off the COVID-19 bottom with force. Saleh points to California-heavy Kura Sushi USA as one target. Also, Papa John's, he said, will benefit from the regional dynamic as the concept had less exposure to the West Coast and Northeast, meaning it didn't benefit as much in 2020 from lockdowns and reduced mobility. "This should improve the sales outlook as the year progresses and lessen the difficult sales comparisons many investors are worrying about," Saleh said.

Again, maybe more so than any year on record, understanding a restaurant chain's outlook in 2021 can't

CHAPTER FIFTEEN

just be restricted to the brand's strength. Understanding the geography and what setbacks were in place in 2020 is going to factor in, good and bad, on a year-over-year basis.

Saleh said food-away-from-home sales should recover, too, thanks to education and hospitality as consumers begin to return to more normalized routines.'

Throughout COVID-19, one relatively stable trend was the optimization of restaurant menus. While some chains used this as a potential differentiator and didn't cut back, most did. They reduced items outside their core in an effort to improve efficiency and speed of service, with a nod to off-premises and smaller staffs. Looking ahead to 2021, Saleh said, operators have an opportunity to separate from the field with menu innovation, pivoting away from each other for the first time in decades—rather than in the same direction.

In other terms, COVID-19 might have struck the final blow for the "all things to all people," mindset that sprung up in the 2000s as brands of all ilk tried to serve a mysterious and fast-approaching millennial generation.

Saleh expects Wendy's to leverage its salad platform to drive sales, while McDonald's completely abandoned the offering. The exception, however, will likely be chicken, with the chicken sandwich wars escalating in the early part of 2021 when McDonald's launches its new Crispy Chicken option. Even with virtual chains flooding the fray by the handful, chicken has shown no real indication of eclipsing peak demand during COVID-19. Not only does the product fit off-premises and in-store targets, but it tends to be operationally simple (customers don't get too crazy with builds and add-ons) and generally carries a healthier perception than burgers.

Where Popeyes fits in this next act and which marketing campaign emerges is hard to say, but you can't deny the chain started a movement that will linger into 2021 he said.

Another common theme, and one often tied to menu optimization, is cost cutting. Saleh said a lasting benefit of COVID-19 will be greater efficiency and higher-operating margins as restaurants reduce expenses and learn to operate with a leaner infrastructure.

Saleh predicted restaurant and food distribution operators will reach pre-COVID-19 profit levels with 90–95 percent of past sales given respective simplification and cost-saving efforts. Additionally, higher digital sales will be another

CHAPTER FIFTEEN

enduring impact of coronavirus as ordering practices remain sticky and customers become accustomed to convenience.

Once a customer orders-ahead for pickup, with the convenience and customization possibilities, why would they go back? More likely, digital adoption of the past year will only solidify different restaurant occasions. Takeout/curbside, for instance, will serve a much more defined journey. What this could mean, especially for full-service restaurants, is an urgency with key pre-pandemic challenges—the need to separate and differentiate in-store dining so that it justifies the speed/price trade-off guests can have with fast food and delivery. Experience and service were always hallmarks of the full-service experience. Now, they're survival terms.

Broadly, higher digital sales should provide greater operating efficiency and some welcome offsets to rising wages for restaurants, namely quick-service brands. Saleh said fast casuals like Chipotle, Shake Shack, and Starbucks will see more of a lift in 2021 than traditional quick service or casual-dining concepts. Like most things, the culprit is whitespace. You've seen it already with Chipotle and its

CHAPTER FIFTEEN

digital ascension of the past two years. The opportunity was more incremental because of how much room there was to gain. Just look at the "Chipotlane" drive thru. Recent units are generating sales as much as 25 percent higher (10 percent is the average for comp units). Those restaurants welcome 60 percent of sales through digital. But vividly, the biggest change is that digital mixes two-thirds order-ahead with Chipotlanes, thus boosting profitability. Typically, the breakdown is nearly even for Chipotle between delivery and takeout, with delivery splitting 65 percent marketplace and 35 percent in-app.

In the case of Starbucks and Chipotle in particular, digital and accessibility opened the door to high-tier growth, with Starbucks saying it expects to open 22,000 locations in the next decade. Chipotle thinks it can get to 6,000 total.

BTIG signaled US Foods a "top pick" for 2020 based on the company's view of the independent restaurant landscape, its exposure to other foodservice channels, profitability channels, profitability gains, and longer-term market share opportunity. But let's focus on the independents angle.

CHAPTER FIFTEEN

Case-volume figures and industry sales benchmarks suggest many of US Foods' restaurant customers are generating positive cash flow at current sales levels, according to recent earnings reports. Saleh said these sales and cash flow levels suggest independent restaurant closures will likely be in the high-single digits.

If that were true, it would come way under some dire projections tossed about during the pandemic.

Saleh said restaurants, chain and independents, can achieve roughly breakeven profit and cash flow with 75 percent of pre-COVID-19 sales volumes. "While the pandemic took many operators by surprise earlier this year, we believe most restaurants adapted to the new off-premises environment, engaging third-party delivery providers, implementing takeout, and offering outdoor dining options," Saleh said.

According to industry tracker Black Box Intelligence, same-store sales fell 55 percent in April, but were down just 7.5 percent in October and 10.3 percent in November (higher case numbers, more restrictions). This suggests, Saleh said, despite COVID-19's impact, restaurant cash flows were negative for about three months in March,

CHAPTER FIFTEEN

April, and May, before turning positive in June/July. He added the pivot to off-premises allowed industry trends to materially recover from the lows in April, and helped stave off mass restaurant closures.

Although same-store sales will surely backtrack in coming months due to winter weather and COVID-19 resurgence, coupled with lockdowns, Saleh doesn't believe sales levels will fall below what is required to maintain positive cash flow.

For a sample, in the week ending November 29 2020, per Black Box, comps sales were the worst experienced since mid-July, which marked three consecutive weeks where year-over-year sales growth declined compared to the previous week. But to Saleh's point, the key there is "since mid-July." It's not "since mid-April." And it's Saleh's that thought you won't ever hear that comparison again.

Also, quick service and fast casual achieved positive comp sales growth in that same week. Off-premises sales as a percentage of total restaurant business increased for three consecutive weeks, Black Box said, with the highest increases happening in full-service restaurants.

CHAPTER FIFTEEN

And on the varied recovery point, the regions with the best comp sales results were the Southeast, Florida, Texas, and the Southwest. Weather seems to now be a bigger factor in restaurant sales, especially since many restaurants have relied more on outdoor dining.

The regions with biggest declines in sales were California, New England, the Western region, and New York-New Jersey. In California, the spike in COVID-19 cases was likely the driving factor behind a steep drop in sales growth during the last two weeks, Black Box said.

UCLA economists issued a forecast that predicted the U.S. would experience "a gloomy COVID winter and an exuberant vaccine spring," followed by stellar growth for years to come.

The forecast, which assumed mass vaccination of Americans would take place by summer, predicted annualized growth in the nation's gross domestic product would accelerate from 1.2 percent in the current quarter to 1.8 percent in Q1 of 2021, then to 6 percent in Q2 and 3 percent growth each quarter going into 2023.

This could signal major business for restaurants trying to bridge the gap today and make to the other side. Leo Feler,

CHAPTER FIFTEEN

a senior economic with the forecast, wrote that the vaccine and "pent-up demand" will skyrocket services consumption.

Going all the way back to April, Datassential asked consumers what the No. 1 thing they missed was. The answer: "dining at my favorite sit-down restaurant" at 41 percent.

"We believe independent restaurateurs are far more resilient and creative than investors give them credit for," Saleh said. "While we expect an elevated level of restaurant closures this year, we believe that figure will be in the high-single digit range, far below dire forecasts of 30 percent or more closures that have circulated amid the pandemic."

Performance Foods recently indicated in a call that it's experiencing high-single digit closures among its customer base, with higher rates in the Northeast and West Coast. That mirrored comments from US Foods as well as Darden, which said it expected industry closures in the 5–15 percent block.

It's impossible to know for sure how this will unfold. The National Restaurant Association recently said 110,000 locations are closed either permanently or long-term.

CHAPTER FIFTEEN

There's no question federal aid—or a lack thereof—will play a role in the final picture. The Independent Restaurant Coalition released a statement regarding the new framework of a $908 billion COVID-19 relief plan that contains no direct aid to independent restaurants and bars. (It does, however, have money set aside for airlines and music venues).

Meanwhile, more than one in five people unemployed from the pandemic, or 2.1 million Americans, are restaurant and bar workers. Also, the industry received less than 8 percent of Paycheck Protection Program funds in the spring as part of the CARES Act.

"Congress' proposed $908 billion compromise bill will be a death sentence for many independent restaurants," said Tom Colicchio, co-founder of the IRC, in a statement. "We're one of the only industries asked by the government over and over again to close our doors, but this bill does not offers any plan to ensure we can fully reemploy our staff in the months ahead. Just 10 weeks of payroll isn't enough to make up for 10 months of lost revenue after we've opened, closed, pivoted, reopened, and closed again."

CHAPTER FIFTEEN

Restaurants continue to push for the bipartisan RESTAURANTS Act. It would establish a $120 billion revitalization fund where independent restaurants and bars would be eligible for grant amounts based on the difference between their revenues in 2019 and 2020. These grants could only be applied to eligible expenses including payroll, rent, supplies, PPE, and debt incurred during the pandemic.

Will the Hospitality and Travel Industry Recover in 2021?

Without a doubt, 2020 was a challenging year for most. Besides lockdowns, many companies let employees work from home permanently. When many business activities were put on a break and supply chains were interrupted, the global economy collapsed. COVID-19's impact on the hospitality and tourism industry has been devastating and unprecedented.

How tough was it in 2020?

The aviation industry

According to the International Civil Aviation Organization, global air traffic dropped from 4.5 billion in 2019 to 1.8 billion in 2020. The financial loss to the industry was $370 billion. Additionally, airports and air navigation service providers reported a loss of $115 billion and $13 billion, respectively. In the U.S., the six largest airlines lost $35 billion in 2020.

Hotels

The American Hotel and Lodging Association (AHLA) estimated that COVID-19's impact on the travel industry in 2020 was about nine times of that from 9/11. Hotel room revenue was cut in half, from $167 billion to $85 billion. Hotels were running at about 44% occupancy in 2020, down from 66% in 2019, although extended-stay hotels and the home-sharing sector seemed to be more resilient during this pandemic.

STR, a leading provider for data benchmarking, analytics, and marketplace insights for the lodging industry, reported a decline of 84.6% in U.S. hotels' gross operating profit per available room (GOPPAR). In 2019, U.S. hotels were running at $245.10 in total revenue per available room and $94.72 in GOPPAR. Such numbers went off the clip to $88.90 and $14.62 in 2020, respectively.

CHAPTER FIFTEEN

Restaurants

The restaurant industry ended in 2020 with about $659 billion in total sales, $240 billion below what the National Restaurant Association estimated for the year before the pandemic. Fast-food or quick-service restaurants, as well as restaurants shifting to curbside pickup and delivery services, seemed to do fine.

The hospitality industry has been devastated by the COVID-19 pandemic, perhaps more so than any other sector. With restaurants struggling to stay open for business and many closing their doors for good, at nearly 40% of all job losses, hospitality unemployment is at four times greater than the national average1 and more layoffs are expected. While these difficult realities remain, we must look to 2021 with the hope of a light at the end of the tunnel, putting an emphasis on holistic risk management strategies to offset costs and help prevent further losses.

As outlined in HUB International's recently released "2021 Hospitality Industry Outlook", the following are top issues we see shaping the hospitality industry, and their implications for risk and insurance:

CHAPTER FIFTEEN

1. Increasing Insurance Rates & Proactive Risk Management

Reduced or vacant properties combined with operators' financial stress will push property insurance, along with commercial umbrella rates, up by 25% to 50% into 2021, and the amount each insurer is willing to write for a particular line is increasingly limited. The industry's financial straits also pose executive liability issues with coverage being driven up an average of 25% in response. Directors' and Officers' (D&O) and Errors and Omissions (E&O) exposures are ramping up with the prospect of more bankruptcies and business consolidations and creditor suits in response. The significant number of layoffs also may trigger Employment Practices Liability actions by employees, and by regulators if payroll tax payments have lapsed.

The best way to control insurance costs is to be proactive to plan ahead to avoid potential losses as much as possible in the first place. It is more important than ever to work with your insurance broker on risk assessments for your business to ensure any potentially costly issues are identified and corrected, like legionella in the water supply or pipes that

CHAPTER FIFTEEN

could freeze due to lack of maintenance staff for necessary protocols. Your broker should proactively review the adequacy of your executive liability coverage for changing circumstances, as well as on practices that improve the risk exposures of executives and boards going forward. The best defense is adequate disclosures, having followed regulations or government recommendations, and following an emergency plan that is regularly reviewed and updated.

2. As restaurants pivot, adequate protection against risk is a key concern.

From the very beginning of the pandemic, restaurants had to quickly develop and provide options to survive the circumstances. That was demonstrated in the immediate wake of the pandemic quarantine period. Restaurants pivoted to delivery and take-out, and kept up the services to stay open. Others have reinvented their business models. The trend toward "ghost" kitchens was hot before the pandemic and has accelerated. These can be urban warehouses containing multiple small kitchens leased by a restaurant or a restaurant's subcontractor for delivery only.

Chances are that delivery services were easily accommodated by third party services like Grub Hub and

CHAPTER FIFTEEN

Uber Eats, which delivered $10.2 billion in carryout meals in 2018. Those that have proceeded with their own drivers should work with their brokers to offset such risks as food safety, customer privacy and data security. They should also be aware of increases in auto coverage in 2021 that might make third party delivery services more attractive.

Another potential risk that restaurant operators face in 2021 is a surge in outsized claims being tracked back to on-the-job contagion, pushing financially stretched health insurers to subrogate them back to workers' compensation (WC) carriers. That could trigger double digit rate increases in WC. Restaurants that have opened to dine-in at any capacity (if and when they had the state's approval to do so) should also conduct risk assessments to audit their coronavirus safety measures, to ensure they meet or exceed Center for Disease Control (CDC) guidelines. Restaurants should also contact their insurance broker for this type of service and additional resources.

Too many restaurants, however, have not been able to withstand the financial pressures of the pandemic. Chain restaurants alone have closed more than 1,500 locations since it started, including such companies as Chuck E.

CHAPTER FIFTEEN

Cheese and California Pizza Kitchen. Those in such straits should check with their brokers on the best way to manage relevant executive liability issues.

3. Transfer risk where you can.

When a business – and industry – is in crisis mode, moving from reactive to proactive mode may be a challenge, but 2021 may be the time to do it. Risk transfer strategies are available. Some are easier than others to put in place.

Strategies like the captive insurance option might be worth considering when the industry is under less financial pressure. Captives allow companies to self-finance their risks, with stop loss coverage assuming the cost of outsized claims. Especially for those with better claims records, the captive strategy can present cost savings and tax advantages over traditional insurance. The captive strategy requires a broker who has experience setting up captives and can provide perspective on the different types and their advantages and disadvantages.

The industry that emerges in 2021 and beyond from the disruption of the pandemic will be not just slimmer, but smarter, demonstrating the resiliency it takes to get through to the other side of uncertain times. It will be a time when

CHAPTER FIFTEEN

meeting health and safety concerns will be paramount – for employees as well as for customers and guests. At the same time, the trend toward buying experiences will accelerate post-pandemic and help reinvigorate travel again. The industry's challenge will be to innovate around it all. An environment like this creates opportunities, but also risks.

Work with an experienced insurance broker and their risk management experts to learn how to develop a risk management program and business continuity plan that will help protect your business and prepares you for the market ahead. A good broker will help position your business' story with insurance carriers, so you get the right coverage and more control over rising premiums.

New research looks at how restaurants and consumers were changed by the events of 2020 and the year of transition ahead.

The report explores crucial areas in which the pandemic forced restaurateurs to adapt quickly, adopting contactless technology, shifting most service to off-premises and outdoor dining, and adjusting labor levels and menus.

The National Restaurant Association's 2021 State of the Restaurant Industry report addresses the devastating impact

CHAPTER FIFTEEN

of COVID-19 on the restaurant industry, documents the altered operational landscape, and captures consumer sentiment, influences and intentions for the coming months.

It also explores several crucial areas in which the pandemic forced restaurateurs to pivot and adapt, quickly adopting contactless technology, shifting most service to off-premises and outdoor dining, and adjusting labor levels and menus.

Based on data from responses to the Association's survey of 6,000 restaurant operators across all industry segments, and a survey of 1,000 adult consumers, the report delivers impact data on sales and traffic, operational trends, food and menu trends, and workforce trends along with consumer purchase preferences and intentions.

The report offers a comprehensive and sobering look at the damage the pandemic caused the industry and millions of its employees nationwide. Several key findings:

The restaurant industry ended 2020 with total sales that were $240 billion below the Association's pre-pandemic forecast for the year

CHAPTER FIFTEEN

As of Dec. 1, 2020, more than 110,000 eating and drinking places were closed for business temporarily, or for good

The eating and drinking place sector finished 2020 nearly 2.5 million jobs below its pre-coronavirus level. At the peak of initial closures, the Association estimates up to 8 million employees were laid off or furloughed

The report offers extensive analysis on trends in several areas:

Operations. Restaurants looked at a number of different ways to retain traffic and generate revenues. Operators focused on building off-premises business, especially in the fullservice segment, with roughly half of restaurateurs devoting more resources to expanding that side of their business since the start of the COVID-19 outbreak in March.

Adding curbside pick-up, in-house and 3rd party delivery and if possible, drive-thru capacity, and upgrading takeout and delivery packaging were just a few of means they used to sustain business. Service styles also changed. In addition to the off-premises focus, a big portion of on-premises dining moved outdoors for as long as the weather permitted. Tech adoption accelerated. Contactless and mobile payment options became crucial. Across all 6 segments—quick service, fast casual, casual, family, fine dining, and coffee and snack—some 40% of operators said they added tech solutions to their businesses.

Food & Menu. With a slowdown in business, and on-premises dining restrictions, many operators reduced inventories, streamlining menus and developing menu items they could make well with smaller crews. Operators also began selling meal kits, bundled meals and even groceries—whatever customers needed and were willing to buy. Customers sought out comfort foods, including burgers, pizza, pasta and Mexican specialties. The report lists best-selling items by fullservice and limited service venues.

Workforce. Before the pandemic, the restaurant and foodservice industry projected it would provide 15.6 million jobs in 2020, or 10% of all payroll jobs in the economy. But the impact of the coronavirus caused staffing levels to fall across all restaurant and foodservice segments, with restaurant employment below pre-pandemic levels in 47 states and D.C. The report emphasizes these three key findings:

CHAPTER FIFTEEN

62% of fine dining operators and 54% of both family dining and casual dining operators say staffing levels are more than 20% below normal.

There are nearly 2 million fewer 16-to-34-year-olds in the labor force, the most prominent age group employed in the restaurant industry workforce.

Restaurants got hit harder than any other industry during the pandemic, and still have the longest climb back to pre-coronavirus employment levels.

Consumer sentiment and intentions. Despite the pandemic, pent-up demand for restaurants remains strong. Customers have become used to ordering takeout, but indicate they really crave in-restaurant dining experiences. Nearly 8 in 10 adult consumers said their favorite restaurant foods delivered flavor and taste sensations that couldn't be duplicated at home, and 6 in 10 said restaurants are an essential part of their lifestyles.

"Our research shows a clear desire among consumers to enjoy more on-premises dining at restaurants than they have been able to get during the pandemic," says Hudson Riehle, the Association's senior vice president of Research. "We've also found that even as the vaccine becomes more

CHAPTER FIFTEEN

available and more customers can return to restaurants, they'll continue to want the expanded off-premises options going forward. Both will continue to be key for industry growth."

The New Year brings hopes to the industry

There are signs of improvement toward containing the coronavirus even with concerns over the variants. First and foremost, fewer people got infected. Daily identified COVID-19 cases dropped from the peak at about 314,000 on January 8 to about 100,000 in the first half of February. Also, the vaccination rate is increasing. Close to 10% of the U.S. population has received at least one dose. Additionally, a clinical trial showed that AstraZeneca's COVID-19 vaccine remained effective against the U.K. variant.

Travelers are hopeful

Some key findings from a survey of Travel Plus of over 5,800 travelers. It appears that close to 70% of the participants want to travel in 2021. Many of them also carried over some of their vacation days from 2020 into 2021. For example,

CHAPTER FIFTEEN

61% feel hopeful about travel in 2021, of whom 83% will take two or more domestic trips and 44% plan for two or more international getaways.

7% are excited about travel.

Europe remains the most sought-after international destination among the Americans (68% of participants), followed by Asia (30%), the Caribbean (28%), and Mexico (25%).

Within the U.S., the West/Pacific Northwest is the hottest region (52%), followed by the Mountains of Idaho, Montana, Wyoming, and Colorado (40%), Southwest (37%), Hawaii (31%), and Northeast (31%).

52% of participants plan to participate in outdoor activities.

68% want to avoid crowds.

26% of respondents carried over 11 or more vacation days from 2020 to 2021; 15% carried over between six and 10 days.

30% of respondents have 21-30 vacation days.

31% of respondents have 31 or more days.

CHAPTER FIFTEEN

While many are making plans for trips, only 15% of respondents purchased tickets for domestic travel, and fewer than 10% have purchased flights for international trips.

Air travel may only see a small improvement in 2021

The International Air Transport Association only predicted a 13% year-to-year improvement in 2021 in a worst-case scenario. The new lockdown restrictions due to the new coronavirus variants could be the reason for such a dim outlook.

According to AHLA's report, hotel occupancy in the U.S. will increase from 44% to 52% in 2021, and further to 61% in 2022. That was still below the 66% level in 2018 and 2019. Room revenue will reach $110 billion in 2021 and $144 billion in 2022, down from $167 billion in 2019. Before the pandemic, 5% of respondents took zero business trip. Such a number changed to 26% in 2020 and 24% in 2021. Recovery is likely to take stages:

Domestic leisure travel will fuel the first phase of recovery.

The second phase of recovery is likely to occur in Quarter 2, 2021, with small and medium events.

CHAPTER FIFTEEN

The third phase of recovery is expected to resume in Quarter 3, 2021, with group and business travel.

Business travel revenue is unlikely to return to a 2019 level until 2024.

Restaurants sales are improving

U.S. restaurant sales are projected to increase 11% in 2021 to $731.5 billion, but still far behind 2019's $864.3 billion. By December 2020, roughly 110,000 restaurants and bars, or about 10% of such establishments, had closed for a long-term or permanently. Additionally, many restaurants have adopted contactless self-service in operations. About 2.5 million restaurant jobs vanished in 2020. It is unlikely these empty positions will be recreated or filled soon.

Restaurant sales to jump 10.2% in 2021, National Restaurant Association says

Sales at U.S. eating and drinking places will jump 10.2% in 2021 to an aggregate $548.3 billion as consumers indulge pent-up demand for restaurant experiences they were denied during the pandemic, according to a forecast released by the National Restaurant Association.

CHAPTER FIFTEEN

That increase would follow a 19.2% drop in restaurant and bar sales during 2020, blasted in the association's 2021 State of the Industry Report as "the most challenging year for the restaurant industry."

The sales rebound will be slightly stronger for full-service establishments, with the association forecasting a 10.7% rise in nominal sales for what is universally regarded as the restaurant sector hit hardest by the coronavirus crisis. Negating the impact of inflation, places offering table service should split a rise of 7.6%, the "real" growth that some equate with traffic gains.

That compares with real growth for the whole industry of 6.7%.

Still, full-service restaurants will fail to reclaim the $85.5 billion they collectively lost in sales during 2020 as states closed dining rooms and consumers sheltered at home. Sales for that sector fell last year by 30%, or roughly a third.

The NRA forecasts total sales for full-service restaurants to top $228.8 billion this year, compared with a total intake of $199.5 billion last year and $285 billion in 2019

CHAPTER FIFTEEN

Limited-service restaurants—researchers' term for quick-service and fast-casual places—will see an 8% rise in nominal sales and a 4% increase in real revenues in 2021, according to the association's data. The sector's total intake will top total 2020 sales for the segment by $23.2 billion, while outstripping the 2019 tally by $4.7 billion, the association says.

The business group that will see the sharpest increase in sales this year is also the one that was hurt most deeply in 2020: Bars and taverns, which the association measures separately from restaurants that serve alcohol. Sales for that category will shoot upward by 80.2% in nominal terms and 77.6% on an inflation-adjusted basis in 2021, the annual report states.

Still, that would leave the sector-wide sales down about 37% from the total generated in 2019.

The restaurant association bases its expectations for 2021 at least in part on pent-up demand for dining out. It cites findings last year that 83% of American adults said they were not eating in a restaurant as often as they'd like

All in all, it seems that recovery will occur as early as the second quarter of 2021 under an optimistic estimation, but

CHAPTER FIFTEEN

this is also contingent on the effectiveness of the vaccines and the vaccination rate. Recovery will take time and in phases, starting from domestic leisure travel. However a full recovery is not expected until 2023 or 2024.

CONCLUSION

There is an obviously urgent and irrefutable need for social distancing today across the breadth of the United States during the new coronavirus pandemic. The sacrifices necessary amid this public health emergency, however, impact some workers and their families and business owners and their families more than others. The U.S. restaurant industry is perhaps the most apt case in point.

Many cities and states took a decisive step to curb the spread of the corona virus by ordering bars, restaurants, and social gatherings, such as weddings and other celebrations often hosted or catered by restaurants, to shutter. There is early evidence that the cities that took this step at the outset are finding success in "flattening the curve" of the outbreak. Closing restaurants and encouraging people to stay home is saving lives, yet millions of workers and owners in the restaurant industry are sacrificing their livelihoods. For those few restaurants and staff still serving food and drink through limited carry-out and delivery

CONCLUSION

services, they are risking their health, too, and will be even more exposed to becoming infected with COVID-19, as governments in states and cities begin cautiously to allow sit-down service.

The restaurant industry had been one of the fastest-growing sectors of the U.S. economy, growing by 30.2 percent since the end of the Great Recession of 2007–2009, compared to 18.6 percent for the rest of the private-sector economy. This growth has occurred in nearly every region of the country, both urban and rural, which makes it unusual in that many other industries tend to grow in single or a few similar regions (think the high-tech sector) and benefit those regions exclusively. The restaurant industry's total revenue in 2019 was $863 billion, representing 4 percent of our country's Gross Domestic Product. It was projected to grow by $36 billion in 2020.

In just the first full month of the pandemic, in March 2020, the U.S. economy shed 714,000 private-sector jobs, 58.5 percent of which were concentrated in the restaurant industry alone (417,300 jobs lost). Final April data on job losses in the restaurant sector will not be available until early May, but the National Restaurant Association

CONCLUSION

estimates that "more than 8 million restaurant employees have been laid off or furloughed since the beginning of the corona virus outbreak in March," or about two-thirds of all workers in the sector.4

The industry consists mostly of small businesses. And the restaurant workforce, though large, is disproportionately composed of low-wage workers, thus finding ways to help restaurant workers maintain their jobs or reclaim them as the pandemic lessens its grip on the nation and the economy begins to recover will help mitigate income inequality. Restaurants, though, are very "high touch" services firms—factors that, all together, leave restaurant establishments and their workers almost uniquely vulnerable to the corona virus and COVID-19.

The need to further assist the restaurant industry is clear. With 11.8 million workers employed in bars and restaurants across the country, the restaurant sector represents a large and important portion of the U.S. service-based economy. The eventual economic recovery after this public health and economic disaster will depend on the ability of consumers to spend money in their local

CONCLUSION

economies, and a vibrant restaurant sector is a critical part of this process.

Restaurant workers themselves are especially vulnerable. Before the shutdown, restaurant workers were paid low wages, lacked employer-sponsored benefits such as healthcare and paid sick leave, and were more likely to be living in poverty. Finding ways for this workforce to remain afloat and attached to its jobs is essential, as is continuing efforts to improve job quality during the recovery.

This issue brief also shows that the restaurant sector is dominated by small businesses, the vast majority of which are much smaller than the 500-employee cut-off for the Paycheck Protection Program. The majority of these small businesses are single establishments that are independently owned by local entrepreneurs who live and spend money in the communities in which they operate. While the restaurant sector has endured the majority of the job losses due to the pandemic, it was less likely to benefit from the support in the CARES Act. In considering additional legislation to help the U.S. economy, Congress should

CONCLUSION

think about ways to better target aid to struggling restaurants.

The U.S. restaurant industry, of course, is more than just a set of numbers. There is a priceless cultural value to these establishments that goes beyond just the size of its workforce or the scope of its economic impact. The industry is a part of the fabric of everyday life in communities across the country, from the small-town diner in rural Idaho to the trendy fusion taco truck in downtown Los Angeles to the family-run Italian restaurant in nearly any city in the United States. Restaurants are complex. There are essential human connections that happen at restaurants between workers, employers, and customers that are simply missing now. Restaurant owners, worker advocates, and nonprofit groups are all working tirelessly to find a way to stay afloat and maintain the prospect of reopening. Congress should do more to extend support to this vital piece of the American economy and culture.

One of the vulnerabilities of the tourism industry is that it is built entirely around a discretionary commodity: the travel. Travel restrictions are often the first action suggested as the most effectual way to diminish the spread of a transmittable

CONCLUSION

disease or pandemic in cases of health emergencies. In consequence, in the case of COVID-19 outbreak, the official rules and governmental restrictions that limit the worldwide travel, have brought catastrophic effects on the global tourism industry.

In conclusion, the corona virus has paralyzed the worldwide economic system. The global GTP growth was infected highly due to the almost general lockdown of the planet. Airlines industry already feels the catastrophic effects of its diachronic enemy – the economic recession. Tourism industry, which depends exceedingly on transport and mobility, may be considered as the 'great patient of the pandemic'. Tens of millions of employees have already faced or are facing losing jobs, and as reflected, the corona virus-induced crisis will cast a long shadow over the hospitality sector.

But even in these critical times, with upcoming crises in the fragile sector of tourism, some hotels succeed to drum up business, from the potential tourists' current needs, and they promote new products like self-quarantine packages. Thus 'quarantined guests' are a new type of hotel clients but only for the big hospitality companies which have the

CONCLUSION

possibility to provide premium isolation with daily healthcare monitoring. Tour operators and hospitality sector stakeholders have to be specialized in smaller groups' host. Furthermore, hospitality managers and tourism sector practitioners must take steps to set up crisis management plans.

Its been a rough time for all of us due to Covid-19. One of the hardest hit industry in the hospitality industry. Millions of people worldwide have been furloughed or laid off. However the incredible resilience and courage displayed by the hospitality community has been AMAZING. Throughout 2020, business owners have been forced to adapt to Covid-19 guidelines, including social distances, revised services, and safety measures. Unfortunately many have had to close their doors, while others struggle to remain financially secure.

Many restaurant owners are having to persevere due to Covid-19 conditions, and it is possible to make it out on the other side. Sometimes the best thing you can do is to keep innovating. Despite all the odds that are stacked against the industry at the moment, many restaurants are finding ways

CONCLUSION

to adapt and thrive, even with all that the coronavirus has thrown at them.

Although no one could have predicted a global crisis like this was heading our way in the year 2020, the restaurant industry however got creative in the midst of the coronavirus.

It is important to note that it is up to you to ensure that the comeback is greater than the setback. The future of the industry relies on your resilience these hard times.

"We're all suffering. But at the end of the day, what makes us stronger is our belief in one another, that we will come together to help one another get back on our feet… this is our time, this is our moment to not go back to politics and Wall street but to move forward. It's more about people than profits. This is our time to move forward and change the system." ----Karen Washington, farmer and founder of Rise and Root Farm and in my opinion that is the only way – forward.

REFRENCES

1. *Bakar, N.A.; Rosbi, S.EffectofCoronavirusdisease (COVID-19)totourismindustry. Int. J.Adv. Eng. Res. Sci. 2020, 7, 4. [CrossRef]*
2. *Yang, Y.; Zhang, H.; Chen, X. Coronavirus pandemic and tourism: Dynamic stochastic general equilibrium modeling of infectious disease outbreak. Ann. Tour. Res. 2020, 83, 102913. [CrossRef*
3. *Oron, D.P.; Topol, E.J. Scripps Research. Available online: https://www.scripps.edu/science-and-medicine/ translational-institute/about/news/sarc-cov-2-infection/ (accessed on 23 February 2021*
4. *Morawska, L.; Cao, J. Airborne transmission of SARS-CoV-2: The world should face the reality. Environ. Int. 2020, 139, 105730. [CrossRef*
5. *Tappe, A.; Luhby, T. 22 million Americans Have Filed for Unemployment Benefits in the Last Four Weeks. Available online: https://www.cnn.com/2020/04/16/economy/unemployment-benefits-coronavirus/index. html (accessed on 23 February 2021).*

REFRENCES

6. Kretchmer, H. *Key Milestones in the Spread of the Coronavirus Pandemic—A Timeline. Available online:* https://www.weforum.org/agenda/2020/04/coronavirus-spread-covid19-pandemictimeline-milestones/ (accessed on 24 February 2021).

7. American Hotel and Lodging Association (AHLA). *Economic Impact of the Hotel Industry Showcases Potential Negative Impact of Coronavirus Pandemic, American Hotel and Lodging Association, Fact Sheet: Oxford Travel Industry Impact Study.* 2020. AHLA. Available online: https://www.ahla.com/sites/default/files/fact_sheet_state_covid19_impacts_0.pdf (accessed on 23 February 2021).

8. AmericanHotel&LodgingAssociation(AHLA).Stateo ftheHotelIndustryAnalysis: COVID-19SixMonths Later. 2020. AHLA.Availableonline: https://www.ahla.com/press-release/report-state-hotel-industry-sixmonths-covid-pandemic (accessed on 23 February 2021).

9. Asmelash, L.; Cooper, A. *Nearly 80% of Hotel Rooms in the US Are Empty, According to New Data. Available online:* https://www.cnn.com/2020/04/08/us/hotel-rooms-industry-coronavirus-trnd/index.html (accessed on 24 February 2021).

10. Sotiris Folinas, Marie-Noëlle Duquenne, and Theodore Metaxas Virtual Economics, Vol. 3, No. 3, 2020

REFRENCES

11. Senbeto, D.L., Hon, A.H., 2020. The impacts of social and economic crises on tourist behaviour and expenditure: an evolutionary approach. Curr. Issues Tour. 23 (6), 740–755. https://doi.org/10.1080/13683500.2018.1546674.

12. Guterl, F., F. Jamali, and T. O'Connor. 2020. The controversial experiments and Wuhan lab suspected of starting the coronavirus pandemic. Newsweek, 4 April. https://www. newsweek.com/controversial-wuhan-lab-experiments-thatmay-have-started-coronavirus-pandemic-1500503.Accessed March 25, 2021.

13. The New York Times, March 13 (updated March 17). https://www.nytimes.com/2020/03/13/world/asia/coronavirus-china-conspiracy-theory.html. Accessed March 26, 2021.

14. Rogin, J. 2020. State Department cables warned of safety issues at Wuhan lab studying bat coronaviruses. Washington Post, April 14. https://www.washingtonpost.com/opinions/2020/04/14/state-department-cables-warned-safety-issues-wuhanlab-studying-bat-coronaviruses/. Accessed March 25, 2021.

REFRENCES

15. *The First P4 Laboratory in China is officially in operation. Xinhua Net, January 5. http://www.xinhuanet.com/politics/2018-01/05/c_129783861.htm. Accessed March 27, 2021.*

16. *Yang, Y.-J., and Y.-H. Tam 2018. Unit 731: Laboratory of the devil, Auschwitz of the East (Japanese biological warfare in China 1933-45). UK: Fonthill Media. Yuan, Z. 2019.*

17. *Current status and future challenges of high-level biosafety laboratories in China. Journal of Biosafety and Biosecurity 1(2): 123–127.*

18. *Land O'Lakes quietly gets rid of iconic Indian maiden mascot by Max Nesterak -April 15, 2020/*

19. *Entrepreneurship, Free Enterprise, and Human Flourishing by Brandon Smith – January 5 2017. https:/atlantic-expedition.org. Accessed March 25 2021*

20. *Free Enterprise, the economy and Monetary policy.https:/ www.dallasfed.org. Accessed March 25 2021.*

REFRENCES

21. 5 facts about partisan reactions to COVID-19 in the U.S. BY TED VAN GREEN AND ALEC TYSON, Pew Research Center APRIL 2, 2020. https/www.pewresearchcenter.com/. accessed March 27 2021.

22. Restaurant Outlook for 2021: Uneven Recovery, but Better Days Ahead consumer trends | December 15, 2020 | DANNY KLEIN. Accessed March 25 2021

23. The Aunt Jemima brand of syrup and pancake mix will get a new name and image. https:/www.NBCNews.com/. Accessed March 26 2021.

24. The Role of Food in Human Culture. https:/www.GlobalGastros.org June 30, 2017. Accessed March 25 2021.

25. The widespread impact of the restaurant industry's shutdown By Gerald D. Davis and Amy L. Drushal June 30, 2020. https:/www.propertycasaulty360.com/. Accessed March 26 2021

REFRENCES

26. *Why food delivery apps are some of the few benefiting from the Coronavirus. By Ankita John. https:/www.emoryeconomicsreview.org/. Accessed March 26 2021.*

27. *Coronavirus: Texas and other states ease rules despite warnings 03 March 2021. https:/www.BBCNews.com/. Accessed March 27 2021.*

28. *Roles and responsibilities of free Enterprise Economy by Alexander Hoffman 2012. Libertas Institute/ online journal/. Accessed March 25 2021.*

29. *Review of Online Food Delivery Platform. https:/www.mdpi.com/. Accessed March 26 2021.*

30. *What the Future of Restaurants Might Look Like, By Kate Krader, Leslie Patton, Jonathan Roeder, and Henry Ren 11 February 2021. https:/www.Bloomberg.com/. Accessed March 27 2021.*

31. *Covid-19: US Supreme Court backs religious groups over New York caps 26 November 2020.*

REFRENCES

https:/www.bbcnews.com/. Accessed March 25 2021.

32. Coronavirus is a Biological Warfare Weapon in an interview with Dr Francis Boyle who drafted the Biological Weapons Act. https:/www.heraldopenaccess.us/. Accessed 27 March 2021.

33. Ksiazek TG, et al. 2003. A novel coronavirus associated with severe acute respiratory syndrome. N Engl J Med 348: 1953–1966. [PubMed] [Google Scholar] Accessed 27 March 2021.

34. Culliton BJ, 1990. Emerging viruses, emerging threat. Science 247: 279–280. [PubMed] [Google Scholar] /. Accessed March 26 2021

35. Anthony SJ, et al. 2017. Global patterns in coronavirus diversity. Virus Evol 3: vex012. [PMC free article] [PubMed] [Google Scholar] Accessed March 25 2021.

REFRENCES

CPSIA information can be obtained
at www.ICGtesting.com
Printed in the USA
LVHW082136111122
732349LV00003B/10/J